The Tanner Lectures on Human Values

THE TANNER LECTURES ON HUMAN VALUES

1981

II

Raymond Aron, Brian Barry, Jonathan Bennett,
Robert Coles, George J. Stigler, Wallace Stegner,
and Michel Foucault

Sterling M. McMurrin, *Editor*

University of Utah Press — Salt Lake City
Cambridge University Press — Cambridge, London, Melbourne, Sydney

Published in North and South America
and the Philippines
by the University of Utah Press,
Salt Lake City, Utah 84112, USA,
and in Great Britain and all other countries by
The Press Syndicate of the University of Cambridge
The Edinburgh Building, Shaftesbury Road,
Cambridge CB2 2RU, and
296 Beaconsfield Parade, Middle Park, Melbourne 3206
Australia

THE TANNER LECTURES ON HUMAN VALUES

Appointment as a Tanner lecturer is a recognition of uncommon capabilities and outstanding scholarly or leadership achievement in the field of human values. The lecturers may be drawn from philosophy, religion, the humanities and sciences, the creative arts and learned professions, or from leadership in public or private affairs. The lectureships are international and intercultural and transcend ethnic, national, religious, or ideological distinctions.

The purpose of the Tanner Lectures is to advance and reflect upon the scholarly and scientific learning relating to human values and valuation. This purpose embraces the entire range of values pertinent to the human condition, interest, behavior, and aspiration.

The Tanner Lectures were formally founded on July 1, 1978, at Clare Hall, Cambridge University. They were established by the American scholar, industrialist, and philanthropist, Obert Clark Tanner. In creating the lectureships, Professor Tanner said, "I hope these lectures will contribute to the intellectual and moral life of mankind. I see them simply as a search for a better understanding of human behavior and human values. This understanding may be pursued for its own intrinsic worth, but it may also eventually have practical consequences for the quality of personal and social life."

Permanent Tanner lectureships, with lectures given annually, are established at six institutions: Clare Hall, Cambridge University; Harvard University; Brasenose College, Oxford University; Stanford University; the University of Michigan; and the University of Utah. Each year lectureships may be granted to not more than four additional colleges or universities for one year only. The institutions are selected by the Trustees in consultation with an Advisory Commission.

The sponsoring institutions have full autonomy in the appointment of their lecturers. A major purpose of the lecture program is the publication and wide distribution of the Lectures in an annual volume.

The Tanner Lectures on Human Values is a nonprofit corporation administered at the University of Utah under the direction of a self-perpetuating, international Board of Trustees and with the advice and counsel of an Advisory Commission. The Trustees meet annually to enact policies that will ensure the quality of the lectureships.

The entire lecture program, including the costs of administration, is fully and generously funded in perpetuity by an endowment of the University of Utah by Professor Tanner and Mrs. Grace Adams Tanner.

Obert C. Tanner was born in Farmington, Utah, in 1904. He was educated at the University of Utah, Harvard University, and Stanford University. He has served on the faculty of Stanford University and is presently Emeritus Professor of Philosophy at the University of Utah. He is the founder and chairman of the O. C. Tanner Company, manufacturing jewelers.

STERLING M. McMURRIN
University of Utah

THE ADVISORY COMMISSION

DEREK C. BOK
President of Harvard University

HAROLD T. SHAPIRO
President of the University of Michigan

DONALD KENNEDY
President of Stanford University

CONTENTS

PREFACE TO VOLUME II

Volume II of the Tanner Lectures includes those delivered during the academic year 1979–80, together with a lecture by Professor Barry given at Harvard University early in the academic year 1980–81. The other lectures for 1980–81 will be published as Volume III.

Arms Control and Peace Research

RAYMOND ARON

THE TANNER LECTURES ON HUMAN VALUES

Delivered at
Clare Hall, Cambridge University

November 22, 1979

RAYMOND ARON studied philosophy at the Ecole Normale Supérieure and at the Sorbonne. Following the *agrégation de philosophie*, he studied in Germany, especially the phenomenologists Husserl and Heidegger and the sociologists, primarily Max Weber. Before the war, he published books on German sociology and philosophy of history and an *Introduction to the Philosophy of History*. After the war, he combined a journalistic career as columnist for *Figaro*, from 1947 to 1977, and now the *Express*, with teaching at the Sorbonne and finally at the Collège de France. His best-known books are *The Opium of the Intellectuals*, *Eighteen Lectures on Industrial Society*, *Peace and War among Nations*, *Essay on Liberties*, *Penser la guerre*, *Clausewitz*, and *In Defense of Decadent Europe*.

The juxtaposition of the two notions *arms control* and *peace research* may at first sight surprise the reader. The first notion implies theoretical and practical research into the ways first, of reducing the risk of war, and nuclear war in particular; second, of reducing devastation if in spite of everything war were to break out; and third, of reducing the cost of armaments and slowing down the arms race. The second notion encompasses all studies relating to the causes of wars and, in more general terms, all the situations and practices dangerous to peace.

The classical period of arms control, a conception of American origin, occurred during the later 1950's and the early 1960's. It developed in response to the strategic and technical studies carried out on nuclear arms and their impact on diplomacy and war. The peace research institutes which proliferated mainly during the 1960's were often in opposition to the American institutes, which concentrated chiefly on nuclear weapons and strategy. The research centres which use the word 'peace' in their titles do not limit their focus to the two European blocs, to American and Soviet strategy, or to nuclear weapons. The inequality among nations and the world economic order also come under their scrutiny insofar as they are causes of conflict, and at any event manifestations of violence — 'structural violence', as the adherents of this school choose to call it.

In other words, arms control specialists tend to be primarily interested in nuclear weapons and the dangers of war related to them. Peace research specialists, on the other hand, tend to broaden out their investigations to cover all forms of armaments and violence. Of the two schools, only the first has exercised any influence on statesmen and the course of events. Some of the ideas thrown out by academics and think-tank researchers have been

taken up and put into practice. The SALT I and SALT II agreements, for example, spring from the school of arms control. And
the debate provoked by SALT II raises questions concerning the
basis of arms control itself.

*   *   *

The French term *maîtrise des armements* conveys the original
intention of *arms control* rather better than the English expression.
Arms control implies neither disarmament, verification, nor inspec-
tion, but a refusal to give in to the dynamic of the arms race. It
implies the will to become again, as Descartes put it, both master
and possessor of nature — or in this case, arms. Disarmament is
not necessarily the aim, since its chief objective is to prevent war,
and it has not been established that disarmament invariably helps
to prevent it. For example, in retrospect, most people would
admit that, faced with Hitler in 1935, rearmament would have
been preferable to disarmament. The theoreticians of arms control do not adopt the thesis that wars are a result of the arms race.
They study the means by which, in a given situation, the risk of
war can be prevented from increasing through either an excess or
an insufficiency of arms. The balance of terror is better safe-
guarded by a few hundred rather than by a few dozen intercontinental missiles.

The theory of arms control, almost self-evident in its principles, would not have been of any special interest in itself if the
conjunction of superpower rivalry and the existence of nuclear
weapons had not presented what might be a perfect example of
'arms control'. The supporters of this theory take as a starting
point that a genuine and fundamental political consensus between
the United States and the Soviet Union is out of the question.
They also hold that both rivals hope to avoid a nuclear conflict.
Starting from these two premises, arms control consists in fixing
the relationship of force between the two superpowers at a level
compatible with both the *desire of each side to get the better of*

the other in confrontations if possible, and their *common desire* not to destroy each other. The stumbling block, and perhaps the contradiction, inherent in this theory lies in the clash between the *obviously antagonistic goals* of the two powers and their *assumed common interest*. Is it really possible to agree on a limitation of armaments favorable to the nonuse of nuclear weapons without, on another level, political or military, favouring one or other of the protagonists?

The first steps in arms control were expressions of *the common purpose*, which, by their nature, did not excite much controversy. The best example is the telephone hot line. It is important, in the heat of a crisis, that the two heads of state be able to communicate directly. Dialogue is not enough to guarantee a solution, but it offers a better chance for avoiding the worst. A second agreement attributable to arms control is the partial suspension of nuclear tests. Common human interest justifies the ban on tests within the atmosphere, so as not to pollute the air we breathe and to avoid radioactive fallout from which other populations would suffer. The comprehensive test ban would slow down or prevent the deployment of new or better weapons.

But the ban has also served another purpose of arms control: to hinder what is called the proliferation (or dissemination) of nuclear weapons and the enlargement of the atomic club. I don't propose to analyse the basis of this theory in detail here: I would simply like to make the point that the ban does embody certain political implications. The first powers to employ nuclear weapons are attempting to reserve this weapon, monstrous or decisive, for themselves — which invites the question, from a preoccupation with peace in general or from self-interest?

Other measures — the renunciation of chemical and biological weapons, and the nonmilitarisation of space and ocean bed — caused no stir. The agreement regarding the nonmilitarisation of space has been partially respected so far: no bombs have been put in space (it has not presented any apparent military advantage).

But it is widely known that the Soviets have carried out experiments in the destruction of satellites and that the Americans, in turn, are working on similar projects.

*   *   *

The first arms limitation agreement was signed by Leonid Brezhnev and Richard Nixon in 1972, together with a declaration laying down the mode of conduct to which the two signatories subscribed. The two signing states committed themselves to restraint (the favorite word of the Secretary of State at the time). They would not try to take 'unilateral advantage' at each other's expense. The link between arms limitation and the diplomatic conduct of the two superstates did not bring about a visible change either in Moscow or in Washington. The same mixture of limited cooperation and permanent opposition still marks their intercourse. (The two superpowers, according to the theory, agree on the ceiling of strategic nuclear arms imposed on each of them in the hope of slowing down the arms race in this field and creating a stable situation that should reduce the risk of war and the actual use of these weapons.)

This treaty and a second, which has still not been ratified by the Senate, have only done away with or, rather, impeded the development of a single system of weapons: antiballistic missiles, or what the Americans call ABM. The Soviets had already installed an ABM system around Moscow which, according to the Americans, was of doubtful efficiency. Meanwhile, the Americans were in the process of setting up their own system which the military leaders hoped to deploy at least around Washington and to protect the silos of intercontinental missiles. According to Henry Kissinger, when Lyndon Johnson brought up the question of a common abandonment of ABM, Premier Kosygin replied that he had never heard such a stupid proposal. But a few months later the Soviets were eagerly underwriting that very proposal: the conscious and determined decision to give up all defence against missiles, or, in other words, to *guarantee the vulnerability* of the territory of the two superpowers. Each of the two reserved the right to protect one site. The United States, at least, has not used that right.

The abandonment of ABM, whatever its accidental cause, had one lasting significance in that it revealed the inspiration behind arms control. What was the objective of the SALT negotiators? Stability: another word for equilibrium but with its own connotation. According to press commentators, the relationship between the two great nuclear powers would be stable on the day when neither of the two would be tempted to have recourse to these weapons, knowing that the reprisals would be equally destructive to themselves. This assurance of reciprocal destruction is reinforced by the *absence of defence* and by the *vulnerability of the cities*, but, at the same time, by the *invulnerability of the weapons of retaliation*. From here one passes from stability to the idea of *mutually assured destruction*, also known as MAD. Nuclear weapons, according to this doctrine, have no other function than to prevent their own military use.

The writers of the *New York Times*, for example, argued against the technology of the MIRV's (multiple independently-targetable re-entry vehicles). To the Soviets, the massive increase in the number of nuclear warheads would constitute a threat because it reinforced American counterforce capability. Without any doubt, the Soviets would go on to do the same, increasing the number of their launchers or their warheads. Either one of the two would ensure a substantive superiority for itself and put the opposing forces in danger; according to this hypothesis, stability would be compromised. Another possibility, far more probable, would be that the two camps would regain the same stability and the same strike capability, but on a higher level of both expenditure and number of weapons. Events confirmed the second alternative. But the academic strategists had never accepted such a simplistic interpretation of deterrence during the 1960's.

If it is demanded of the nuclear force of the United States only that it should be able to inflict enormous devastation on the aggressor at a second strike, the task of those in power is singularly simplified. The 41 submarines, each carrying 16 MIRV'ed missiles, alone can inflict untold damage on the Soviet Union (and not even that number is necessary). However, such an action against enemy resources would be more or less suicidal, because it would call down upon American cities an equivalent catastrophe.

In other words, the theory of arms control, in this form, implies a strategic doctrine. If one defines stability as the invulnerability of the main forces of the two superpowers, arms control should aim not only at stability, but at the elimination of all counterforce capability. For the counterforce capability of one camp presupposes the vulnerability, if only partial, of the enemy force. This explains why some statesmen of the United States, Robert MacNamara in particular, seemed both to want and to fear the counterforce capability that they still possessed by the early 1960's. MacNamara repeatedly advised the Soviets to protect their missiles better and to reinforce their silos. His reasoning was that the Soviets would be tempted to strike first if they thought they were at the mercy of an American first strike.

Via these arguments, arms control leads to what the strategists call the *minimum deterrent*, the capacity to deter the adversary from a nuclear attack against one's own territory. But with or without arms control both the United States and the Soviet Union already wield this minimal deterring power. Years of negotiation would not have been necessary to arrive at this kind of stability — a partial stability, limited to a single level of strategic nuclear weaponry. Is this kind of partial stability in conformity with the strategic doctrine of American diplomacy? Is the minimum deterrent sufficient to guarantee the security of the allies of the United States? Stability at one level, restricted to one type of weaponry, does not, by itself, stabilise the overall relations between the two superstates.

*   *   *

Beyond the abandonment of ABM, SALT I fixed a ceiling on the number of intercontinental missiles the two superpowers were allowed to own. The Soviets were allotted a ceiling around 40 percent higher than the Americans, who, thanks to MIRV technology, owned a far higher number of nuclear warheads. The Senate ratified SALT I without much resistance. It did, however, demand that the subsequent treaty should re-establish equality in the number of the two superpowers' intercontinental missiles.

The intercontinental ballistic missile systems of the United States and the Soviet Union present such structural differences that trying to determine equality or parity or equivalence leads to endless discussion. The negotiators finally agreed on the total number of strategic nuclear missiles (2,400 and subsequently — from January 1, 1982—2,250), the total number of land-launched missiles equipped with MIRV's (820), the total number of MIRV'ed missiles (1,320), and the maximum number of nuclear warheads inserted in a single heavy missile (10).

In SALT I, there was one ceiling for land-based missiles, another for SLBM's. In SALT II, there remains a ceiling for all intercontinental missiles, but inside this total global number of launchers each one of the two signatories retains the right to determine the composition of the aggregates, the percentages of ICBM's, SLBM's, and bombers. On the Soviet side, the proportion of ICBM's is 62 percent, on the American side only 40 percent. SALT II attempts to slow down, if not to stop altogether, the renewal of arms and quantitative progress by specific measures. The original internal volume of an ICBM silo launcher should not be increased by more than 32 percent; there is the interdiction against increasing the launch-weight or the throw-weight of the heavy ICBM, flight testing or deploying new types of ICBM's (with the exception of one light model), the interdiction against increasing the number of reentry vehicles for the ICBM, SLBM, etc.

There is still today a passionate debate about SALT II, advantages and dangers. It is not my purpose to go into the details of the controversy in order to discuss the consequences of the treaty for Europe. I shall concentrate on the key objections of the adversaries of the treaty, leaving aside also the uncertainties of verification.

The Soviet heavy launcher, the SS-18, can carry up to ten nuclear warheads. The ceiling on the SS-18 is fixed at 308. If the nuclear warheads of these heavy launchers have the firing accuracy that the Americans think they do, they could destroy at a single blow almost the entire United States force of Minutemen, other land-launched missiles, and airfields. These are the most accurate missiles, the best adapted to counterforce. In response to a hypothetical destruction of the American land-launched missiles, the President of the United States could only use either the submarine-launched missiles or the bombers, equipped with cruise missiles or not, at the risk of triggering mutual destruction, the devastation of the industrial system, and a senseless orgy of violence.

SALT II's supporters do not deny that towards 1983 the Soviets will indeed have the capacity to destroy some 90 percent of the United States' land-launched missiles, whereas under the treaty the United States would not have the equivalent capacity to destroy the Soviet land-launched missiles. As of June 12, 1979, the United States had at its disposal, in addition to 1,054 land-launched missiles, 656 submarine-launched missiles (including 496 equipped with MIRV's), and 573 heavy bombers. Whatever the effectiveness of a Soviet first strike, it could not take away from the United States its capacity for massive reprisals. But having once destroyed the American land-launched missiles in a first strike, the Soviet Union would still have more than enough missiles to lay waste the territory of the United States.

In theory, this sort of stability at the level of strategic nuclear weaponry should weaken the deterrent effect of these weapons in relation to all acts of aggression, with the exception of the most serious of all those directed at the vital interests of the country and the integrity of its territory. In other words, the desired effect of the doctrine of mutually assured destruction is in the direction of a neutralisation of these weapons. And, at the same time, conflicts at a lower level, even armed ones, become less improbable.

Furthermore, has this so-called stability really been established at the level of intercontinental missiles? Is the unequal vulnerability of the Soviet and American land-launched missiles really compatible with stability? Once again, according to all the experts, whether for or against SALT II, the Soviets, with their heavy missiles, will in two or three years' time have the capacity to eliminate the system of American land-launched missiles at a first strike, whereas the Americans will not be able to do the same. In other words, the Soviets are supposed to have a first strike capacity superior to that of the Americans. Does this superiority have serious implications? Most people will hesitate here: the very idea of such a war is so repellent, the scenario so improbable, that it is difficult to take these macabre calculations entirely seriously. If one enters into these analyses, Soviet superiority depends on the inaccuracy of the SLBM. The next SLBM, the Trident, could be just as accurate as the ICBM and be fired at the remaining Soviet land-based launchers without aiming at the cities. (Even during the time of planned massive retaliation, the Americans did not target on the cities, but at military or economic objectives. Still, the collateral destruction would have been, and, in spite of improved firing accuracy, would still today be enormous.) Soviet superiority consists in launching-weight and throw-weight, the megatonnage which improves the counterforce capability.

What effect does the uncertain stability of the intercontinental nuclear forces have on the relationship between the two superpowers? Here also the reply is far from clear cut. Nuclear weapons cannot fail to have an influence on those in power, on both sides, encouraging them to be prudent. But Henry Kissinger himself has gone back on the remark he made once to journalists during an interview: "In the name of God, what does superiority mean in this field?" Should genuine equality at the level of intercontinental weapons be established, the relative force in other areas, and in Europe in particular, takes on an increased significance. The West can no longer count on the threat of escalation. Nor can it count on its superiority on a higher level to compensate for its inferiority at the lower levels. Put more explicitly, it can neither count on tactical nuclear weapons to weigh against its inadequate number of divisions nor make up for the number of Soviet medium-range missiles through the number of its intercontinental missiles. For Europe, 'theatre' weaponry thus becomes an essential element of security.

The Americans have proposed what is in effect a prolongation of SALT I into SALT II, which will deal with so-called 'gray areas'. Without discussing the problem at length, I shall express my skepticism. The negotiations of SALT I and SALT II neither modified the programmes of the two signatories nor prevented the development of the offensive missiles the Soviet Union wanted to produce. By limiting the enlargement of launching silo volume, the American negotiators hoped to avoid the mass production of heavy missiles. They failed; the Soviet experts were able to insert heavy missiles into their launching silos without enlarging them. In the negotiations concerning Europe, what could the American–Europeans trade off against the tanks, the guns, the planes, the SS-20's of Soviet weaponry? Quantitatively, the Soviet side is superior in all fields. On what basis would stability be founded?

Beyond that, during the SALT negotiations discussion had already been complicated by distinctions made between the various types as well as numbers of missiles. As a result of the heterogeneous natures of the two different systems, the notion of equality has been brought into question. And furthermore, inequality in first-strike capacity has finally been agreed upon, deriving from the technical and perhaps strategic choices of the two parties. In any negotiation on theatre weapons, it would be difficult to ignore the basic differences in the two sides' approach to strategy. NATO, a fragile coalition of democratic governments, is by nature incapable of taking initiatives. If war does break out in Europe, the offensive will necessarily come from the East. And in so narrow a theatre of operations, the offensive takes on a decisive importance, as shown by the wars in the Middle East. How important is the number of planes and even of tactical nuclear weapons if the nuclear warheads of the SS-20's can, at a blow, destroy a few hundred points crucial to the defence of the West?

The doctrine of arms control assumed a common wish on the part of the two great superpowers not to destroy each other — that they would not use nuclear weapons against each other. But, in the case of Europe, Soviet military treatises anticipate a lightning strike, with the simultaneous deployment of both conventional and nuclear weapons. The West does not know which kind of war it should be preparing for.

I arrive here at a conclusion that you will perhaps find too categorical: that the doctrine of arms control has been a failure so far.

1. First of all, it has not helped to reduce military expenditure, or even caused a reduction in the sums spent on nuclear weapons. The ceilings laid down leave margins for both the production of new launchers and their improvement. Since SALT I, the Soviets have deployed many new systems: ICBM, SS-16, -18, -19, SS.N.18 SLBM; the Americans have MIRV'ed their Minutemen II and III and Poseidon. Jimmy Carter had promised to produce 200 MX and the Trident after the ratification of SALT II. Ronald Reagan will probably do more.

2. The negotiators have been overtaken by the speed of technical progress. Counting launchers is a crude yardstick; the

diversity of missiles and their possibilities, the differences in strategic attitudes make stability a more complex matter than simply counting the number of weapons.

3. The Americans took as a starting point the hypothesis of a common desire on the part of the superpowers not to destroy each other. This hypothesis is indeed a highly probable one. But there are two ways of achieving the aim of avoiding war: parity or superiority. The Americans originally bet on superiority, and it may be that the Soviets are now wagering on superiority in turn. In their treatises, the Soviet strategists refute the Western theory that neither camp can win a nuclear war. They maintain that even nuclear war would not be an exception to Clausewitz's maxim that war is the continuation of state policy by other means. Nuclear war, they affirm, which could be avoided, would, if it were to break out, mark the final episode in the struggle between the two socioeconomic formations, socialism and capitalism. Do they really believe it? No one knows.

4. Even supposing that an approximate parity were to be established at the level of intercontinental missiles, the relative neutralization of those arms would not necessarily entail the same consequences for both camps. Everything would depend on the relative forces at lower levels and in other theatres of operation.

Some members of the arms control community will object that the arms race would have been worse without SALT. It is true that ABM has been prevented, but is this an achievement or a cardinal error? The idea was to stop first the defensive and then the offensive arms. The increase of offensive arms, the heavy missiles, numbers of warheads, continued. It is true that SALT II limits the freedom of the two sides on certain points, for example the mobile missiles. But, here again, with an exception: the Soviets have already produced, tested, and deployed the SS-20, an intermediate-range missile which threatens the entire NATO defense system. The cost of MX will be increased because mobile launchers have been excluded by SALT II (in order to make verification possible). Even without ratification of SALT II, the new administration will avoid systems which would make verification impossible.

Should we, in the opposite direction, place the responsibility for the degradation of the balance of power between the superpowers on arms control? I do not think so. At least, the responsibility of arms control is a limited one. In any event, the Soviet Union possessed the means necessary to reach some sort of parity with the United States: the financial resources, technicians, and industry. The leaders of the Communist party do not stint when it comes to armaments: neither money nor the best brains are spared in the pursuit of military absolutes. It may be that their obsession with arms control causes the American leaders to forget the balance of power and remain passive in the face of the Soviet accumulation of armament.

Henry Kissinger said recently that "rarely, in history, has a nation accepted so passively such a radical change in the military balance. It is not the consequence of SALT, it is the consequence of unilateral decisions extended over a decade and a half, of a strategic doctrine adopted during the sixties, of the bitter domestic divisions growing out of the war in Vietnam, and of the choices made by the present administration . . . ." The doctrine of arms control did not dictate the clauses of SALT I, any more than it did the attitude adopted by the United States between 1973 and 1978, when the extent of Soviet military strength and the deployment of the SS-16, -18, -19, and -20 came to light. The leaders of the United States judged their nuclear force sufficient to remain an efficient deterrent. But as the negotiations drew to a close, the senators could not fail to appreciate the modification of the balance of power.

Arms control had assisted in the decline of American power and helped to conceal it. SALT II, all in all, enshrines and ratifies the decisions taken unilaterally by the two sides. The Soviet Union has spent and manufactured more. The United States has contented itself with the land-launched MIRV'ed missiles of the 1960's and adhered to the 'triad' theory: the capacity for massive reprisals on a second strike and a reduced counterforce. The American strategists assumed that the first strike would come from the East, and in order to assure the invulnerability of the missiles put the majority of them to sea. The Soviets were not afraid to suffer a first strike.

*   *   *

Arms control is inspired by a doctrine and defines its goals. The peace research institutes are of an altogether different nature. That is why the following observations on these institutes are of quite a different nature from those that I have developed in the preceding pages. The directives issuing from arms control, which are, in a certain sense, operational, are open to criticism because they have observable results which bring its very principles into question. Peace research, which is purely academic in essence, does not lead to any practical application, unless one considers it borne out by general propositions, which are always open to contestation.

The literature on peace and war is immense and has grown even faster since the last war. A plethora of different disciplines has been put to the test. Historians, sociologists, economists, psychologists, and psychiatrists have pooled their efforts. But the fact remains that we don't know much more than we did before. We have no basis from which to deduce principles for action.

Take one example: armament or the arms race. Are we in any position to state that the arms race necessarily ends in war? As long as one defines the term in a sufficiently broad and vague way, one could say that the great wars of modern times have been preceded by arms races. But whether the states increased their military budgets because they were preparing for war or whether war was brought on by the accumulation of arms is another matter. In the case of neither world war is the answer straightforward.

As to the war of 1939, the most plausible reply is that the rearmament of the Third Reich was determined by Hitler's diplomatic projects. The West was slow to respond, but in the end did rearm, fearing the Führer's ambition.

The military budgets of the great European nations increased in the years immediately preceding 1914, during what is called the 'armed peace'. But these budgets remained relatively small in terms of gross national product. They did not weigh insupportably upon the finances of the different states or upon the standard of living of the populations. Diplomatic tensions raised fears of an armed conflict and politicians took precautions. France's 'loi de trois ans', the subject of furious polemic, was intended to diminish the inferiority of the French army in relation to that of the Germans, despite the difference in numbers between their two populations.

One can speak of an arms race today, but not without certain reservations. The United States devotes 5 percent of its GNP to the national defence budget. In western Europe the percentage hovers around 3.5. Estimates for the Soviet Union vary between 11 and 15 percent, equivalent, in percentage terms, to two or three times that of the United States. In absolute terms, military expenditure is considerable — more than $100 billion in the United States. This expenditure arouses the imagination and also the indignation of people of good will who weigh the value in real wealth — food, education, industry, and health — that the money could be spent on rather than missiles, submarines, and tanks. But this expenditure does not crush whole peoples or give vogue to the sentiment that it would be better to have done with it all rather than endure this endless terror.

Leaving aside the futile questions: who is responsible? and who began it all? we should remember two facts, peculiar to their era, which contribute to the so-called qualitative arms race. Like all industrial products, arms can be improved. Because of this, all states feel more or less obliged to renew the machines of war, obsolescent rather than worn out, before they have even used them. The SS-18 outclasses the Minuteman III. In countless ways the struggle between the armour and the sword continues on land and sea, in air and space.

A second historical fact explains the arms race today: the strategic groundplan that emerged from the last war. On one hand, the intercontinental missiles face each other over oceans and peoples; and on the other hand, the Soviet army, equipped for the offensive, is stationed right in the heart of Europe. This state of affairs makes it probable that in time of war there would be no time to mobilize. The decisive battle would be waged with active, not potential, forces. Even more than before 1914, the military consider the first battles to be decisive. The trend towards professional armies is partially explained by the conception of a probable war.

Peace research institutes more often than not deplore the wastage of resources devoted to armaments. But they haven't, to my knowledge, found either an original method of disarmament or an unknown cause for the arms race. Nor have they proved that the states which arm themselves the most, the Soviet Union and the United States, are dragged by their defence budgets towards an inevitable war.

Let us move on from the explanation of wars by the arms race to a theory which still carries weight in certain circles: that capitalism becomes imperialism and that this, in turn, provokes war. By definition, it runs, the capitalist countries are unable to agree upon the division of the planet and are animated by insatiable greed. But whatever the relationship between the so-called capitalist economy and war, experience does not in any way allow us to imagine that war will disappear with capitalism. The tension between the Soviet Union and the People's Republic of China, and between Vietnam and Cambodia, at the very least suggests the general proposition that ethnic rivalries and historical conflicts survive revolutions and remain equally alive even when governments profess the same ideology. Furthermore, the great wars of the century set against one another nations which belonged to the centre of the world market. It was they who had the most to fear and the least to hope for from struggles which pushed them to the extremes of their available resources.

Certain of the peace institutes have brought into vogue a particular representation of the capitalist world: at the centre the industrialised or wealthy nations, and on the periphery the nations of the third world, from which the states of the world obtain the raw materials necessary for their industries, and part of their surplus value, through the intermediary of the multinational companies. This distinction between the centre and the periphery is reproduced within each state. The centre of the central states levies the surplus value from its own internal periphery and leaves a part to it. In the same way the centre of the peripheral states profits from a share of the surplus value it takes from its internal periphery, while pleading integration in the world market — often to its own interest.

This interpretation does not seem to me to make an important contribution to the comprehension of war and peace. It helps to explain national wars of liberation, although the desire for liberation, in the sense of rejecting a foreign colonial power, is also fuelled by elemental sentiments. At any rate, in the twentieth century it is the war between the states of the centre which has devastated the planet: the claim that it is no more than a quarrel over booty is far from convincing. Since 1945, Japan and West Germany have proved that they did not need conquest to prosper, and that they could take for themselves a large part of the external surplus value without reducing the other central states to slavery.

The distinction between the centre and the periphery suggests a representation of the world of the states comparable to the Marxist representation of every collectivity. A minority of exploiters appropriates the surplus value, taken directly from the workers. In the states of periphery, a double exploitation is working at the expense of the workers: the centre exploits its own periphery and lets the world centre exploit the entire peripheral collectivity. The privileged classes by definition take for themselves a part of the profits that agricultural and industrial enterprises have engendered. The multinational companies, insofar as they transfer their profits, cream off the periphery's surplus value to spend or invest elsewhere. Viewed from a neoclassical standpoint, the same facts would appear in a new light, with one main difference: are the profits of foreign investors always the fruit of exploitation? Are they always contrary to the interest of the developing country? Do the prices at which the industrialised states buy primary products from the peripheral states really represent a form of exploitation? It is not possible, in the context of a conference, to analyse the concept of exploitation, object of controversy between the neoclassical and Marxian schools. I will only make the problem explicit.

Before 1973 the price of oil stood at a level that is commonly thought of today as unjustified, despite the fact that the cost of extraction in Saudi Arabia was and is extremely low. Today, operating like a cartel, the producers can fix prices and manipulate production so that an on-the-spot market rise at Rotterdam can cause an increase in prices fixed on contract.

And if one considers market prices as a norm, the argument is the same: regarding raw materials, there is nothing to stop one of the producers from cutting back production or one of the consumers from abruptly releasing available stocks onto the market. Brazil, for example, acting despite the number of other producers, now knows how to manipulate the coffee market legally, without a cartel, by controlling the supply in order to control prices.

Such research, which has only a remote or indirect connection with peace, plays an important part in the studies of some peace research institutes. Whether or not the structure of the capitalist world market is unjust, it has not determined the great wars. It has perhaps accelerated the revolt of the colonised countries, and it probably fuels diplomatic and commercial disputes between the governments of the third world and the wealthy nations. But it was not the source of the two great wars of the century, and it is not at the root of the rivalry between the two great powers, between Vietnam and Cambodia, between India and Pakistan.

The peace institutes, it must be admitted, are often anxious to single out or to define a real peace, as distinct from an 'absence of war'. In his treatise on politics, Spinoza made the distinction. Peace should be more than an absence of war. In the field of international relations, peace is often not more than the absence of war. The peace treaty imposed by the victorious state is tolerated by the defeated because of the lack of force to change it. There are many instances where the peace treaty is only an armistice. Regarding the so-called economic order, it is today commonly affirmed that it is unjust and imposed by the centre upon the periphery. From this view one deduces the concept of 'structural violence'; the world market appears as a manifestation of violence, more or less the equivalent of war.

This kind of analysis errs in the opposite direction from that of the arms control specialists who concentrate on a particular type of weapon, as if the nonutilisation of intercontinental missiles were the same as the nonutilisation of all kinds of arms. Those analysts who see structural violence in the world market imagine that in combating that kind of violence they are working for peace. Both parties are deceiving themselves: the theoreticians of arms control because they isolate a single kind of arms, and the peace research specialists because they extend the concept of war indefinitely.

The partisans of arms control start from an idea which is in fact justified: that nuclear weapons possess such a potential for destruction that it is not unreasonable to attempt to prevent their use, while resigning ourselves to non-nuclear wars. Some specialists in peace research start from the false premise that peace requires justice. In fact, peace has been imposed when and where an imperial power has dictated it or when enemies, exhausted by their fighting, have either found a way to reconciliation or perceived the threat of a new common adversary. Periods of peace based on equilibrium often have been no more than prolonged armistices. The struggle for justice within nations or between them justified in and of itself, is not always a pacific action — it eventually leads to violence.

*   *   *

I do not claim to judge the peace research institutes. I have wanted simply to recall that we know little about the causes of war when it comes to making practical use of such knowledge in order to maintain the peace. I have briefly isolated two theories still in vogue concerning first the arms race and second international economic ambitions.

I have neither condemned arms control, because there are many forms of it, nor have I suggested that SALT II should not be ratified. I have not wanted to enter into the debates of today. Any judgment for or against ratification should require a complete study of the text and analysis of the political as well as the military considerations. My purpose has been to make clear the paradoxes of the doctrine of arms control.

Some facts are obvious, irrefutable. We recall the official goals of arms control. Reduce the risk of war: I see no improvement. Reduce the destruction if, in spite of everything, a war should occur: the destruction would perhaps be even worse because the superpowers have eliminated their means of defence and increased the means of offence — the number of warheads and the throw-weight of the heavy missiles. Reduction of military spending: since SALT I, both sides have increased their budgets for strategic weapons, the Soviet Union much more than the United States. Jimmy Carter had promised a massive increase of spending on the MX and the Trident if SALT II were ratified. Ronald Reagan will do it with or without ratification.

Why the spectacular failure? I have exposed some reasons which I will summarize in different language.

Is real agreement regarding the balance of military forces possible between states which remain fundamentally hostile to each other? They could agree against nuclear proliferation, but each one of them is in search of a parity favorable to it.

Beyond this primitive reason, I would mention technical progress. The first yardstick is the number of launchers, but you may put many warheads in any missile. Then comes firing accuracy, which transforms the efficiency and function of the missiles. The missiles become more vulnerable and, at the same time, battle-field weapons (warheads of low yield). 'Equivalence' becomes more and more difficult to establish. One has to take into consideration the pay-load, the throw-weight, the accuracy of the missile, and the yield of the warhead.

The third argument, the most political, the most instructive, is the fallacy of partial stability. Partial stability might compromise global stability, especially because of the asymmetry between the two camps. I even distinguish three styles of asymmetry:

1. Nuclear weapons have not necessarily the same place in the defence systems of the two camps; the Soviet camp maintains its superiority in the domain of conventional weaponry. Equivalence at the highest level may bring about the inferiority of one side in the global balance.

2. The asymmetry of the two nuclear systems makes equivalence at least equivocal. The Soviet camp is superior in throw-weight, in megatonnage; the American in number of warheads. Which is more important? What are the consequences of the Soviet capability of destroying the land-based launchers, the ICBM's? How does the nuclear strategic balance influence the minds of the statesmen and the course of diplomacy?

3. The present accuracy of the missiles gives the camp which strikes first an enormous advantage. The political asymmetry between a fragile coalition of democracies and the unified control

of the Eastern armies determines, in advance, who will strike first. Are the Pershing II and the cruise missiles invulnerable enough to balance the SS-20?

There may be a fourth asymmetry. Do the Soviet military leaders consider the use of nuclear weapons in battle normal, inevitable? For what sorts of hostilities do they prepare their troops? And do the political leaders really adhere to the doctrine revealed in the books of their generals, according to which a nuclear war could be won like any war of the past?

Thirty years ago we tended to believe that the states would modify their behaviour in response to the threat of nuclear arms. Instead, these arms have been integrated into the course of ordinary international relations, with one new element, the fear of escalation to extremes and nuclear wars. The states, the cold monsters, have not changed, they have become more prudent. Scientific studies on war, conducted by institutes of polemics, peace, or strategy, have made no decisive contribution to the task of the statesmen. It is up to the statesmen to know whether the SALT negotiations are politically desirable, however modest their military results. And it is up to them also to know whether SALT is necessary for detente, or whether detente must lead to SALT, or whether detente is necessary to peace.

I have focussed on two questions: are states which are basically hostile to each other able to come to an essential agreement about the relationship between their forces? My reply is no. Have we learnt the causes of war and the means of preventing it? Here again, my reply is no. Since complex societies have existed, this has been the historical condition of mankind. So far technology has turned weaponry upside down, but not men. Should we be surprised? Should we despair? Neither surprised nor despairing. The human adventure, horrible and glorious, goes on.

Do Countries Have Moral Obligations?
The Case of World Poverty

BRIAN BARRY

THE TANNER LECTURES ON HUMAN VALUES

Delivered at
Harvard University

October 27, 1980

BRIAN BARRY was born in London in 1936. He read philosophy, politics, and economics at Oxford and also received the D.Phil. there for a thesis written under the supervision of H. L. A. Hart. Before crossing the Atlantic in 1975, he held positions in a number of English universities, including, latterly, those of Professor of Government at the University of Essex and Official Fellow of Nuffield College. After a year each at the University of British Columbia and the Center for Advanced Study in the Behavioral Sciences in Stanford, he joined the faculty of the University of Chicago, where he is Professor in the departments of political science and philosophy and of social sciences in the college.

Professor Barry is the author of *Political Argument, Sociologists, Economists and Democracy*, and *The Liberal Theory of Justice*. He is currently working on a book to be entitled "Don't Shoot the Trumpeter, and Other Essays on Social Justice," and one that will take up the themes of the lecture published in this volume. He was founding editor of *The British Journal of Political Science*, is presently editor of *Ethics*, and is a Fellow of the American Academy of Arts and Sciences.

I do not think that I need to say much about either the timeliness or the importance of the subject of this lecture. In September 1980, for example, in a specially convened session of the United Nations General Assembly, the rich countries of the world stonewalled all the demands of the poor ones for the implementation of the so-called New International Economic Order. And it is plain that these demands, although rebuffed in the United Nations and UNCTAD, are not going to disappear, but are destined to form a central part of the international agenda for the rest of this century and beyond.

Although the subject is of such practical import, I should perhaps explain that my own interest in it arose originally out of a purely speculative problem. It occurred to me several years ago that we might discover something interesting about the concept of justice itself by looking at situations other than the usual ones of contemporaries in a certain society. I therefore began to study justice between generations and between countries. However, although I still find the intellectual puzzles that these topics throw up as fascinating as ever, I have very gradually arrived at some substantive views that are, I think, somewhat at odds with those of most people in the world's rich countries, including (and, indeed, especially) this one. And it is in the role of an advocate, rather than that of a completely detached philosophical analyst, that I appear before you tonight.

The actual demands of the poor countries, as represented for example by the Declaration on a New International Economic Order passed by the United Nations General Assembly in 1974, or the Charter of Economic Rights and Duties of States adopted in 1975, are a heterogeneous collection of points of widely varying generality and importance. And the justificatory theory within which these demands are presented is the now-standard United Nations one of asserting a "right" corresponding to each demand. This is, of course, a style of rhetoric not unknown in the USA, but in either the domestic or the international context it seems to me to have very little to contribute to rational discourse. In my view all it can be taken as claiming is that there is some valid reason for meeting the demand, but it does nothing to explain what that reason is. The statement of a specific right ought to come at the end of an argument, rather than being presented as if it were one.

For these reasons, I shall not in this lecture be offering a defence of either the content proposed or the reasoning offered for the New International Economic Order. But on one central and crucial point I shall be supporting the claims of the poor countries as they have been developed in various international bodies in recent years: namely, I am going to argue that, as a matter of justice, rich countries should be transferring resources to poor ones on a substantial scale.

The idea that justice requires the continuous and systematic redistribution of resources *within* countries is now a commonplace, even if not a wholly unchallenged, one. The same idea applied to the world as a whole is, however, still generally regarded as fairly wild. It will be my object here to try to make it more familiar — to domesticate it, if you like. It is, in fact, my view that only by cultivating a schizoid mentality is it possible to combine a belief in the justice of domestic redistribution and the notion that international transfers are a matter purely of humanitarian aid rather than one of the just distribution of resources. Of course consistency can be achieved in either of two ways. Professor Nozick, for example, would suggest that we retain the collective entitlement of rich countries to what they produce (or whatever they receive in exchange for what they produce) and extend the same doctrine of "what we have we hold" to the domestic rich. I shall, however, be pursuing the opposite tack and suggesting that the principles of justice supporting internal redistribution also support international redistribution.

At this point, the following challenge is liable to be made: am I not overlooking the essential differences between the domestic and international contexts? Is it not these differences that render the concept of justice inapplicable between countries? I shall begin by taking up this challenge in relation to a core conception of justice, the most universally acknowledged and I think the most indisputable. This is the notion of justice as reciprocity, the idea that benefits should be requited, equal value exchanged for equal value, and the like. I shall first acknowledge that this concept does require a context — a normative order — if it is to have application. I shall then, however, suggest that the international sphere is enough of a normative order for justice as reciprocity to apply in it in at least some matters. And then, having, I hope, established that justice as reciprocity does apply to international economic relations, I shall ask what redistribution of resources between countries it calls for. I should perhaps say now that the implications I shall find are rather limited. However, in the second half of the lecture, I shall go on to set out a second, complementary, principle of justice that I shall try to show has more far-reaching implications. I shall conclude with a few remarks on the question of the relation between justice and self-interest in international affairs.

Having laid out my strategy for the rest of the lecture, let me now come back to the challenge that I said had to be met before we could proceed further. Putting the point in as simple a way as possible, and leaving out all the qualifications that might be introduced in a more leisurely treatment, the argument to be considered is that justice as reciprocity requires stable expectations, and that in the international sphere, unlike the domestic sphere, there is no basis for these. The first part of the argument is valid. As David Hume observed, a single act of benevolence, if it succeeds in actually going good, requires no practice underlying it. But a single act of justice (and justice for Hume was largely a matter of respecting property rights and keeping contracts) cannot be understood, let alone unequivocally recommended, in the absence of an institutional framework. In other words, if I simply want to do you a good turn, that presents no problems. But if my idea is that one good turn deserves another, I have a reason for doing you a good turn only if I have cause to believe that you share this principle and will act on it when the time comes for you to do your bit.

All this, then, is fair enough. But the second part of the proposition is unfounded — at any rate if asserted as being true across the board. International affairs are not a pure anarchy in which nobody has any reason for expecting reciprocal relations to hold up. In economic matters, particularly, there is a good deal of room for stable expectations. A firm that sells something abroad, or signs a contract to obtain something from a foreign country, does not have — generally speaking — much greater fears of default than it does with trading partners in its own country.

Of course, it is true that states do not have a "common power to keep them in awe," as Hobbes said. But what is the significance of this? The only relevance here is to actual expectations. You can produce an *a priori* argument that effective norms require a central source of sanctions, but if it appears not to be so, then that should settle the matter.

It is also true that you cannot *absolutely* count on some contract not being repudiated, but it is equally true within a country that there might be some change of regime that would invalidate existing contracts. Absolute certainty is not to be had in this life. But in fact, because of the adverse implications of tearing up international contracts, revolutionary regimes are often quite punctilious in observing external agreements even if they recast the domestic economy. I conclude therefore that the background conditions for justice as reciprocity to operate do exist in the international sphere. International relations may be an anarchy in the technical Hobbesian sense but not in any more interesting sense.

It may, of course, be said in defence of the Hobbesian thesis

that the ugly reality is laid bare at time of war. I do not see why
war should be considered more real than peace. But there certainly is a long tradition to the effect: *Inter armes silent leges.*
Here I have some reluctant sympathy with the Hobbesian analysis,
to this limited extent: I do not think that moral constraints are
out of place in warfare, but I do think that justice has a relatively
limited role to play. The strongest moral reasons for not fighting
a war in a barbaric fashion are derived from humanity, not justice.
For the obligations of humanity — although they have the drawback of leaving much room for judgement as to what they require
in a specific situation — are universally binding. But the obligations of justice are derived from various conventions, controlling
the treatment of prisoners of war, for example, or outlawing certain kinds of weapons. Thus justice in war is justice as reciprocity
and here the weakness of reciprocity in the absence of appropriate
contextual conditions does seem serious.

Let me go back, however, from warfare to economic relations.
If I am right in saying that the conditions for the application of
justice as reciprocity do hold in the international economic sphere,
what implications does this have for the distribution of wealth
between countries? The answer is, I think, that the implications
are rather limited.

I shall distinguish three aspects of justice as reciprocity. One
is keeping contracts. A second is fair exchange. And the third is
the duty of fair play. Of these, contract obviously has no revisionary tendencies in itself. It underlies the whole system of economic relationships, but says nothing about the *content* of contracts. The second, fair exchange, says that equal value should be
exchanged for equal value. It can be used to criticize the actual
content of contracts and is thus potentially revisionary. But it runs
into the traditional problem of the "just price." That is to say, is
there some independently-specifiable criterion for a fair rate of
exchange between different commodities?

I do not think that all aspects of this question are totally intractable. If I paint watercolors for a living and sell them for $50 each to a dealer who turns round and sells them for $1,000 each, it seems pretty uncontroversial that I am not getting an adequate return on my efforts. The relation between the royalties on a barrel of oil before 1973 and the price at which that barrel of oil found its way into the hands of the consumer in an industrial country was about like that. Banana producers, it has been estimated, are still in about the same position, as they get only about ten percent of the final price. If their take doubled, the final price would go up only by ten percent, so their revenues would probably almost double too. It is not surprising that commodity-exporting countries have in recent years taken an increasing interest in the amount they receive as a proportion of the final price and have sought to secure a higher ratio.

But none of this, of course, touches the main issue. The OPEC countries, obviously, have not simply gained a higher share of a fixed final price, but by pushing up their own take have pushed up the final post-tax prices in the industrial countries several times over. But is the price now more or less just than it was? I must confess that that does not seem to me an intelligible question. This is not to say that commodity prices are beyond rational discussion from a moral standpoint — or even the standpoint of justice in particular. But it does imply that justice as fair exchange does not have much to contribute to such a discussion. In my view we have to start from some desirable end-state and work backwards to the prices it implies rather than imagine we can define justice in terms of the exchange of equal values. Thus, it might be said that higher copper prices would be just because we have a duty to future generations to conserve resources. Or it might be said that higher copper prices will make the copper-exporting countries richer, and that would be a move in the direction of justice since they are mostly relatively poor (though not among the poorest). But we have to produce some independent argument that it is just to conserve resources or that justice would be served by transferring resources from relatively rich to relatively poor countries. Where such judgements about justice could come from I will suggest later.

The third type of justice as reciprocity that I mentioned is the duty of fair play. This is the duty to do one's part in some mutually-beneficial enterprise. Now, the crucial point about justice as fair play is, it seems to me, that it presupposes the existence of some mutually beneficial practice already in existence. Given that such a practice exists, we can use the idea of a duty of fair play to criticize those who fail to contribute to it. But we cannot use the concept of justice as fair play to argue for the bringing into existence of mutually beneficial institutions where they do not exist now.

Therefore, the scope of justice as fair play in the international sphere is very limited. It could be used to criticize "free riders" on international agreements concerning pollution of the atmosphere or the oceans, or restrictions on fishing or whaling in international waters, where such agreements actually exist. But so long as such mutually beneficial agreements do not exist, the case for them should be argued from collective advantage rather than from justice. Justice comes in only once they do exist, to provide a reason for compliance (and then only so long as others comply).

This negative conclusion can be challenged. I doubt if I can hope to make both the nature of the challenge and the nature of my reply fully intelligible to anyone unfamiliar with the literature, but I will say something anyway. Charles Beitz, in his excellent book *Political Theory and International Relations*, argues as follows: since the international economy forms a single unit, because of the degree of interdependence between national economies, we should treat the whole world as, morally speaking, a single society. If so, John Rawls's theory of "justice as fairness," which is said by him to apply to a "society," should apply to the whole world, with the implication that economic arrangements should be such as to make the worst off people in the world as well off as they could be.

The problem with this argument is, as I see it, that it is either insufficient to establish its point or it is unnecessary, depending on the aspect of Rawls's theory we follow up. If we fasten on the idea that each person should do his bit in an enterprise of mutual benefit, we get out justice as fair play, but not, in the world as it is, much in the way of a duty to redistribute from rich to poor, because institutions corresponding (say) to social security within a country do not exist.

On the other hand, if we emphasize Rawls's idea that justice is whatever rules would be chosen from behind a "veil of ignorance" designed to eliminate knowledge of personal or external advantages, it is hard to see why the existence of actual cooperative relationships would be either here or there. If Rawls's arguments for the difference principle — making the worst off as well off as possible — are valid at all, then it would seem that we can argue immediately that they should be applicable globally.

However, if we go in that direction we immediately have to ask: why should we accept that principles chosen behind a veil of ignorance as specified by Rawls are just? How does this tie in with any recognizable conception of justice? This is, of course, a big question; but the essential point for the present is that the idea of justice as fair play will not itself carry the weight. What we need, then, are independent arguments to persuade us that it is just to set up institutions that take no account of personal and social advantages, and thus avoid the intrusion of what Rawls describes as "morally arbitrary" features. Such arguments, however, lead us away from justice as reciprocity altogether. And Rawls, in writings subsequent to *A Theory of Justice*, has increasingly moved in this direction himself.

Rawls's idea of the "morally arbitrary" is a powerful one, and, although I do not agree with all the implications that he draws from it, I do think that it leads us in the direction of an alternative conception of justice to that of justice as reciprocity. I am going to call it justice as equal rights, and I will develop an argument for it as the next point in this lecture.

To begin with, I think it is fairly easy to see that justice as reciprocity cannot be adequate in itself because it already presupposes some more fundamental criterion of distribution. Contracts presuppose prior property rights; fair exchange is morally significant only if the parties have a title to what they exchange (if I steal your bicycle and sell it back to you, how much credit do I get for not overcharging you?); and we can talk about cooperation for mutual benefit only if we have some baseline for measuring benefits in the absence of cooperation.

What we are looking for, then, is some distributive principle that will tell us something about basic entitlements. The one that I shall put forward is by no means original — if it were I would have less confidence in it. It can be traced back directly to an influential article by H. L. A. Hart called "Are There Any Natural Rights?" But the basic idea can be traced back further — to Kant, for example. My object here, in any case, is not to recount its history but to try to make it as persuasive as I can. However, I will start by outlining Hart's own approach, because I think it helps to clarify the essential logic.

Hart argued that if there are any special rights arising out of the actions of people (paradigmatically, contracting with one another), there has to be a general right to equal liberty. For it makes no sense for people to be able to *change* their rights if there is no baseline from which they change them. This is, of course, the point I have already anticipated in suggesting that justice as reciprocity cannot be a complete theory of justice.

Now, stated this baldly, the argument may seem like a piece of legerdemain. And it is, I think, correct to say that Hart offers no definite reason why the *general* right must be an *equal* one. However, one can surely make an argument to the effect that, if we are talking about a right independent of what people do, it is hard to see on what basis it can be *un*equal. This will not satisfy the kind of racist who says that some people have superior claims not in virtue of anything they have ever done but simply intrinsically, in virtue of who they are. But it should be good enough for anyone else.

But what does this equal right cover? At this point, I want to strike out on my own and suggest that it should be taken as covering anything having the characteristic that nothing anyone does gives that person any special claim on it. As a prime example, I would offer the case of natural resources, considered in themselves lying in the earth's crust or wherever. Is there anything that, in the absence of some convention or rule, constitutes an act of appropriation? In this land of devout Lockeans I expect the answer "By mixing one's labor with it." But in fact, Locke's fundamental premise was that the earth was given to all men in common, and the "mixing one's labor" criterion for appropriation was put forward as a way of trying to show how one avoided the conclusion that "men must starve," in the absence of universal consent. Now, as a practical way of putting into effect the equal right principle, the Lockean system would perhaps be acceptable under the very restrictive conditions stipulated by Locke. I want to leave open at this point the question of how to implement the principle that the earth is "the common heritage of mankind." The principle itself seems to me pretty hard to deny. In practice, we tend to notice the arbitrary nature of the principle of national sovereignty over natural resources only in the most extreme cases, such as countries in the Persian Gulf with small populations and large oil revenues. But once cases like that set us thinking, I would hope that we would see that the principle itself is without any rational foundation.

Natural resources provide a relatively straightforward application of the idea that what nobody can make any special claim on everybody has an equal claim on. But of course most of the disparities in national prosperity are not accounted for by the abundance or lack of natural resources. They flow, rather, from differences in the stock of productive capital, in the infrastructure of transport and communications facilities, and in the training and education of the work force, the abilities of managers, and so on. Where does our principle fit in here?

It seems to me that there are three points to be made in this connection, each of which has quite different implications, and that somehow we must give weight to all three in arriving at a final judgement. The first is that there is no country that is well off by world standards (say an annual income of $4,000 per head or more) in which the current generation can claim all the credit for their prosperity. In every such country *either* the level of income arises from large oil revenues divided among a relatively small population *or* it owes a great deal to inherited human and physical capital. In other words, saying "we deserve it because we worked for it" is never strictly true, unless the "we" is tacitly extended back to earlier generations.

The second point is that, in spite of the importance of inherited advantages, we should still be willing to give people credit for making efforts themselves. Not everybody can become a world-class swimmer. You need an appropriate physique and access to a swimming pool, and it no doubt helps to have good coaching, supportive parents, and all the rest. But out of all the people who have those advantages, only a few actually put in the necessary hours of practice. Perhaps, as Professor Rawls suggested in *A Theory of Justice*, even the ability to make an effort is the result of some favorable combination of genes and environment — but the fact remains that the effort has to be made. Capital equipment and a skilled work force do not produce anything unless the work force applies itself to the equipment with a certain diligence. If, say, British workers want slower assembly lines and longer tea breaks than German workers, it seems perfectly reasonable that they should also accept a lower material standard of living, and I would hypothesize that one of the reasons for the lack of noticeable discontent in Britain with the country's relative (though not absolute) decline in per capita income in recent decades is that this is widely recognized, at least at an intuitive level.

The third point is a very difficult one to deal with in a short space of time, but I will say something about it all the same. It may be argued that we are making a mistake if we focus our attention exclusively on the present generation and say that their good fortune in inheriting an effective productive structure is something for which they cannot claim any special credit. For inheriting a productive structure is not like sitting atop a huge lake of oil. It is man-made even if not by those currently alive. If we say that it arises from the efforts of previous generations of people in that country, does it not follow that they should be able to determine the beneficiaries of their efforts? This suggestion raises a host of difficult questions. How should posthumous wishes be treated? What *did* past generations expect to happen as a result of their efforts? And to what extent were their efforts directed at making life easier for their descendants anyway? Because time is short, I shall finesse these questions, for the present purpose, by saying that I think it would be hard to come up with answers to them that would imply an absolute right among the present generation in any wealthy country to enjoy exclusively the advantages they inherit.

Different people will no doubt be impressed to different degrees by the three points I have just raised, so they will tend to come out in rather different places when it comes to drawing implications from them for the obligations of rich countries to poor ones. I shall, however, suggest two minimal recommendations that seem to me to follow from the principle of equal rights — minimal in that they leave current property relations intact and merely make incremental changes in the distribution of the benefits arising from those relations. The first, which flows from equal rights to natural resources, is an international severance tax on the extraction of natural resources, the proceeds to be distributed to resource-poor countries. And the second, which flows from the extension of the principle to inherited advantages, is an international income tax, levied on countries with a per capita GNP of (say) $4,000 a year and up, and distributed to countries with (say) annual incomes of $1,500 a head or less. It seems to me that these two forms of tax must have the effect of redressing injustice by moving things in the right direction, though there remains room for disagreement as to how far they should go and whether additional measures would be desirable.

In order to proceed, I shall take it that justice does require international transfers from resource-rich to resource-poor countries, and from countries with high average incomes to those with low average incomes, and then address two issues that arise. The first question is this. It may be recalled that I said earlier that justice, unlike humanity, had institutional and normative presuppositions. Justice as reciprocity entails the existence of an ongoing set of normatively-controlled relationships. One does not advance the cause of justice as reciprocity by conferring benefits that are not, when the relevant time comes, reciprocated in whatever is the appropriate way.

What about justice as equal rights? Now, the notion of justice as equal rights does not in itself, it seems to me, entail the existence of institutions for its application. An exchange of apples now for oranges in the future requires an institution of promising. But to divide equally an apple between two people with an equal claim on it requires no more than a sharp knife. Clearly, however, the full implementation of a system of global transfers based on the two criteria that I have proposed would indeed require the existence of institutions that do not now exist.

What follows from this? Obviously that they ought to be brought into existence. This sounds, perhaps, a hopelessly utopian thing to say. I cannot here undertake to analyse this charge in any detail. But let me offer two remarks. First, the institutions do partly exist, imperfect and inadequate as they may be. I point for an example to the increase in Special Drawing Rights for poor countries that has been carried through in the International Monetary Fund. The poor countries propose to put this on a regular basis rather than regard it as a one-off change. The rich countries have recently blocked this, but it seems clear that a mechanism for the regular and systematic transfer of funds could be worked out without any revolutionary transformation of the international monetary order. The second observation I want to make is that we should adopt a sensible time perspective in judging the feasibility of large-scale changes. We should be thinking in decades and even centuries. Within countries, the welfare state and redistributive taxation have come about as the administrative capacity of the state and the accepted ideas about its role have developed *pari passu* over the past hundred years. I can see no reason why the same should not happen in a wider sphere. Indeed, by those domestic standards, the growth of international institutions in the past thirty years is rather fast. And so too is the rise in the idea of international redistribution itself, from something almost unheard of in 1950 to the common currency of North–South exchanges in 1980.

There is a second aspect of the proposal for international transfers that I want to take up, and that is that I make countries rather than individuals the units of redistribution. The taxes will, I assume, be levied on countries, which will then collect them through their own tax systems; and they will be paid to countries, where they will operate in effect as a relaxation of constraints on imports.

The objection that is liable to be made to this is that in principle justice should be regarded as a relation between individuals. States may have to be accepted as intermediate instruments in the move towards a just world economic order, defined at an individual level, but no more than that. The implication drawn from this is usually that countries that do not use the additional resources in an equitable way internally should not receive them.

My answer to this is that it fails to appreciate the difference between justice and humanity as grounds for making transfers. Humanity is a principle that is indeed to be defined at the individual level, because a transfer either relieves suffering or not, and suffering is a predicate of individuals. A transfer which increases resources (either of an individual or a collectivity) but which does not relieve the suffering of some person or persons has not achieved its end. Hence, incidentally, the attraction to donors of aid with strings or in kind rather than cash. By contrast with this, justice has as its subject-matter the distribution of resources. It is concerned with the way in which rights and powers are allocated. And rights, powers, or resources may be attributes of collectivities as well as attributes of individuals. There is therefore no incoherence in saying that justice may be defined over two — or indeed any number of — levels. We can talk about the justice of distribution between countries, and also the justice of distribution within countries. There is no a priori reason for supposing that a just distribution between countries can be deduced directly from considering what would be a just distribution among four billion or so individuals, regarded as if they were not the members of various collectivities (including countries) with decision-making power over the disposition of various resources.

In this context, it is worth noting that in practice we do not really think about the distribution of income *within* countries as a distribution among individuals but among families (except when we are not thinking concretely and individualistic ideology takes over). In no country, for example, does social policy treat someone as indigent even if he or she has no personal income at all, so long as he or she is married to and living with someone who does have a substantial income. In practice, we do adopt a two-level approach. Social policy is concerned almost exclusively with the distribution of incomes among families (either in wages or social benefits), and the distribution of those resources within families is left pretty much to those families. If we regard families as decision-making units entitled to some autonomy as to their internal arrangements, I can see no reason why we should refuse to extend the same standing to countries.

That is not to say that no international pressure on states is ever warranted, but again the domestic parallel holds. If a man spends all his wages on drink with the result that his wife and children go without food and clothing, that is not simply his business but the public's. But the appropriate reaction is *not* to refuse to pay him his wages or renege on debts that are owed to him. Yet the proposal that transfers should be denied to poor countries with inequitable internal arrangements is exactly analogous to that. Countries are, if I am right, owed transfers as a matter of right, and there is no more reason for withholding transfers than there is currently thought to be for refusing to pay for imports from such a country. (There is also no less — withholding transfers would be legitimate where the freezing of assets would be.) The advisability or otherwise of international intervention to press for greater justice within a country is left open by what I have said about international justice. It certainly is not ruled out.

I have deliberately eschewed any appeal in this lecture to self-interest as a reason for rich countries making transfers to poor ones. It may appear to some people that this dooms the case I have made to futility. I do not believe this. Let me in conclusion very briefly say why.

It is a matter of record that, although a number of industrial countries have reduced the proportion of their GNP going to foreign economic aid in recent years, the most precipitous decline has occurred in the USA's contribution, which has now fallen to less than one fifth of one percent of GNP. And the USA is a country in which the case for foreign aid has been almost exclusively argued for in terms of the American national interest. Conversely, the countries which have actually improved their record in recent years — Scandinavia and the Netherlands — are those in which aid to poor countries has been presented most strongly as a moral obligation. This provides some simple empirical support for the proposition that, as a sheer matter of practical politics, moral appeals may be more effective than appeals to self-interest.

The fact is, I think, that it is genuinely uncertain whether or not the self-interest of rich countries, either individually or collectively, calls for substantial economic transfers to poor ones. This is partly a question of the difficulty of establishing causal linkages on the scale and over the time-span required. Suppose that it is claimed (as it sometimes is) that the continuation of the status quo with respect to transfers will lead by the end of the century to "turmoil in the third world." How exactly does poverty lead to turmoil? To what sort of turmoil? And how would that affect the rich countries, on a variety of assumptions about the measures they might take to defend themselves against adverse consequences? Similar problems arise through the whole catalogue of possible effects.

But there is a deeper reason for uncertainty, and this lies in the inadequacy of the concept of interest when it is confronted with an issue of this nature. The concept of self-interest works best in contexts where a choice has to be made within a well-defined framework. Given my tastes, aspirations, and circumstances, should I take this job or that one? But in choosing whether or not to make serious transfers to the poor countries, we are choosing between alternative worlds that will increasingly diverge as time goes on, and choosing not just for ourselves but for our children and their children, whose tastes, aspirations, and circumstances will be different in those different worlds. The supposed definiteness of the question dissolves, and in the end we can do little more than ask "Which world would we prefer for ourselves and our descendants?" And when the question is posed in those terms, I think that the attractions of a less unequal world are not to be despised.

Let me finally raise the question to a higher level of generality. I am far from underestimating the force of economic self-interest in human affairs. But, for better or for worse, large-scale collective action normally arises in response to ideas rather than interests. This is often for worse rather than better. Take your pick of the worst blots on human history — the Spanish Inquisition, the Holocaust, or almost any war in the past two centuries — and it will be hard to conclude that with rational, self-interested people on all sides they could have occurred. Bertrand Russell used to say that, if people would really pursue their interests intelligently, the world would be a lot better place than it is. And there is much to be said for that view.

But since in fact people are swayed by ideas as well as by interests, it is as well that there is a brighter side to the picture. General ideas can give rise to movements that are liberating rather than destructive. The best example is the anti-slavery movement in Britain and America. British parliaments voted first to ban the slave trade (which was quite lucrative) and then to abolish slavery everywhere in the British Empire, with compensation from tax revenues for slave owners. As far as the USA is concerned, I have no wish to blunder into the historical minefield of "the causes of the Civil War." But I hope it is reasonably uncontroversial to say that the revulsion against slavery in the North made the pre–Civil War settlement increasingly fragile.

In both countries, the opposition to slavery was, I think, almost entirely based on the moral sentiment that it was wrong. World poverty is not as dramatic an issue as slavery. And a longer, more complex, train of moral reasoning is required to arrive at the conclusion that the coexistence of desperate deprivation in some countries alongside superfluity in others is a moral indecency of the same order. I do believe, however, that, if such a conviction can be inculcated in enough people, we have reason for hoping that results will follow. Anyway, I hope so.

Morality and Consequences

JONATHAN BENNETT

THE TANNER LECTURES ON HUMAN VALUES

Delivered at
Brasenose College, Oxford University

May 9, 16, and 23, 1980

JONATHAN BENNETT was born in New Zealand in 1930 and educated there and at the University of Oxford. He taught at Cambridge for twelve years, for eleven more in Canada, and since 1979 has been Professor of Philosophy at Syracuse University. He has written a good many articles — including, on moral philosophy, 'Whatever the Consequences' and 'The Conscience of Huckleberry Finn' — two books on the philosophy of mind and language, and three on early modern philosophy. He collaborated with Peter Remnant in a recently published edition and translation of Leibniz's *New Essays*, and is currently writing a commentary on Spinoza's *Ethics* and a book on moral philosophy which is closely related to his lectures in this volume.

I. KILLING AND LETTING DIE

I want to express my gratitude to the Principal of Brasenose and Mrs Nicholas, and to the Fellows of Brasenose, for the warming hospitality they have extended to my wife and myself; to Professor Tanner for his magnificent benefaction; and to all of you for being here. For me this time in Oxford — my first solid visit since I graduated from here exactly twenty-five years ago — is a heavily charged occasion. Added to the pride and anxiety which go with being the Tanner Lecturer, there is the joy of simply being in Oxford, and the complex set of emotions — known collectively as nostalgia — which are stirred by looking back across half a lifetime. In my case those emotions are strongly coloured by the fact that of my Oxford contemporaries the four who were dearest to me are all dead — have all been dead for many years now. One of the things I am doing in returning here is to celebrate the memories of Donald Anderson, Robin Farquharson, John Lemmon, and Richard Selig.

*   *   *

In this lecture I shall offer to make clear, deeply grounded, objective sense of a certain contrast: I call it the contrast between positive and negative instrumentality, and it shows up in ordinary speech in remarks about what happens because a person *did* do such and such, as against what happens because he *did not*.

The line between positive and negative instrumentality lies fairly close to some others which are drawn by more ordinary bits of English. For instance, the difference between positive and negative instrumentality in someone's dying is cousin to the difference between killing a person and letting him die. The latter distinction has the advantage of being already encoded in plain untechnical English; but it also has drawbacks for the sort of moral philosophy I want to do, as I shall now explain.

First, I want a genuine distinction — something which marks off two mutually exclusive species; and my second desideratum is that the two be jointly exhaustive of a genus which I call that of 'prima facie responsibility' for a state of affairs. I want it to include every case where a person's conduct makes him in some way and to some degree responsible for a given state of affairs. This is to be decidable in advance of considering whether he should be excused on grounds of mental incompetence, unavoidable ignorance, or whatever. Just because those matters are so morally important, I want them to have their own separate day in court; so I don't want the line I am drawing to get tangled up with them anywhere along its length.

Third, because the distinction is to separate out two classes of situation so that we can do some basic moral thinking about them, it must not depend for its initial application on our having already done some of the moral thinking. So it must be defined in terms which have no moral content in their meanings: if they turn out to have moral import, that will emerge later as a matter of substantive moral judgment; it will not be there all along as a matter of meaning.

Fourth, the line to be drawn should be statable in terms which are clear, objective, and deeply grounded in the natures of things. I do not want it to be one whose application to particular cases is at the mercy of controversy; or even at the mercy of agreed linguistic intuitions if these are not backed by a decent degree of clarity about what they are intuitions *of*. That is a matter of degree and is vague, but it will get a little clearer as I go along.

Those desiderata are better satisfied by the line between positive and negative instrumentality — the difference between 'because he did' and 'because he didn't' — than by any other distinction which might be regarded as a rival to it. I shall mainly discuss one rival, namely the line which has causal verbs on one side of it and corresponding phrases about 'letting' things happen on the other side — felling and letting fall, misleading and letting go astray, spoiling and letting deteriorate, killing and letting die. This line is worse for my purposes than the line between positive and negative instrumentality because it satisfies none of my four desiderata.

First, it separates two non-overlapping classes of verbal expression, but not two non-overlapping classes of event. There are killings which get described as lettings die (such as pulling the plug on the life-support system of a terminal patient), and there are lettings die which get described as killings (such as killing a houseplant by not watering it).

Second, the two are not jointly exhaustive of the genus 'prima facie responsibility'. There are cases where something happens because I did not do A, but where, since I did not know that it was liable to happen, it is improper to say that I 'let' it happen. If I didn't know, then perhaps I am not morally accountable for its happening; but that is a matter for subsequent moral discussion which I don't want to be preempted by the very terms in which my line is initially drawn. And, on the other side, there are cases where something happens because I did do A but where the relevant causal verb is not applicable — although she died because of what I did, I didn't kill her but merely hired or forced someone else to kill her. Again, there are moral issues about the difference between that and outright killing; and again I want to set those aside for later consideration rather than building them into the initial distinction.

Third, along some of its length the line between doing and letting happen — e.g., killing and letting die — reflects prior moral judgments. For example, if a houseplant dies of drought, and would have survived if I had watered it, the question of whether I *killed* it depends largely upon whether it was my job, my responsibility, to water it. That is the sort of moral input or moral taint which I want to keep out of my basic distinction.

Fourth, and last, there is controversy about parts of the borderline around killing and letting die, and even where there is agreement, there is sometimes not enough clarity about what the underlying principles are. For instance, we speak of pulling the plug on someone's respirator as a case of 'letting' him die because we see his dying as something which is tending or trying or straining to happen, and we see what we are doing as the mere removal of an obstacle to that process. I cannot find that that way of viewing the situation corresponds to anything in the objective world which I would be prepared to make room for in my moral thinking. I might have to withdraw that remark: someone might reveal what lies behind those removal-of-an-obstacle intuitions, and show it to be fit to bear a heavy moral load. Until such a revelation comes along, however, I add this to my charge-list against the distinction between doing and letting happen.

There are similar drawbacks to most of the other terminology that is commonly used to mark distinctions which, since they partly coincide with the positive/negative line, could be regarded as rivals to it.

For example, the meanings of 'refrain' and 'forbear' are too restricted: either of these terms, when combined with any of its plausible partners, yields a distinction which is not exhaustive of the genus. If we take the line between 'because he did A' on the one side and 'because he refrained from doing A' on the other, we shall be excluding cases where he did not do A but did not *refrain* from doing it either, because it never entered his head to do it, or because it occurred to him to do it but he felt no inclination that way; and similarly with 'forbear'.

The situation with 'omit' is different, but no better. It seems that you can 'omit' to do something without feeling a pull towards doing it; but you can't properly be said to 'omit' to do something unless you prima facie ought to have done it; and so we have a substantial moral taint in the language of act/omission if the latter term is properly used.

When people contrast 'active' with 'passive' euthanasia, they may be pointing to the positive/negative line which interests me. If they are — and indeed even if they are not — they are using 'passive' in a manner which seems not to stand up to critical scrutiny.

Worst of all is the verb 'to cause'. There are idiomatically natural ways of using it to draw something close to the positive/negative line. If something happens because I did do A, it will very often be natural to say that I *caused* it to happen; and if it happens because I did not do A, it will often be natural to say that I didn't cause but *allowed* it to happen. But I cannot turn this to account in theory-building, because I cannot see how to make these idioms put their feet firmly enough on the ground.

If we tie the word 'cause' to any of the most promising philosophical theories about causes — e.g., Mackie's about INUS conditions, or Lewis's counterfactual analysis — then it won't do anything like the work of positive instrumentality. For according to those theories, if the door slams because I do not grab it, my not grabbing it can easily qualify as a cause of its slamming.

Those theories, however, concern 'cause' as a noun or a verb used in relating one event to another — 'e causes f' or 'e is a cause of f'. When 'cause' is used to draw something like the positive/negative line, it is being used as a verb with a *person* as subject — 'He causes the door to close'. These uses of 'cause' have, so far as I know, no plausible, strong, clear philosophical theory to back them up: we seem to have to steer pretty much by our intuitions. And if we are to be guided by nothing but the linguistic proprieties, we shall find that plenty of negative cases will still be cases of someone's 'causing' something to happen, so that there will again be overlaps between causing things to happen and, for instance, allowing them to happen; and, worse still from my point of view, the criteria for whether a given negative instrumentality is a causing or not are themselves partly moral.*

* Judith J. Thomson, *Acts and Other Events* (Ithaca, N.Y.: Cornell University Press, 1977), p. 215.

Even if there were not that moral taint, the reliance on largely unexplained linguistic intuitions is for me a large drawback to the use of the verb 'to cause' in basic moral philosophy. I mentioned this a few moments ago, but should say a little more about it. What I am rejecting is the idea of taking unexplained linguistic intuitions as components in the hard data of my moral theorizing. If someone proposes, as a basic moral principle, something to the effect that it is worse to cause the death of an innocent person than to allow such a death, I don't know how to think about this except insofar as I am clear about what the difference is between causing a death and allowing one. Some people, on the contrary, are pre- pared to accept such a principle in advance of being clear about where it will lead them; for them, the pursuit of clarity about causing is part of the process of moral discovery. It is presumably because there are such people that we find, in the morally oriented literature on causing, ordinary-language semantics intertwined with moralising: writers take their stand on who causes what, as a way of jockeying for moral position. I don't mean to sneer at this, and when I revert to it at the end of my third lecture I'll indi- cate one respectable basis for taking this approach to such matters. But it is not my approach. Rather than holding firm to a principle using the verb 'to cause', and exploring the verb's meaning in order to discover what I am morally committed to, I would regard any unclarity over what 'to cause' means as automatically limiting my commitment to any moral principle containing it.

As I said, I favour the contrast between positive and negative, between 'because he did' and 'because he didn't'. As a point of reference for discussion of this contrast, let me introduce three very short stories. In each, a vehicle is on ground sloping down to a cliff top; and in each, there is a course of events which culmi- nates in the vehicle's falling down the cliff. My interest is in the role in the different stories of someone I call John.

A. John gives the vehicle the push which starts it rolling, and then nothing can stop it.

B. The vehicle is rolling when the story starts. There is a rock in its path which would stop it. John kicks away the rock.

C. The vehicle is already rolling. There is a rock near its path which would, if interposed, stop it. John does not interpose the rock.

The line which interests me falls between A and B on the one side and C on the other. In both A and B, the vehicle is destroyed because John did do such and such, while in C it is destroyed because he did not do such and such. The line between doing and letting falls differently, because most people say that in B John, in removing the rock, 'lets' the vehicle go to its destruction as he does also in C, that being just the sort of thing I dislike about the verb 'to let'.

These days, moral philosophers with an interest in theoretic foundations shy away from the positive/negative distinction, apparently because they are nervous about the concept of a negative action. Although I have no need for that concept, I shall say a little about its prospects.

Whether there can be a coherent concept of 'negative action' depends on what one's underlying ontology of actions, and thus presumably of events generally, is like. If Kim and Goldman are right, then actions are abstract entities and can perfectly well be negative. Really, Kim's 'actions' are *facts* about agents: just as the fact that John does not interpose the rock is distinct from the fact that John keeps both his feet on the ground, so Kim will say that John's non-interposition of the rock is one action and his keeping of both his feet on the ground is another. And, just as facts can be negative, so can actions if they are the finely-sliced, abstract items that Kim makes them out to be.

If, on the other hand, Lemmon and Quine are right, actions are concrete chunks of space-time, so that the phrase 'John's non-interposition of the rock at time T' is just one name for the totality of what John is up to at time T, this being an entity which may also answer to such descriptions as 'John's keeping both feet on the ground at T'. There is no chance of making that entity negative in itself: negativeness is always *de dicto*, not *de re*; but the totality of what John is up to at time T is a *res*, a concrete particular thing, and cannot be negative. It answers to some negative descriptions, but then so does everything.

Bentham's celebrated account of negative actions seems to have fallen foul of this point. The only way I can make sense of what he wrote is to suppose that he took actions to be concrete chunks of space–time while also thinking that a subclass of them are negative; so that to pick out the members of the subclass we must be able to peer at the totality of what a man is up to at a given time and declare *it* to be negative, negative in itself, negative *de re*. Someone with those ideas at the back of his mind will be apt to conclude — as apparently Bentham did — that such an item can be negative only if it consists in the extreme of inaction, i.e., in a state of affairs which brackets the agent with corpses and fence posts and pebbles: "Acts . . . may be distinguished . . . into positive and negative. By positive are meant such as consist in motion or exertion: by negative, such as consist in keeping at rest; that is, forbearing to exert one's self in such and such circumstances." * Of course Bentham doesn't stick to this disastrous account. He says, for instance, that the non-payment of a debt is 'a negative action', without asking whether the defaulter keeps stock-still at the time when he should be paying up. Still, there the official account sits — 'by negative, such as consist in keeping at rest'. I think it is the result of a doomed attempt to use 'is negative' as a monadic predicate which applies to actions understood as concrete particulars.

In my opinion we shall not have a worthwhile ontology of events and actions unless their identity conditions lie between

* Jeremy Bentham, *An Introduction to the Principles of Morals and Legislation*, ch. 8, sec. 8.

Kim's and Quine's, so that a given bit of space–time can contain more than one event (which is all Quine allows) without any risk of having to accommodate the infinity of events which Kim threatens to cram into it. Davidson seems to be hoping for an intermediate position, though he has never found one. If someone does, we shall have to look at the details before we can know whether it allows for negative events or actions.

Anyway, as I said, I dispense with negative actions. In situation C, it doesn't matter whether John performs a negative action; the important negative item in C is a *fact*, namely the fact that John does not interpose the rock.

There are plenty of negative facts about his conduct in situation B also — he does not dance a jig, does not join the army, and so forth — but in B there is no negative fact about his conduct which, combined with the impersonal facts of the situation, guarantees that the vehicle will go over the cliff. If I tell you about the rolling vehicle with the rock in its path, and add only some negative fact such as that John does not stand on his head, you cannot tell from that what will become of the vehicle. Whereas in C the negative fact that John does not interpose the rock is all we need, given the impersonal circumstances, to know that the vehicle is doomed. In each case the crucial question is: what is the weakest fact about John's conduct which suffices for the vehicle's destruction? In B it is a positive fact, while in C it is negative.

That indicates in a rough way how I distinguish 'because he did' from 'because he didn't', or positive from negative instrumentality. At least it shows how I use the concept of a negative fact and liberate myself from the concept of a negative action.

But that leaves me with the enormous problem of explaining what it is for a fact or a proposition to be negative. It is easy to classify sentences as negative or not; but that is no help to me, since the very same proposition may be expressible in sentences of both sorts — e.g., the proposition that George *is not* in the armed forces any longer, or *is* now a civilian. In short, granted that negativeness won't fall from propositions down onto actions or events, can I prevent it from floating off propositions up onto sentences? If I can't, my concept of negative instrumentality will be revealed as language-dependent: what happens in situation C will involve John's negative instrumentality if we describe his conduct as his *not* interposing the rock, but it will come out as positive if we fake up some non-negative sentence which means the same. For instance, let us give the word 'permit' a meaning such that 'x permits y with z' means that x does not put z in the path of y; and then we can say that in situation C the vehicle is destroyed because 'John permits it with the rock', which is not a negative sentence. Such a concept of negative instrumentality, being at the mercy of choice of wording, would not be worth having; and rather than persist with it I would prefer to go back and try to revive one of the other candidates.

But I don't capitulate. I cannot offer — and suspect that there cannot be — a general theory of proposition-negativeness. But I can produce a very limited one which is nevertheless broad enough to support an account of negative instrumentality. As well as being limited, it will be shallower than one might have hoped: its shallowest roots won't run deep enough to let the whole account belong to abstract logic or fundamental metaphysics; but they will get below the surface of the language and will give to the resultant line between kinds of instrumentality a good deal more depth and objectivity than I can find for any of its rivals.

The underlying idea has occurred to philosophers as different as Kant and Ayer (I refer to Kant's notion of an 'infinite' proposition and Ayer's 'Negation' paper in his *Philosophical Essays*). It is that a negative proposition is just an extremely though not entirely contentless one — a proposition which says enormously much less than its contradictory. It is the idea that a negative proposition sprawls across nearly but not quite the whole of logical space, is true at nearly but not quite all possible worlds.

That idea, as it stands, is indefensible. But there is a limited adaptation of it which does work, and which is all I need. To introduce it, I should first explain why the idea cannot be rescued in its full generality.

Let us represent logical space — or the totality of possible worlds — by a square, each point in which represents one possible world, one complete way things might be. Then any proposition P is represented by the set of points representing worlds at which P is true. Thus

<blockquote>Roses are red and violets are blue</blockquote>

is represented by the set of all the points which represent complete descriptions of worlds at which roses are red and violets blue; and that set can be thought of as a subregion within the square. It in turn is part of the larger region corresponding to

<blockquote>Roses are red,</blockquote>

and is indeed just the intersection between that and the region which represents *Violets are blue*. Within this way of representing things, it is quite clear what is going to count as a representation of one proposition's saying more — having more content — than another; it will be the former's having a smaller area than the other. If P entails Q and not vice versa, then in a good sense P has more content than Q; and they will be drawn as in Figure 1, which manifestly gives P less area than Q. The link between amount of content and smallness of area is also embodied in the

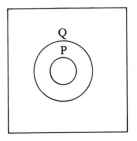

FIGURE 1

fact that each *point* in the square represents a proposition which
chatters on until it has said the whole truth about some possible
world.

So far, so good: if one area contains and is not contained in
another, you don't need a metric to tell you that the former is
bigger than the latter — sheer topology is enough. But the Kant–
Ayer idea about negative propositions requires a metric for logical space: we have to be able to compare the regions assigned to
two propositions of which neither entails the other. Specifically,
we need a basis for saying not merely that P and not-P divide up
logical space between them, but further that the line falls not like
that in Figure 2, but rather like that in Figure 3. No one has
found a general procedure which will settle the question for each
contradictory pair of propositions. It obviously cannot be done
by counting possible worlds, for in every interesting case there
are infinitely many of those — i.e., the same number of those —
on each side of the line. I believe that there is no general solution
to this problem, and that a fully general concept of negative
proposition cannot be had through the Kant–Ayer idea — and
therefore, I am pretty sure, cannot be had at all.

Suppose we set our sights a bit lower. Let us take a square
which represents not the whole of logical space, but just the
totality of possibilities with respect to one particular thing *a* at
one particular time T. The points on this square represent propositions of the form   Fa at T

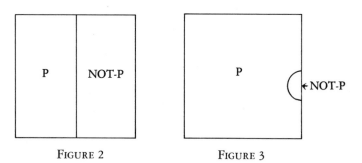

FIGURE 2   FIGURE 3

where 'F' stands for an absolutely specific statement about *a*'s state at that moment. A line across that square represents a pair of propositions which are complementary within the square, though they are not strictly contradictories because each of them entails the existence of *a* at T. For example, *John's right hand moves at T* and *John's right hand does not move at T*, where the square represents the possible conditions of John's body, or perhaps of John's right hand.

It will help me to explain what I'm doing — though it isn't theoretically required — if I thin out the propositions represented on the square by restricting the values of F to predicates concerning motion. That is, each point proposition is an absolutely specific statement about whether and how the object *a* is moving at time T.

That doesn't immediately help to show how a line can fall unevenly across a square, for it still leaves us with equal numbers of point propositions on the two sides of the line. Suppose we have the square for John's body at T, and take the complementary pair *John's right hand moves at T* and *John's right hand does not move at T*: there are infinitely many ways of being in movement with your right hand moving, and infinitely many ways of being in movement with your right hand not moving; and so once again the count will be the same on each side of the line. This difficulty will always arise except where one member of the complementary pair is itself a point proposition or a finite disjunction of them; but such propositions are of no interest to moral philosophy. So I shall ignore them, attending only to complementary pairs each of whose members corresponds to a region of the square rather than to a finite set of points. And so, as I said, it is no use counting point-propositions as a way of getting the line between a complementary pair to divide the square unequally.

As a start towards showing what *can* make a line fall unequally across a square, I shall first show how two mutually contrary propositions can be entitled to equal-sized regions of a square, i.e., can deserve to be represented as in Figure 4, rather than, for instance, as in Figure 5, or in some manner which implies nothing metrical. I suggest that the former of those diagrams is the right one if P and Q differ only in that they attribute *different but equally specific* modes of motion to the object *a*. Thus, if P says that at time T *a* is drifting in the direction NE (plus or minus 1.5°) at a speed of 5 m.p.h. (plus or minus 1 m.p.h), and Q says that at that time *a* is drifting SW at 7 m.p.h. (with the same plus-or-minus riders), then we have two equally specific attributions of movement to the same thing at the same time. I regard this as providing a good sense for the claim that the two propositions have the same amount of content and thus should be represented by equal-sized regions of the square.

It works with motion but won't work with everything. If, say, I had a square full of propositions about *a*'s colour at time T, I could assign propositions equal areas only if I knew whether, for instance, 'shocking pink' and 'royal blue' are equally specific; but I don't know that, and we have no objective basis on which to decide it. But because we have objective measures for space and time, we have them also for movement, and thus for degree of specificity of kinds of movement.

Now, at last, I can say how a complementary pair of propositions can divide the square unequally. Let P be any proposition represented by a region within the square. Let $P_1, P_2, \ldots, P_n$ be a set of propositions, pairwise contraries, each of which entails P;

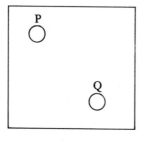

FIGURE 4

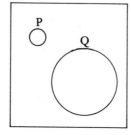

FIGURE 5

so they are propositions which state various different more specific ways in which P could be true. That can be represented as in Figure 6. Since those little propositions do not overlap with one another, and there are many of them contained within P's area, it follows that each has only a tiny fraction of the area occupied by P. Now it could be that one of them, P_k, occupies an area equal to that of P's complement, i.e., equal to that part of the square which lies outside P, as in Figure 7. This would be so if P_k and $\bar{P}$ attributed different but equally specific modes of motion to the same object at the same time; for that, by my criterion, would make them equally contentful; from which it would follow that $\bar{P}$ was enormously much more contentful than — that is, was represented by a very much smaller region than — P. From this I infer, now bringing in as much as I can save of the Kant–Ayer idea, that relative to this framework P is negative and $\bar{P}$ is not.

Now I shall set the scene for applying this to the notion of instrumentality. I take someone to be instrumental in the obtaining of a state of affairs S if S does indeed obtain, and if the person's conduct makes the difference either between S's being impossible and its being on the cards, or between its being less than inevitable and its being inevitable; that is, it either hoists S's probability up from 0 or hoists it up to 1. It could do both at once, making the whole difference between probability = 0 and probability = 1 for the state of affairs S; and to keep my exposition simple I shall confine myself to that strong kind of instru-

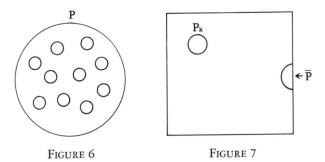

FIGURE 6   FIGURE 7

mentality. So I take it that in situation B, the vehicle is certainly all right if John doesn't dislodge the rock and certainly doomed if he does; and analogously with situation C.

If someone is in this sense instrumental in S's obtaining, his instrumentality can be simply represented on a logical-space square. We construct a square representing all the ways the person could have moved at the relevant time, with each point in it representing one completely specific, absolutely detailed proposition. There is a unique line across the square which has on one side of it all and only the propositions which satisfy the condition:

> If it were the case that . . . , S would obtain,

and on the other side of it all and only the ones satisfying the condition:

> If it were the case that . . . , S would not obtain.

For example, in situations B and C there is a line through John's possible-conduct square with all and only the vehicle-is-destroyed movements on one side and all and only the vehicle-survives ones on the other.

Now, I say that in situation B — where the vehicle is destroyed because John dislodges the rock — what makes John's instrumentality in the vehicle's destruction positive is the fact that the line between his vehicle-is-destroyed options and his vehicle-survives ones looks like that in Figure 8. That is, of all the ways

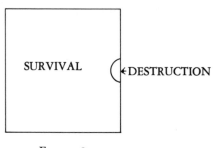

FIGURE 8

in which he could have moved, only a tiny proportion were such as to lead to the vehicle's destruction; virtually all of them would have had its survival as a consequence. In contrast to that, situation C looks like that in Figure 9. Here, almost any move John could have made would have had the vehicle's destruction as a consequence; only a tiny fragment of his possible-conduct space contains behavioural possibilities which would have resulted in the vehicle's surviving.

If you don't find this obvious, then here is a procedure which should convince you that I'm right about B; and then it will be a routine matter to adapt it to C as well. Consider the proposition *John dislodges the rock*, and think about the different physical ways he could do this: a few dozen pairwise contrary propositions would pretty well cover the possibilities, each of them identifying one fairly specific sort of movement which would get the rock dislodged. Thus, the region of the square containing the vehicle-is-destroyed propositions can be divided up into a few dozen still smaller regions, each associated with some specified kind of movement of one or more specified parts of John's body. Now, each of those little propositions can be paired off with what I'll call an 'echo' of it on the vehicle-survives side of the line — that is, with a proposition which has the same amount of content as it, and is indeed very like it except that its truth would not in the circumstances result in the vehicle's destruction. For instance, if on the vehicle-is-destroyed side we have a proposition attributing to John

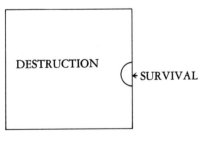

FIGURE 9

a kind of movement with his left foot, let its 'echo' be a proposition attributing to him a remarkably similar movement of that foot but with (say) the direction differing by just enough for this to be a movement which in the circumstances would not dislodge the rock and so would not doom the vehicle. In general, for each little proposition on the 'destroyed' side of the line, let its echo be one whose truth would make it look as though John were trying to dislodge the rock but had lost his sense of direction or his sense of timing or the like. Of course, the 'echo' propositions are to be pairwise contraries so that their regions don't overlap. So the drawing is like Figure 10. The pockmarks represent the echo propositions. Their combined area is the same as that of the vehicle-is-destroyed area; and it is perfectly obvious that they take up only a tiny proportion of the total vehicle-survives area. Each echo proposition attributes to John some movement which is physically rather like a rock-dislodging movement — now think of all the others which are not in the least like rock-dislodging movements!

That, then, is my case for saying that in B John is positively instrumental in the vehicle's being destroyed; and it is child's play to rerun the argument to get the conclusion that in C he is negatively instrumental in this. The facts about the use of the word 'not' (he *does* dislodge the rock, he *does not* interpose the rock) have nothing to do with it.

This, I submit, squares pretty well with the majority of our

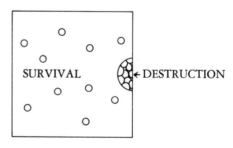

FIGURE 10

confident intuitions about whether someone's instrumentality is positive or negative — i.e., whether it is a case of 'because he did' or rather one of 'because he didn't'. It depends utterly on the concept of the possible *movements of a body*: that provides the objective measure of degree of specificity, which is needed for two contrary propositions to have the same amount of content, which is needed in turn for one proposition to have much less content than its complement in a given square.

The restriction to bodily movements does not, so far as I know, exclude any important kind of moral situation. In assuming that the options confronting the agent are all describable in terms of how he could move, I don't think I am leaving out anything that matters.

A point which used to be much stressed is that there is no simple match-up between kinds of movement and kinds of action. But I have no need to deny that. All I need is that, given the impersonal facts of a situation, a full enough account of how the agent moves will imply an account of what he does, i.e., of what actions he performs. It just doesn't matter for what I am doing that a kind of movement which is a rock-dislodgment in one setting might be a goal kick in another.

The emphasis on bodily movement could generate the accusation that although I have established *a* distinction between positive and negative instrumentality, it turns out to be a trivial affair and not what people ordinarily have in mind when they say, for instance, that sins of omission are not as bad, other things being equal, as sins of commission. That is a serious and important charge, which will be the topic of the last part of my second lecture. I have no time to go into it now.

Another objection which has been brought against my account, and which also involves the stress on bodily movement, holds against the account something which I think is one of its merits. I shall explain.

We are to classify a person's instrumentality in S's obtaining by looking at his possible conduct square to see how much of it is occupied by S kinds of movement and how much by non-S kinds. What about the possibility that he should make no movement at all?

In most actual situations, relative to most values of S, the person's remaining immobile would belong on the roomy side of the S/non-S line. For instance, in situation B where John dislodges the rock, if he had kept still that would have the same consequence, so far as the vehicle is concerned, as his doing any of the other things which did not get the rock dislodged. And in case C John's immobility would have been one of the many ways of not interposing the rock. In short, for most interesting values of S in most actual situations, stillness will be one way of being negatively instrumental.

But not quite always. We can construct a case where if the person stays quite still, S will inevitably ensue, whereas if he makes any movement at all non-S will certainly obtain.

Here is an example. Henry is in a sealed room where there is fine metallic dust suspended in the air. If Henry keeps utterly still for two minutes, some of the dust will settle; and if it does, some is bound to fall in such a position as to close a tiny electric circuit which . . . well, finish the story to suit your taste, but make it something big; and let's call its occurrence S. Thus, any movement from Henry, and S will not obtain; perfect immobility, and we shall get S.

I could keep my account of instrumentality silent about this case by confining it to ways of *moving* and not letting the proposition that Henry keeps still appear anywhere on his possible conduct square. Then he will not be 'instrumental' in my sense, because his ways of *moving* do not divide into non-empty S and non-S subsets, since all the ways he could move would have non-S as a consequence.

That tactic will not do. If my concept of instrumentality is to cover every sort of prima facie responsibility for upshots, then it must cover Henry's immobility in the situation where this makes him responsible for S. So I must allow the possible-conduct squares to cover every way of moving including the null way which consists in immobility.

What my account says about Henry, then, is that if he moves he is negatively instrumental in S's obtaining, whereas if he keeps still he is positively instrumental. Henry's immobility is the sole item on the S side of our line across his possible modes of motion; everything else lies on the non-S side; and so this is a case where stillness would be a positive instrumentality and any movement would be a negative one.

I do not dispute that if Henry keeps perfectly still, he *lets* the dust fall by not creating the currents which would *keep* it in the air; but that is just one of those results which distinguishes letting from negative instrumentality and makes me want to focus on the latter.

What is there to be said for my way of drawing the line? I contend that there is everything to be said for it — i.e., that one should not think of immobility as necessarily bracketed with non-doing, non-interference, etc., and my analysis helps to show why. Why indeed should anyone think otherwise? I can think of two possible sources for this belief.

1. Someone who is infected by the idea of intrinsically negative concrete actions might be led, as Bentham was, to think that immobility is a perfect paradigm of negativeness, so that if Henry gets a result by keeping quite still we must say that this is a negative instrumentality if anything is. The idea might be that in cases where the person does move, we can call his instrumentality 'negative' in a secondary sense, meaning that, relative to the upshot we are interested in, his movements had the same result as his immobility would have had; but where he actually is immobile we have primary negativeness in all its glory. But all of this is quite worthless because it relies on the notion of negativeness *de re*, negativeness as a monadic property of concrete actions and events.

2. Some people protest that, whatever you say about instrumentality, *Henry does not move* just undeniably is a negative proposition. If there were solid theoretic grounds for saying this, I should bow out gracefully: that is, I would still distinguish instrumentalities in terms of precisely the same distinction between propositions, only I would not name the latter distinction in terms of the word 'negative'. My concern, after all, is not with that one English word, but with a whole way of looking at some material — a way which I think is profitable, however it is worded.

Still, let us ask what the credentials are for this claim that *Henry does not move* is a negative proposition.

It is clear enough, I hope, that if we are considering only the possible conduct of Henry at time T, then *Henry moves at T* is on my account a negative proposition. (I mean by that that it is negative relative to that frame of reference, i.e., is negative as compared with the complementary proposition *Henry does not move at T*. My theory gives me no way of saying of any proposition that it is negative *sans phrase*.) If it seems to you insanely wrong to classify *Henry moves at T* as in any way negative, then look at it in this way. We have a square divided into tiny subregions, each representing some fairly specific way in which Henry could conduct himself with respect to motion or rest; and the proposition that Henry moves points to one tiny subregion and says *Not that one.*

What is to be said on the other side? I find no shortage of people on the other side, but a great dearth of arguments. Indeed, the only argument I have seen is one by Leibniz which so thoroughly fails as to constitute positive support for my view. It occurs in the *New Essays*, after Leibniz has quoted Locke's expressed doubts 'whether rest be any more a privation than motion', to which Leibniz responds: "I had never thought there could be any reason to doubt the privative nature of rest. All it involves is the denial of movement of the body, but it does not suffice for movement to deny rest: something else must be added to determine the degree of movement, since movement is essentially a matter of more or less whereas all states of rest are equal." But it is simply false that 'it does not suffice for movement to deny rest'. When a philosopher as good as Leibniz permits himself such a flatly false premise as that, this is evidence that he has got himself into an untenable position. On my theory of the matter, of course, he has produced the makings of an argument for classifying not 'x is at rest' but rather 'x is moving' as negative.

Before concluding, I want to throw a short bridge between this lecture and my next one.

The distinction which emerges from my analysis is obviously without moral significance. If someone is prima facie to blame for conduct which had a disastrous consequence, the blame could not conceivably be lessened *just* by the fact that most of his alternative ways of behaving would have had that same consequence. That much is obvious; but of course there is more to be said, and in my second lecture I shall say some of it.

If my positive/negative distinction lacks moral significance, I can show, using that as a premise, that there is no moral significance in any of its rivals either. In conclusion, I now present that argument as applied to the distinction between doing and letting happen, with special reference to killing and letting die.

First, let us set aside positive instrumentalities which are not killings, and negative ones which are not lettings die, because the relevant probabilities are too low. If my opening the gate at the railway crossing hoists your chance of being hit by a train from 0 to 10%, then if you are hit by a train I am positively instrumental in your dying, but I have not killed you. And if my not giving you a certain medicine raises from 0 to 10% your chance of dying this week, then if you do die this week I am negatively instrumental in this, but I have not let you die, even if I have the requisite knowledge, responsibility, and so on. These matters of probability are of great moral importance, but they cannot bring moral significance to the killing/letting-die distinction since they fall between killing and positive instrumentality in the same way as between letting die and negative instrumentality.

Next, we should set aside positive lettings die, such as letting a climber fall to his death by cutting his rope, or letting a terminal patient die by unplugging his respirator; and set aside negative killings, such as killing your baby by not feeding it. Of several reasons for setting these aside, the simplest is that in these cases the very same conduct is both a killing and a letting die; and so they cannot be in question when someone says that, other things being equal, killing is worse than letting die.

What remain to be considered are negative lettings die and positive killings. My argument on them runs as follows. My premise is that negative instrumentality in someone's dying is no better in itself than positive; and the desired conclusion is that letting someone die is no better in itself than killing him. To get from premise to conclusion I shall argue for two lemmas: that letting die is no better than the relevant negative instrumentality, and that the relevant positive instrumentality is no better than killing. Slide the premise in between those two and the conclusion rolls smoothly out.

Lettings die are negative instrumentalities marked off by special features which tend to increase moral weight and certainly do not lessen it. If I am negatively instrumental in a premature death, the addition of facts which imply that I *let* the person die will tend to make my culpability greater, not less; for they are facts such as that I had the relevant knowledge, had some responsibility in the matter, and so on.

So much for the first lemma. The second is more complicated.

Killings of the kind we now have to consider are a species of positive instrumentality in people's dying; they are marked off by two differentiae which must be examined separately.

One is the absence of an intervening agent. I can be positively instrumental in your dying by forcing or persuading someone else to kill you; but in that case I don't kill you. To get any moral leverage out of this differentia, one would have to argue that there is some exculpatory force in the plea 'I didn't kill her; I merely hired someone to kill her'; and I don't think anyone will be game to defend that.

The other differentia is the absence of intervening coincidences. This is less well known than the first one; it came clear to me only quite recently, in conversation with David Lewis; and I'll need a moment or two to expound it. Start with a positive instrumentality which is also a killing, though not a typical one. I kick a rock which starts a landslide which crashes into a lake and sends out a wave of water which drowns you as you stand in the stream fishing. In this case I kill you; and if my kicking the rock raised the chance of your dying in that way either from 0 or up to 1 then I am positively instrumental in your death. Now alter the story a bit: the kicked rock starts a landslide only because it happens to coincide with a crash of thunder; the wave goes your way only because it happens to reach the junction at one of the rare moments when the control gates are set to the left; and the water catches you only because by chance that is the moment when you are hastily wading across the stream. The fact that the causal route from my movement to your death involves several intervening coincidences seems to imply that in this case I do not kill you; yet if the probabilities are right I am positively instrumental in your dying when you do. If I am wrong about killing, then this second differentia doesn't exist and my argument was completed a minute ago. If I am right, then killing someone involves more than being positively instrumental in his dying — it requires also that the causal chain run through a stable and durable structure rather than depending on intervening coincidental events. But it seems clear that this difference in itself makes no moral difference. Of course if the causal chain involves coincidences, I may have been unable to predict that my conduct would have your dying as a consequence; and predictability is a highly morally significant matter. But it is a likely concomitant of the event-coincidence feature, and not of its essence. So there is nothing in this second differentia which supports the idea that killing is worse, other things being equal, than positive instrumentality in deaths.

Putting the bits together, then: letting die is no better than negative instrumentality, etc.; that is no better than positive instrumentality, etc.; that is no better than killing; and so it is a mistake to think that letting die is less grave, other things being equal, than killing is. The further exploration of that thesis will be the task of my second lecture.

II. OUR NEGLECT OF THE STARVING: IS IT AS BAD AS MURDER?

I hold the not altogether uncommon opinion that, other things being equal, it is no better to be negatively than to be positively instrumental in something bad's happening; your conduct is no worse if the calamity occurs because you did not do A than if it occurs because you did do B. What led me to this view, and is still my reason for it, is a certain account of what the difference between the two sorts of instrumentality amounts to when it is made clear and objective. I can also argue that if that difference lacks moral significance then so also do those between commission and omission, acting and refraining, causing and allowing or letting, and so on, except where these are used as vehicles for moral judgments already made.

But I am addressing myself directly to the positive/negative distinction and not to any of those others. If you think about letting people die, for instance, you will have to deal not only with negative instrumentality in deaths (as when someone is let die by not being fed), but also with positive instrumentality in people's not getting artificial life support (as when someone is let die by having his respirator disconnected). I cannot find that moral thinking is helped by bringing these very different matters together, as they are brought together by 'let'. Anyway, I am concerned with only one of them — i.e., with the line between poisoning and not feeding, or between disconnecting a respirator and not connecting it.

I believe that that distinction is morally neutral. I mean by this that it *never* makes a moral difference, the only alternative being that it *always* makes one. What is in question is the moral significance of a universal, and I don't see how the answer could be that sometimes it has significance and sometimes it doesn't. To claim moral significance for it is to imply that if something bad happens in consequence of how I behave, the fact that it happened because I did do B rather than because I did not do A is a reason for increased severity of moral judgment on my conduct — perhaps outweighed by other considerations, but still a *reason* for a certain moral conclusion. And reasons are essentially universal: what sometimes gives a reason for X always gives a reason for X.

You will easily think of counter-examples to that, but they will concern *derivative* reasons, whereas my topic is the thesis that the kind of instrumentality is a source of *basic* reasons for moral judgments. For example, if a state of affairs involves a person's being lonely and unhappy, that is a basic reason for judging it to be a bad one and would always be a reason for such a judgment. In contrast, if I were to stay up for half of tonight I would be tired tomorrow; that is a reason for my not staying up, but only because I am committed to a philosophical discussion tomorrow; so it is a derivative and not a basic reason, and in other circumstances it might well have no force or might even go the other way. With basic reasons — ones whose force does not depend upon particular contingencies — I stand by my claim that what is ever a reason is always one.

Some philosophers seem to take a position according to which the positive/negative distinction, though it does not *always* make a moral difference, *sometimes* does so in a manner which cannot be called derivative — a manner which does not involve its being the occasional vehicle of something else which does make a moral difference. The idea seems to be that positive/negative can *combine* with another item which is not itself morally significant to form a morally significant whole — as a chemical compound can have a property not possessed by any of its elements. That chemical analogy, however, is not a substitute for clear explanation, and I have never seen a version of this idea which is clear enough to be discussible. Until one is given, I must perforce drop it and focus on the clash between those who think that positive/negative always makes a moral difference and those who think that it never does.

That clash ought to be fairly easy to adjudicate, since either position could be established by just one example — find just one case where positive/negative does, unaided, contribute a moral difference, and you have established the moral significance of the distinction; find just one case where it contributes nothing, and you have established its insignificance. That *is* the theoretical situation; but in practice it doesn't help much, because it is so hard (on the one side) to be sure that an agreed moral difference *is* being contributed by positive/negative alone, or (on the other) to be sure that there really is no moral difference between the two options which differ only as positive to negative.

I shall say a good deal about the former kind of difficulty. But first I should mention the latter. Tooley and others have argued for the moral neutrality of the difference between positive and negative instrumentality by adducing particular cases of matched pairs of villainies: one man poisons his wife out of hatred and greed, another's wife takes poison by accident and, out of hatred and greed, he withholds the antidote; and we are invited to judge them to be morally on a level, and to infer that the difference between positive and negative instrumentality has no moral significance. The trouble with this is that when the seas of wickedness are running so high, we cannot possibly trust ourselves to detect every little drop of moral difference.

On the other hand, we can't use examples where there is

nothing moral at stake, for the question is about whether the difference in kind of instrumentality affects adverse moral judgments. We could avoid being distracted or dazzled by the intensity of moral concern by comparing a case where the door closes because I do push it with one where it closes because I do not pull it; but that is useless because it has no initial moral content for the positive/negative difference to work on. Later on I shall produce a pair of examples which I think will overcome both halves of this difficulty; but it is not my chief present purpose to convince you of the moral neutrality of the difference between positive and negative instrumentality, and if that were my purpose I would not try to achieve it through examples.

From here on, I shall assume the neutrality thesis, as I call it, and proceed with two tasks: to explain why the thesis might seem wrong even if it is not; and to apply it to the question of whether our negative instrumentality in the deaths of people who die because we do not save them, although we could, makes us no better than murderers.

If the answer comes up that we are as bad as murderers, that will convince most of you that the neutrality thesis is wrong. It would worry me too; but I would not count it as decisive, for I do not offer the neutrality thesis as reconcilable with all the plain man's moral convictions. Just because I have an argument for it, I am prepared to let it modify my moral views and to urge you to let it modify yours.

Still, a sufficiently intolerable theorem refutes a theory, and the conclusion that we are no better than murderers in respect of starving Cambodians might be such a theorem. Something which would *certainly* refute the neutrality thesis — I think everyone thinks — would be its permitting a surgeon to kill one healthy person in order to get the organs needed for organ transplants to save five people who would otherwise die. Since this is a choice between positive instrumentality in one death and negative in five, and since five are worse than one, must we be judging that positive instrumentality in a death is worse than negative? Judith Thomson has shown that the answer is No. She compared that transplant case with one where a runaway trolley is hurtling down a hillside on a track leading to a point where it will kill five people unless someone throws a switch which will divert it to a place where it will kill only one person, who would otherwise have been safe. This is also a choice between positive instrumentality in one death and negative in five: *modulo* the positive/negative distinction it is indiscernible from the transplant case; yet we judge it very differently.

The moral is that if you want to refute the neutrality thesis by producing a case where an undeniable moral difference must be attributed to a moral asymmetry in positive/negative, make sure that the difference doesn't come from something else instead. If your moral response to the trolley problem differs in direction, or even just in intensity, from your response to the transplant case, then the latter must have special features to which you are giving moral weight, and positive/negative may have nothing to do with your attitude.

The biggest morally significant difference which tends to accompany the positive/negative difference has to do with amount of *cost*, taking this to cover everything which might make a given item of conduct unattractive to the person concerned: pain, difficulty, expensiveness, boringness.

The basic notion here is that of someone's *incurring cost*. A person is incurring a greater or lesser cost at a given time depending upon how far what he is then doing is painful or expensive or otherwise unattractive to him. Now, it could not be true that one tends to incur greater cost in positive instrumentalities than in negative; for at any moment when I am positively instrumental in the obtaining of one state of affairs I am negatively instrumental in the obtaining of others. For example, at the very moment when my name goes onto a bit of paper because I do write it, the door slams because I do not hold it, water stays in a glass because I do not spill it, and so on.

But we can also speak of a *task* as costly, meaning that it cannot be carried out without incurring cost. I here take 'tasks' to include plans, projects, schemes, obedience to orders and laws and rules, and so on. And tasks, unlike particular items of conduct, *can* be divided into positive and negative: if I am ordered to write my name on a bit of paper, my task is positive; if I am ordered not to grab the door, my task is negative. And positive tasks tend to be costlier than negative ones.

It is a familiar point: we all know that rules or orders which tell us not to do certain things are in general easier to obey than ones telling us what to do. And we can understand a little better why this is so by invoking my analysis of the difference between the two sorts of instrumentality. The crux is that the proposition that someone *does* do A puts his behaviour within a quite small part of the range of all the modes of conduct which are open to him at the relevant time, while the proposition that he *does not* do A puts his conduct outside such a relatively small area and into the large remainder. The picture is as shown in Figure 11, with the square representing the logical space of his possible modes of conduct, and — for instance — *He does hold the door* being represented by the tiny bit while *He does not hold the door* is represented by the rest. To tackle a positive task is to try to squeeze your behaviour into a designated small area, and there is some chance that you cannot do that without incurring some kind of cost — i.e., that every way of behaving which lies in that area

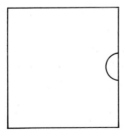

FIGURE 11

is painful or difficult or morally objectionable or whatever. On the other hand, a negative task requires you only to keep your conduct out of a certain small area and within the large remainder; and the latter's size increases the chances that you can stay within it somehow without incurring much cost. Compare being banished to Liechtenstein with being banished from Liechtenstein.

The difference in cost is quite distinct from the difference in kind of instrumentality, even if the two tend strongly to be correlated. So any views you hold about the basic morality of positive versus negative should be independent of your views about the basic morality of costs and benefits. If I can be instrumental in some good's coming to someone else, the cost to me may be too high for that amount of benefit — and perhaps too high for any amount of benefit — and this is a judgment that may be made without reference to what kind of instrumentality is involved. That is why it is wrong to say, as one writer has, that the neutrality thesis 'leads straight to an ethic so strenuous that it might give pause even to a philosophical John the Baptist.' That implies that someone who accepts the neutrality thesis must be blind to facts about cost-benefit ratios; and that is nonsense. Anyone is entitled to hold that a given cost is too high, either absolutely or for a given benefit; there is no impediment to this from the neutrality thesis.

My own practical thinking about cost-benefit ratios reflects my having an agent-relative morality: in weighing the pros and cons of a possible line of conduct, I hold myself entitled to give extra weight to a cost or benefit which is to accrue to someone with a special relation to me. The most special relation of all is identity — I am entitled to put my thumb on the moral scales on behalf of my own interests — but I extend this to my offspring, my parents, my closest friends, and so on. This is not to offer as a moral 'principle' something which refers to me in particular. What I have is a genuinely universal principle, in the manner of Kant or Hare, which allows each person to bias the scales in favour of his own near and dear. It does not name anyone, but quantifies over everyone.

I believe that most of us have some such principle, but we probably differ a good deal in our views about which relations justify how much tilting of the moral scales, and indeed about which justify any amount of tilt — except that we will agree that identity is one of them. Without such a principle, there is no bearable answer to the question I want to put before us, namely: Does the neutrality thesis imply that we are morally no better than murderers because of our negative instrumentalities in the deaths of starving people in the third world? If we cannot use the excuse that we are only letting them die, not killing them, what excuse have we? Precious little excuse, it seems, unless we are morally entitled to tilt the moral scales on behalf of ourselves and our near and dear.

In estimating costs and benefits, I think with Bernard Williams that we should emphasise a person's 'commitments' — those long-term projects and undertakings which give his life its shape and point. In estimating the cost to someone of relinquishing some activity, for instance, we should ask not only how much good it does and how much he enjoys it, but how far it is what his life is *about*, how far it is what makes sense of him as a person with a history. This, for me as a deliberating agent, is a thought not only about *my commitments* but about *commitments*: if some plan of mine threatens not merely the comforts and pleasures of another person but the lifelong activities to which he is principally devoted, that ought to have great weight with me. My own commitments weigh more with me than his do, but only because of that general slope towards myself which also makes my pleasures count with me more than his do. Williams seems to hold that the slope is steeper with commitments than with other valuables, perhaps holding that they are not valuables at all but something deeper; but I see no reason to agree with him on either point.

The stress on commitments, incidentally, cuts across the line between positive and negative instrumentalities. One tends to think of one's life-plans as pulling one away from positive instrumentalities, i.e., as excuses for negative ones: it is because of my devotion to philosophy that I do not take up farming, say. But they can also pull one away from negative instrumentalities, i.e., serve as excuses for positive ones: if some deeply cherished long-term project of mine requires me to act so as positively to cause harm to others, then a general stress on the importance of such projects will provide some excuse for my conduct. According to the neutrality thesis, if I can be excused for not bringing someone a benefit because to do so would jeopardise my career, then other things being equal I should also be excused for positively preventing his getting the benefit if that was needed to fend off a threat to my career. Near the end of the first chapter of *Walden*, Thoreau says: 'Probably, I should not consciously and deliberately forsake my particular calling to do the good which society demands of me, to save the universe from annihilation', thus representing himself as infinitely committed to his 'particular calling'. He won't drop it in order to spend time and energy saving the universe instead; but if his mind is clear he should also refuse to forsake his project if it is itself the universe-destroyer.

These remarks are not an argument for the neutrality thesis. They are merely a warning against thinking that by stressing the importance of deep projects and commitments you can make trouble for that thesis. The view that projects are morally crucial can be held in a form which is symmetrical with respect to the difference between positive and negative instrumentality, or in a form which is not. If you want it in the asymmetrical form you must stand up for positive/negative asymmetry as a distinct moral doctrine: you can't derive it from an emphasis on projects.

Summing up so far: if we are excusable for our relative neglect of the needy, it must be because we are entitled to give that much special weight to our own interests and those of our near and dear — with 'interest' so construed as to put great weight on something like Williams' notion of a commitment or lifelong project.

The conclusion I have so far come to is uncomfortable. Even if I may tilt the moral scales in my own behalf, does this entitlement go as far as the premature deaths of other people? And do murderers have it too? Am I saying that we are as bad as murderers, but that they are better than they are made out to be? No, there is more to be said. The comparison between not giving food to someone and shooting him dead — with which adherents of the neutrality thesis are often triumphantly confronted — raises too many questions at once. It cannot be usefully discussed without more clearing of the undergrowth; and in the rest of this lecture I shall do some of the clearing. I shall not get right back to the comparison between ourselves and murderers, but I hope to make that comparison easier to think about accurately.

The ensuing discussion will have another motivation which I now explain. I shall later present a pair of cases which differ as positive to negative and in no other way that matters, in the hope that you will find them to be morally on a par. Really, each is a continuum of cases, with a sliding ratio between cost to the agent and benefit to the patient. For some cost-benefit slopes you will condemn the conduct on both sides; for others you will approve it on both sides; and you may agree that the break-even point comes at about the same place on each side of the positive/ negative divide.

If my cases are to carry conviction, I must ensure that apart from positive/negative they do not differ in any way which might make you think — rightly or wrongly — that there is a morally significant difference between them. I shall discuss four such items: they have occurred to me while thinking about how we can live with our neglect of needy people, and in presenting them I am continuing that discussion as well as preparing for my examples.

One concerns the fact that our moral thinking about costs and benefits is affected by whether a cost consists in a lowering in one's level of welfare or merely in its not rising when it might have; and whether a benefit is an increase in one's welfare level or merely a non-lowering of it when it might have gone down. In contemplating a cost to me as the price of a benefit to you, it might make a difference — independently of what the amounts are — if my cost is a loss while yours is a gain, rather than, for instance, my cost being a non-gain while your benefit is a non-loss. This matter is richly present, all tangled with the difference between positive and negative instrumentality, in the language of 'harm' and 'help'. But I cannot go into that now.

This matter cannot help us to defend our neglect of the third world needy. It *might* do so if we could help only by lowering our own welfare level, and if the benefit would always be a raising of theirs, though even that would not be impressive if the levels were far enough apart to begin with. Anyway, it is not true, for many countries need first the arresting of a steady downward slide in their level of welfare. And at our end, some of us become richer as the years go by, so we could incur further costs without reducing our level of well-being, merely holding it steady when it might have risen.

The second of my four considerations concerns *rights*. If I kill a child in Cambodia, its right to life is violated, but if I let it die — do not save its life with a gift of food — I do not violate any of its rights. Or so it is usually maintained. Sometimes very bad arguments are given for this, but the conclusion is broadly correct. The concept of a moral right has a considerable positive/ negative asymmetry: my right to speak is a right not to be silenced, not a right to have my laryngitis cured; my right to freedom is a right not to be imprisoned, not a right to be rescued from an underground cave; and so on. But this does not automatically refute the neutrality thesis, and so it doesn't help with our problem. If we combine the neutrality thesis with the view that the concept of a moral right is asymmetrical as between positive and negative, what follows is not a contradiction, but just the conclusion that corresponding to any positive violation of a right there is a possible negative instrumentality which, though it would not *be* the violating of a right, would *be just as bad as* the violating of a right.

That shows that in this area the concept of moral rights is not an irresistible force. But is it perhaps an immovable object? Suppose that someone contends that to kill a person is to violate his right to life, whereas to let him die is neither to violate his right to life nor to do anything as bad as that; what can I say in reply? Really, only what I have already said in my argument for the moral neutrality of the difference between killing and letting die. Someone who holds that there is a morally significant difference between rights-violations and their negative analogues ought, I contend, to show what is wrong with my argument to the contrary — I mean the argument given in my first lecture. If he won't do that, that may be because he agrees that positive/negative does not *always* make a moral difference, but holds that it can combine with other morally inert elements to form a morally significant compound, and that one such compound is the concept of a moral right. It would be foolish of me to say in advance that nothing along these lines can be made to work; we can only wait until it has been presented in enough detail for discussion of it to be profitable.

The rights theorist might reply that he has no intention of — and sees no need for — a general theory about how moral significance can emerge from conceptual combinations of morally inert elements. He would then presumably be taking his stand on strong moral intuitions which he was prepared to retain, without supporting theory, in the face of opposing arguments. Between such an opponent and myself there is a fundamental disagreement about how moral philosophy should be done — a disagreement which I mentioned early in my first lecture and shall return to late in my third. At this point, there is no time to do anything except salute and pass on.

That is all I want to say about rights.

In trying to make a moral comparison between positive and negative instrumentality, one runs into such facts as this. If I kill someone, e.g., by poisoning him, there is a finger pointing from me to him as the person I kill, and a finger pointing from him to me as the person who kills him. Those seem to be two large differences between this and my negative instrumentality in the deaths of people in Chad; and that pair of differences constitutes the third and fourth of my four considerations.

It seems natural to think that when someone dies in Chad, there is no finger pointing straight at me: he would have lived if I had helped him, *or* you had, *or* you *or* he *or* she had; so that my role is disjunctive in some way which reduces my responsibility.

Although that is a natural line of thought, it is just wrong. It is true that he would have lived if it had been the case that

I helped him *or* you helped him;

but now turn that right-side out, and make it say why he died, namely because

I did not help him *and* you did not help him.

The crucial statement about our negative instrumentalities is conjunctive: we were in this together, each doing his negative bit; so there *is* a finger pointing straight at me. There is also one pointing straight at you, but that does not lessen my responsibility. At any rate, we don't ordinarily think it does, for instance when there is a conjunction of positive instrumentalities, as when one 'provo' plants the bomb and a second detonates it. Morally speaking, there is no safety in numbers.

A simple pair of examples might help. Common to both is an electric circuit interrupted by ten switches, each controlled by a different person who has a prudential reason for wanting his switch to be closed as much as possible. The circuit is hooked to an infernal device, so that if current flows through it an atrocity will occur. The source of the current is a dynamo over which none of the people has any control. The story then splits into two.

1. The dynamo is running, and all the switches are open. If the atrocity occurs in this case, it is because *everybody closes his switch*, i.e., because of a conjunction of positive facts about behaviour.

2. In the second version, the dynamo is about to start, and all the switches are closed. If the atrocity occurs in this case, it is because *nobody opens his switch*, i.e., because of a conjunction of negative facts about conduct.

If you are one of the ten people in case 2, you may feel that the finger of blame should not be pointed straight at you; but I contend that there are ten fingers of blame, one of which is all for you, just as in situation 1, where this is more obviously the case.

Even if you grant all this, you may wonder whether I ought to say that you are 'instrumental' in the atrocity's happening, in either of the two cases. Well, I take a person to be 'instrumental' in something's happening if his conduct put it on the cards (made the difference between probability$=0$ and probability>0), or made it inevitable (made the difference between probability<1 and probability$=1$). So in the case where you do not open your switch, that fact about your conduct makes the difference between there being no chance that the atrocity will occur and there being some chance. Of many changes that can be rung on this theme, I will mention only one, namely the strong kind of instrumentality in which a person's conduct makes the whole difference between probability$=0$ and probability$=1$ for the upshot in question. The killing of a person by shooting him might be like that — an instant raising from 0 to 1 of the probability that he will die in the next few minutes — but that is not the special prerogative of positive instrumentalities. It is easy to think up negative cases which have that same feature — e.g., my second electric story in a version where there is only one switch. But that is all by the way.

Summing up this part of the discussion, then: I hold that there is nothing morally diminishing to be said about the nature of the finger pointing towards me from a person in Chad who died when I could have saved him. Others too could have saved him, but what of that?

I now come to the last of my four considerations — the tricky matter of the finger pointing from me to the victim. For obvious reasons, I want to fix our attention on really bad things which I could have prevented. That compels me to think — as indeed I have in this talk so far — in terms of individual people whom I could have helped, especially ones whose early deaths I could have prevented.

So I do not wish to discuss my failure to give more help to needy people by contributing to programmes which would then spread my benefits as widely as possible, or my failure to institute a wide-ranging programme funded by me alone. I worked out that if I spent $1000 a month on Bangladesh, and there was no wastage or theft or administrative costs, I could, unaided, bring to every citizen of Bangladesh nearly one grain of rice a month. That's the sort of thing I don't want to discuss, because it doesn't lend itself to the sort of comparison I am trying to conduct.

So as not to lose sight of the comparison between killing and letting die, I shall focus on individual deaths which I could have prevented. In respect of each of these, my conduct made at least this much difference to whether the person died then or not: my possible ways of behaving divided into two classes, those on the 'He may die this month' side of the line and those on the 'He will live out the month' side, and I kept my conduct on the former side, giving him a probability >0 of dying in the course of the month, whereas I could have so behaved as to lower that probability pretty well to 0. And my conduct may sometimes have made the whole difference between probability $=0$ and probability $=1$.

For me to have saved all those people would have required enormous wealth, or absolute political power, or a capacity for irresistible moral persuasion. Lacking these, I could not have saved all the people. That they *all* died last year *is* a consequence of my behaviour; but that *most* of them died last year *is not*, because it was not in my power to alter that. So, one might say, each of those deaths was a disjunctive consequence of my behaviour.

It is easy for negative instrumentalities to have disjunctive consequences — states of affairs belonging to some morally homogeneous class of which one could have prevented any one but could not have prevented all. But let us be careful how the facts are expressed. In a chapter which I admire, Jonathan Glover has written: 'One difference between acts and omissions that is of some moral importance [is that] actions take time, while omissions do not. There is no end to the list of a person's omissions, while the actions he has time for during his life are limited. However heroic he is, he cannot do all the good things which, ignoring pressure of time, would be in his power.' * That is wrong. My omission to raise my arm during the past hour has taken me exactly an hour; my omission to climb Mount Everest will take me a lifetime. Also, when a number of good things are severally but not jointly in my power, the obstacle is not always one of time. It could instead be that each would require all my money, however much that might be, or that one would require me to die a virgin while the other would require me to father seven children — the obstacle to doing both of those not being a temporal one. The real reason why omissions are so numerous is that one engages in so many of them all at once: they stretch out through time just as commissions do, but they can be piled ever so much higher.

As I was saying, it often happens that we could have done

---

* Jonathan Glover, *Causing Death and Saving Lives* (New York: Penguin Books, 1977).

any one of some set of things but could not have done them all. On the positive side of the line, disjunctive consequences seem not to occur except in cases which are contrived and not interesting. I am going to assume that the disjunctive-consequence idea properly belongs only on the negative side of the line.

Since there are people of whom I could help any but not all, the question arises: 'Whom am I to help?' If it cannot be all, there must be selection. And, rightly or wrongly, we care about how the selection is made: we resist letting our benefits go arbitrarily to one person or group rather than to another. I suggest that this explains why it is sometimes said that one is more strongly obliged to help 'a starving person whom one meets on the street' than to help 'a starving person in a distant land' or — as I have heard a philosopher argue — more strongly obliged to help someone known by acquaintance than someone whom one knows only by description. Each of these opinions has strenuous implications for the moral effects of, say, a brief stopover in Bombay. What really underlies them, I suggest, is the idea that my obligation to help someone in need depends in part on why I am to consider him in particular as a recipient of my help. Granted that he is not related to me by kinship, friendship, or the like, my response to his need will depend in part upon whether it is laid before me by a natural, uncontrived course of events, or whether instead it is before me because I have — or some relief agency has — arbitrarily selected this from a large number of morally equivalent cases. In the former case, his need will press in on me much more strongly than in the latter.

Why are we like this? Perhaps it has something to do with how things are put to us by our consciences. The conscience is a considerably imaginative faculty, at least in some of us; our victims can visit us in the night, so to speak, filing past with promises to meet us at Philippi. The parade may be a long one; but it cannot be a disjunctive one, with each fist being shaken on the condition that the others are not; and so if the deaths of my victims are all disjunctive consequences of my neglect, there is no parade; and this may help me to sleep soundly. You may find this disgraceful; or you may think — as I am inclined to — that it reflects something so deep in our natures that we had best accept it, align ourselves with it, build it into our moralities. But my immediate point is just that this *is* how we are, and that is a fact which I cannot ignore in constructing my promised pair of illus-trative cases.

Here is the negative instrumentality case. There is a village in southern Africa which is about to lose its water as a result of damming operations higher up the river. The lives of the villagers will now be much worse unless they get a well: this will require capital for equipment and drilling, and a good annual sum for maintenance. All of this could be provided by 10% of my income from now until I retire; and I know that if I did make this sacri-fice it really would bring durable benefit to the villagers, with few bad side effects. Furthermore, the village's needs have come to my attention in an unarbitrary manner: while engaged in ethological field work, I stayed in the area for long enough to become fully acquainted with the village's plight and the attempts that had been made to remedy it, though I formed no friendships with the villagers. I am rightly sure that if I don't provide the needed help, nobody will. Thus, if I don't give over my money, I am nega-tively instrumental in the village's downward slide.

The positive instrumentality story has the same village, with the same needs and dangers, but my relation to them is different. In this story I am threatened with a 10% loss of income, though I can make up for it by pressing my claim to a trust fund which would bring me level again. If I do press my claim I shall suc-ceed; if I don't press it, then the fund will go to provide and maintain a well for the village; and if the village does not get that money it will not get any. If I launch my lawsuit, then, I am posi-tively instrumental in the village's downward slide.

In each story, up/down works in the same way — the cost to

me is a going down, the benefit to them would be a not going
down. In each there will be few enough beneficiaries that each
would benefit appreciably from the proposed conduct, and there
is evidence that no incidental mischief would be done by it. In
each, there is an unarbitrary, natural, uncontrived reason why I
should be concerned with benefit to these people rather than to
any others; that is the finger pointing from me to them.

What about the finger pointing from them to me? In the positive case there is one, because it is *my* action (not someone else's)
which blocks the money from going to them, while in the negative case nothing picks out me (not someone else) as *the* one who
let them down. It would be different — you might think — if
nobody else *could* provide the particular help they needed. It
would indeed make a difference, for in that case only one finger
would point; but in the story as I have told it, there is a finger
pointing at me, and I have argued that it doesn't affect *my* moral
situation if there are also fingers pointing at others. So long as I
am sure that nobody else *will* help the village, why should it
matter whether I think that nobody else *can*? Anyway, the finger
pointing at me is different from most, and perhaps all, the fingers
pointing from the village towards other potential benefactors:
the very same circumstances which make these villagers a special
case for me make me a special case for them. Looking from the
standpoint of my resources at the world of need, this village is
picked out by the fact that an intimate knowledge of its needs has
naturally come my way. Looking from the standpoint of the
village's need at the world of potential benefactors, I am picked
out by that very same fact.

The stories can be further detailed in various ways, yielding
cost-benefit slopes of varying degrees of steepness. Perhaps my
loss of income would change the direction of my life and my
dominant activities; perhaps there would be a reduction in comfort, but nothing worse than that; or . . . and so on. And there
is a similar scale on which we can adjust how bad life would be

for the villagers without the well and how good it would be with it.

Try the stories out for yourself, adjusting those parameters, first in one way and then in another, though always in the same way for each. You may find that your moral response is about the same to each member of any given positive–negative pair — that a cost-benefit slope which makes the lawsuit disgraceful makes not handing over the money disgraceful, and that one which makes it permissible for me to keep my money to myself also permits me to press my claim to the trust fund.

To the extent that you respond in that way, this is evidence that your own moral thinking already embodies the neutrality thesis, even if you thought it didn't. I have constructed this pair of cases through a plodding attempt to eliminate every difference that might be thought morally significant except for that between positive and negative instrumentality. When that at last stands alone — not in a drenching downpour of moral disapproval as in Tooley's cases, and not in stories which are too skimpy for moral thought to get any grip on them — it doesn't look morally significant, does it?

But I am not finished, because there is a grave difficulty about this whole line of argument. Suppose that I replace the second story by one in which I have given my accountant full power of attorney, and I learn that through a misunderstanding he thinks it is right for him to sign away 10% of my income to be sent to the village for its well; and I 'phone him up and tell him not to do that. In the comparison of that with the first member of the pair, in which I am handling my own money and I merely do not send the money to the village, I take it that no one thinks that there is the faintest moral significance in the difference between the two. But I do not produce this pair of cases in triumph: the victory comes so easily that one must suspect that the point has somehow been lost.

You might think that that pair of cases would be all right

except that the positive/negative difference is drowned, as it were, by the presence of the overpowering fact that in each case the money is *mine.* I don't want to explore that suggestion: ownership involves rights, and rights — I unfashionably think — are best avoided when one is doing fundamental moral philosophy. Anyway, it is easy to change the examples so that, although they still exhibit the trivial-seeming positive/negative contrast which I'm now talking about, they involve money which is not mine, though I can control who gets it. I shall not go into this in detail, and shall stay with the trivial-seeming pair of examples which is now before us.

I had better admit right away that I do regard these 'trivial' examples as establishing the neutrality thesis. I avoided them at first because I wanted to give you examples which would inspire more confidence; but I do in fact regard the trivial examples as constituting a perfectly good challenge to anyone who thinks there is moral significance in the difference between 'because he did' and 'because he didn't'. Still, I am not being truculent about this, because of course I still have a problem. I am unworried by the person who says that sometimes positive/negative does provide a basic reason for a moral discrimination while sometimes it doesn't, since that is a conceptual mistake about the nature of basic reasons. But I must take seriously the person who says that these trivial examples merely show that I have not been talking about the same positive/negative line as do those I have set myself against. Developing this idea, it could be said that in the 'trivial' pair what I do in each case is *not give* my money to the village, which is a negative fact about my conduct even if my way of *not giving* the money is to *tell* my accountant not to give it.

This brings me to the crux, which is the need for some objective basis on which to draw the positive/negative line. Of course it cannot be done just according to whether the relevant sentences contain a word like 'not', for that yields no single line through the cases: compare 'He did stay home' with 'He did not go out'. My account of the difference, as I indicated earlier, rests on the idea of a line which cuts very unequally through all the things the person could have done; but that points to the need for a metric for the area of logical space that the line is cutting through — some way of counting 'kinds of things he could be doing' which will let us say that there are far more of them on one side of the line than on the other. My solution to that, in terms of which I do all my thinking about these matters, is earthily physical: I go by the different equally specific ways in which the person could move his body. Most normal intuitions about whether a fact about someone's conduct is positive or negative — whether it is really a 'he did' or a 'he didn't' — square pretty well with this movement-of-body criterion. For example, if my accountant is going to sign away my money, the ways I could prevent him can be divided into a relatively small number of equally specific kinds of movement with my pen or larynx; each of those could be mapped off against an equally specific kind of bodily movement which would not stop the money from being signed over; and with all those mappings completed there would still remain, unmapped, the vast majority of ways in which I could have moved at that time. That is the force of saying that in stopping him from signing the money I am doing one of the relatively few things I could do which would have that effect; whereas if I do not stop him, I am doing one of the vast majority of things I could do which would have the money's being signed away as a consequence. And it is what underlies my judgment that if I stop him I am positively instrumental in the money's staying with me and thus in the village's downward slide. In the other member of that pair, where my accountant is not involved, a similar argument shows that if I do not sign away my money I am negatively instrumental in the village's downward slide: this is because most of the movements I could make would not get the money headed away from me and towards them. That is why the pair do illustrate the difference between positive and negative instrumentality in the village's downward slide.

Now, someone who finds that pair of cases trivial, and maintains that whether it is a matter of my not signing, or of my forbidding my accountant to sign, the dominant fact each time is the negative one that I do not so conduct myself that the money gets to the village — someone who says *that* owes us his account of how he is drawing the line between positive and negative instrumentality, or between act and omission, or between acting and refraining, or whatever. How can he do that?

His best chance seems to be through some variant on my idea of an uneven cut through the kinds of things I could do. He might say that what matters is the range of things I could do with regard to the money, and that these divide into such equal-sized kinds as investing it in bonds, spending it on pleasures of the flesh, giving it to my children, spending it on a swimming pool for myself, donating it to Oxfam, and giving it to that village in southern Africa. On this account of the matter, giving it to the village would just be *so conducting myself that it gets to the village*, with no special attention being paid to what physical movements are needed for this to happen, and thus with no regard to whether it would be a matter of my signing a document or rather of my not blocking my accountant's signing. I imagine that you find that an intuitively natural view of the matter; so do I. But what are our intuitions based on? What criteria guide our decision that 'so behaving that the money goes to the village' is to count as one kind of conduct, on a par with such other single kinds as 'so behaving that the money is invested in stocks in my name', and 'so behaving that the money buys me a swimming pool' and so on?

I have been unable to find any which do not themselves rest on prior moral judgments. The only positive/negative line I can find which is not defined in partly evaluative terms, and which rests on something deeper than sentences, is mine in terms of kinds of bodily movement. But others may be forthcoming. Or it may be counter-argued that the place of positive/negative in our moral thinking, though important, does not require that it have deep roots in the objective world. I don't deceive myself that this work of mine is the end of anything; but I hope it may help to start something.

III. INTENDED AS A MEANS

In this lecture I shall exhibit some difficulties about a certain distinction which is thought important by many moralists — namely that between what you intend to come about as a means to your end and what you do not intend although you foresee that it will come about as a by-product of your means to your end. This has a role in most defences of the Doctrine of Double Effect, and is one source for the view that terror bombing is never permissible though tactical bombing may sometimes be — i.e., that it is never right to kill civilians as a means to demoralizing the enemy country, though it may sometimes be right to destroy a munitions factory as a means to reducing the enemy's military strength, knowing that the raid will also kill civilians. In the former case — so the story goes — the civilian deaths are intended as a means; in the latter they are not intended but merely foreseen as an inevitable by-product of the means; and that is supposed to make a moral difference, even if the probabilities are the same, the number of civilian deaths the same, and so on.

First, let us look at two kinds of causal structure:

1. movement ———→ means (bad) ————→ end (good)
2. movement ———→ means (neutral) ——→ end (good)
   ————→ by-product (bad)

The item on the left is the movement the person makes — the 'basic action' whose upshots are in question. The other terms name particular events, and I add evaluations of them as a reminder of why these structures are supposed to be of moral interest.

In helping myself to that pair of diagrams, I am pretending to know more than I do about the identity of events; but I shall steer clear of problems about that by taking only examples which the diagrams do uncontroversially depict.

Some moralists say that a type 1 situation is worse than a type 2 one, but they are hard put to it to give reasons for this. A vague impression of reasons is sometimes conveyed by saying that in type 1 situations the bad is 'directly' produced while in type 2 ones it is not; but there is no good sense in which that is true. A type 2 case must admittedly have at least one event between the basic action and the bad event; but a type 1 case could also have an intermediate event, or a dozen of them for that matter. There is no essential difference between the two types in respect of what leads up to the bad event: the essential difference is in what flows from it; and it seems absurd to express that difference by saying that in one case but not the other the production of the bad event is 'direct'. Anyway, think for a moment about the claim that the tactical bomber in dropping live bombs onto the heads of the civilians does not 'directly' kill them!

A more usual position amongst those who morally contrast the two types of situation is not that type 1 is inherently worse than type 2 but that it is worse to intend to bring about a type 1 situation than to intend to bring about a type 2 one. That view about intentions is my chief topic in this lecture; but first I want to say two things about this use of it — that is, about the position of someone who forbids terror bombing but not tactical bombing because of an underlying judgment about the corresponding intentions.

My first remark is that this is a much odder position than is commonly recognized As a rule, if it is worse to intend to bring about X than to intend to bring about Y, that is because X is worse than Y; but here the moral difference is supposed to be introduced by the intention, rather than existing at the intention level only because of a difference at the level of events in the

world. Still, this is only an oddity, not an absurdity; and I shall
say no more about it.

My second remark is a warning against a misunderstanding.
The moral position we are confronted with has two elements. One
is a prohibitory rule which, for certain sorts of good and bad,
forbids us to produce the good by means of the bad but does not
forbid us to produce it by means which also produce the bad. The
other element is the moral judgment that it is worse to intend to
produce the bad as a means to the good than to foresee that the
bad will happen as a by-product of your means to the good. That
judgment is supposed to help justify the scope of the prohibitory
rule, but I do not take it as being, itself, such a rule. That is, I
do not see the position we are considering as including a rule
which forbids us to intend certain things.

In my opinion, it is a mistake to think of first-order morality —
morality for the guidance of deliberating agents — as making any
use of the concept of the deliberator's future intentions. The
morality I consult as a guide to my conduct does also guide my
intentions, but not by telling me what I may or may not intend.
It speaks to me of what I may or may not do, and of what are or
are not good reasons for various kinds of action; and in that way
it guides my intentions without speaking to me about them.

The concept of intention has a role in second-order morality,
i.e., in guiding judgments on people in respect of past actions.
How much I blame someone depends in part on his intentions in
acting; and if it is I who am in the dock then it is my intentions
that I must consider. But they are my past intentions, and I treat
them as external objects of judgment like anyone else's. Nothing
in this is remotely like consulting a moral rule which forbids me
to have such and such an intention.

Some moralists have been quite unclear about this. I have presented the view that a certain prohibitory rule is partly justified
by a moral fact about intentions, this being the best I can do for
the means–ends part of the Doctrine of Double Effect. But that

may be too charitable to some adherents of that doctrine. Some of them, some of the time, write as though what were prohibited is the having of that kind of intention, i.e., as though they gave the concept of intention a place in first-order morality. One consequence of that mistake will be mentioned later on, but the mistake as a whole is not something I can go into here.

My central concern, as I said, is with the thesis that it is worse to intend to produce something bad, even if only as a means to something good, than it is to foresee that the bad will result as a by-product of one's means to the good. I am interested in this only if it is maintained even when the degrees of good and bad are the same, and the probabilities are the same. It is the thesis that the terror bomber is in a worse frame of mind in intending to kill ten thousand civilians as a means to lowering enemy morale than the tactical bomber is in when he intends to destroy a factory and confidently expects his raid to have the side effect of killing ten thousand civilians. Some writers take examples where the numbers of deaths, or the levels of probability, are different; but I shall filter out such differences as those and look for the moral significance of the difference in intention, taken on its own.

Let us see what truth there is in the statement that the terror bomber does, while the tactical bomber does not, intend to produce something bad — specifically, to produce the deaths of civilians. It must be a weaker sense of 'intend' than that given by 'pursue as an end', i.e., as something sought for its own sake; for neither of our bombers need regard civilian deaths as intrinsically desirable. But it must be stronger than 'foresee as an inevitable upshot of one's conduct'; for both of our bombers foresee the civilian deaths.

The only way I can see of driving a wedge between the two is by invoking the view of intentions which is found in G. E. M. Anscombe's book: this is now the dominant opinion in the relevant parts of philosophy, and I am sure it is correct.* The core

---

* G. E. M. Anscombe, *Intention* (Oxford: Blackwell, 1957).

of it is the idea that intentions are explanatory of conduct: what you intend is determined by which of your beliefs explain or give your reasons for your behaviour. That immediately distinguishes our two bombers, for the terror bomber is in some way motivated by his expectation that his raid will produce civilian deaths, while the tactical bomber, though having similar expectations, is in no way motivated by them.

But let us not too rapidly draw any moral conclusions. That there is a moral difference between the states of mind of the two bombers is *not* automatically established just by the fact that one of them intends something bad which the other does not intend.

There is moral significance in what a man intends as an end, what he pursues for its own sake. It would be a bad man who wanted civilian deaths for their own sakes; but neither of our bombers is like that. This is a *sufficient* condition for intending something, and neither bomber satisfies it.

There is also moral significance in what a man is prepared knowingly to bring about. As Aquinas said, in effect: 'If a man wills a bombing raid from which he knows civilian deaths will result, it follows that he wills those deaths. Although perhaps he does not intend the deaths in themselves, nevertheless he rather wishes that the civilians die than that the raid be called off.' And that is highly morally significant. But this is only a *necessary* condition of intention, and it applies not just to the terror bomber who intends the deaths but also to the tactical one who does not. The tactical bomber would rather have civilian deaths than not have his raid, and that is something for which he needs a pretty good excuse. So our question is left standing: is the tactical bomber easier to excuse than the terror one? If so, it must be for a reason which stems from the difference in what they intend, but it is not handed to us on a plate just by the fact that the word 'intend' fits in one case but not in the other. So we shall have to dig for it. Let us try to be more precise about what the difference in intention amounts to.

If intentions are determined by which of the person's beliefs motivate his action, then we should be able to get at them by asking how the behaviour would have differed if the beliefs had differed in given ways. The difference between our two men should show up in their answers to the test question:

> If you had believed that there would be no civilian deaths, would you have been less likely to go through with the raid?

Specifically, the difference should show up in the terror bomber's answering Yes and the tactical bomber's answering No. I am not saying that an intention is just a disposition to be moved by certain beliefs, merely that the difference between these two intentional states is equivalent to the difference between two dispositions to be moved by beliefs. Even that is doubtless only an approximation, but I do not think its inaccuracies matter for present purposes.

The test question is a counterfactual one, and there are different ways of interpreting it. Each man is asked: Would you have been likely to behave differently if . . .? If what? What is the possible state of himself which he is asked to entertain, telling us how he would have behaved if he had been in that state? We know that it is to include his thinking his raid will not lead to civilian deaths; and it had better also involve whatever follows from that by virtue of his working logic, so that it won't also include his believing, for instance, that the raid *will* cause civilian deaths. Now, how else is his supposed state to differ from the frame of mind he was actually in when he launched his raid? There are three possible interpretations.

1. His supposed state is to differ from his actual one *only* in respect of the belief that there would be no civilian deaths and its logical accompaniments — in no other way. In that case, we are leaving the terror man with his belief that his raid will lower morale, and the tactical man with his belief that his raid will destroy the factory. Each of them, then, if faced with the question

'Would you in that case have called off your raid?', will answer No. So this version of the test question does not separate them.

2. His supposed state is to differ from his actual one in the belief that there would be no civilian deaths together with whatever follows from that by virtue of his causal beliefs. On that reading of the test question, the terror bomber will answer Yes, in that case he would have cancelled his bombing raid, for he is supposing himself to believe that there would be no civilian deaths and thus no lowering of morale — for he has the causal belief that morale can't be lowered without killing civilians. But the tactical bomber will also answer Yes, he too would have called off his raid, for he is supposing himself to believe that there would be no civilian deaths and thus no destruction of the factory — for he has the causal belief that the factory can't be destroyed without killing civilians.

Of those readings of the test question, the first supposes too little change in the antecedent state, the second too much. We need something in between, and it is not hard to see what it is.

3. The bomber's supposed state is to differ from his actual one in the belief that no civilian deaths would be caused, together with whatever follows from that, by virtue of his causal beliefs, through a causally *downstream* inference. That is, the adjustments are to concern what results, not what is causally prerequired. So the terror bomber is being supposed to think that there will be no civilian deaths and therefore no lowering of enemy morale; while the tactical bomber is being supposed to think that there will be no civilian deaths, but not to think that the factory will survive — since the factory's fate is not causally downstream from the deaths of the civilians. So the terror bomber will answer Yes, while the tactical bomber will answer No, to the test question.

That is the best I can do to clarify the difference between the two states of mind. That third reading of the test question confers reasonable clarity and undeniable truth on the statement that one man does and the other does not intend to produce civilian deaths.

But it doesn't add plausibility to the claim that this makes a moral difference. Neither bomber would call off his raid if his beliefs changed only in not including the belief that it would kill civilians. Each would call it off if they changed in that way and in every way that causally follows from it. To get them apart we had to specify what causally follows downstream and not what causally follows upstream, and I cannot see why anyone should knowingly attach moral significance to that difference as it appears here.

There is obviously great moral significance in the difference between upstream and downstream from one's own conduct. From the facts about the surgeon's behaviour it is causally inferable that there is a wounding upstream from it (he is stitching up the wound); and that is no ground for complaint against him as it would be if one could infer that there was a wounding downstream from his behaviour (because he was causing it). But that is irrelevant to our question, for in each raid the civilian deaths are downstream from the bomber's basic action.

It has been suggested that there is a difference in respect of what the two men are hoping for, or what they would in the circumstances *welcome*. The terror bomber, even if he does not want civilian deaths for themselves, still wants them — is in a frame of mind where the news of the civilian deaths would be *good* news — whereas the tactical bomber does not want the deaths: he merely thinks they will occur.

There is truth in that, but we must pick carefully if we are to retrieve it without bringing along falsehood as well. The terror bomber will indeed be glad when he hears that many civilians have died, because he needs their deaths for his ultimate aim. But the tactical bomber will also be glad when he hears that many civilians have died, because their deaths are evidence that something has happened which he needs for his ultimate aim. Because the raid will inevitably kill many civilians if it destroys the factory, it would be bad news for the tactical bomber if he heard that few civilians had died, for that would show that something had gone

wrong — his bombs had not exploded, or had fallen in open coun-
tryside. Something which contradicts that bad news is good news.

There is a difference between the two welcomes of the news of
civilian deaths: one man is glad because of what will flow from
the deaths, the other is glad because of what will flow from what
must have preceded them; one is downstream glad, so to speak,
while the other is upstream and then downstream glad. But there
need be no difference in how greatly glad they will be; and so,
as far as I can see, there need be no difference which creates a
moral difference.

It is true that the tactical bomber's wish for the civilian deaths
is a reluctant one: if he could, he would destroy the factory without killing civilians. But the terror bomber too, if he could, would
drop his bombs in such a way as to lower morale without killing
civilians. So there is nothing in that.

It may occur to you that there is some chance of bombing the
factory without killing civilians, whereas there is none that the
terror raid will lower morale unless civilians are killed by it. This
goes with the thought that the tactical man's regret at killing civilians could generate a sane, practical desire for more precise bombing
or for a wonderful coincidence in which all the civilians happen
to be out of town at the time of the raid; whereas the terror man's
regret at killing civilians could only lead to a sigh for a miracle.
That is all true, but only because of a difference in probability
which is an accident of this example; the difference between intending as a means and foreseeing as a by-product is not systematically linked to a difference in probability.

Here is another reason which has been offered as making a
moral difference between the two men. Suppose for simplicity's
sake that each case involves only the death of a single civilian —
you. The tactical bomber expects his raid to kill you; but if it
doesn't, and he sees you staggering to your feet amidst the rubble
of the factory, he may rejoice. On the other hand, if the terror
bomber sees that you have survived his raid, he has reason to drop

another bomb on you, since his purpose will be defeated if you survive. This suggests a difference in how hostile they are: if the terror bomber's plans go awry, he will use his flexibility and ingenuity in ducking and weaving his way *right up to your death*; but not so the tactical bomber.

From your point of view the two cases feel different. But that difference in feeling is hard to justify unless it reflects a difference in the probability of your death; which difference exists only if there is some chance that each bomber's expectations will turn out to be wrong. But the moral doctrine I am examining is supposed to hold even when the relevant upshots are perfectly certain, so that the question doesn't even arise of the agent's using his ingenuity to deal with breakdowns in his plans.

Anyway, why should the difference in how it feels to you reflect a moral difference between the two men? Each of them is prepared to maneuver towards your death: the tactical bomber may work to overcome political resistance to his raid, evade the defences which try to keep him away from you, solve the mechanical problem with the bomb-aiming equipment, and so on, using all his skill and ingenuity and plasticity to keep on a path which has your death on it. It is true that eventually the path to your death forks away from the path to his goal, and his ingenuity goes with the latter and not the former. But he has in common with the terror bomber that he relentlessly and ingeniously pursues, *for as long as he has any reason to*, a path with your death on it. The moral difference eludes me.

It is sometimes implied that the terror bomber is *using* people as a *means* to his end whereas the tactical bomber is not. I shan't take time to sort out that tangle. As a start on it, consider whether the tactical bomber, who is supposed not to be treating people as means, is treating them as ends!

Some writers who think there is moral significance in the distinction between doing or causing on the one hand and allowing or letting on the other believe that this invests our present distinction also with moral significance. I disagree with their premise, for reasons given in my first lecture; but even if it were true, it would not do this work, as I shall now show.

If it were to do this work, the difference between what is intended and what is foreseen would have to contain or involve the difference between what you do or cause or make to happen and what you merely let or allow to happen. Some writers seem to assume that there is not merely an involvement or intertwining but a downright equivalence between these two distinctions. I have found a moral theologian clearly implying that 'the distinction between rendering someone unconscious at the risk of killing him and killing him to render him unconscious' is the same as the distinction between 'allowing to die and killing'. Another moralist slides smoothly in the reverse direction, starting with a mention of 'what we do, rather than what we allow to happen' and moving on, as though with no change of topic, to a mention of 'what we intend, and not the whole range of things which come about as a result of what we do intentionally.'

I submit that this is a mistake. Given that you do something, or actively bring it about or make it happen, it is a further question whether you intend it as a means to your end or merely foresee it as a by-product of your means; and that further question could be asked, though a bit less happily, about something which you don't do or bring about but merely allow to happen. The two distinctions cut right across one another; the belief that they are somehow aligned or intertwined seems to me to have no truth in it whatsoever.

If you are not convinced about this, consider whether you are willing to say that the tactical bomber in dropping bombs right onto people does not kill them but merely allows them to die.

* * *

I am a bit more than half-way through. The lecture now changes gear.

There are problems about how to apply the notion of 'intended as a means' in particular cases, and these are worth discussing even if we think that the notion has no moral significance. For one thing, they are intrinsically interesting; for another, they turn out to have a bearing on the moral significance issue, as I shall show at the end. I turn, then, to some questions about application.

Suppose that in order to save the life of a woman in labour, a surgeon performs an operation in which he crushes the head of the unborn child, thereby killing it. Must the child's death lie within the scope of what the surgeon intended, or can we say that he intended only to change the shape of the head, the death being a foreseen but unintended by-product of the procedure?

Many moralists, especially Roman Catholic ones, do condemn the crushing of the child's head; and some of them think that to do so they must say that the surgeon in crushing the child's head intends its death. By the standard of my test question, that is just wrong: it is possible and even probable that the surgeon does not intend the child to die though he knows very well that it will. In a moment or two I shall come back to that and look at some ways of trying to get around it.

First, I would like to comment briefly on the tangle which some of these moralists have got themselves into. They accept a morality which picks out some kinds of actions as absolutely prohibited, no matter what the circumstances or consequences, one prohibited kind of action being the killing of innocent human beings. Someone who holds to that ought to condemn the killing of unborn babies, no matter with what intention: if you crush the child's head you do kill it, which is to do something of an absolutely forbidden kind; and it doesn't matter whether the death was an intended means or only a foreseen by-product of your means.

On the other hand, if the prohibition of the killing of the innocent is taken literally, it condemns things which some of these moralists want to permit. Suppose for example that the removal of a cancerous womb will certainly lead to the death of an unborn child which might become viable if the womb were left in place for two more months; and that leaving it in place for that long will remove any chance of the mother's surviving. On any tenable account of the concept of action — or of the concept of killing — the surgeon who performs this hysterectomy thereby kills the child. The causal route from his movements to the death is longer and more complex than in the head-crushing case, but what he does is a killing for all that. One common response to this is to say that it is not prohibited because it is not an intentional killing — as though the prohibition were not on killing the innocent but only on killing them where their deaths are something you intend. That puts the concept of intention into first-order morality, where I maintain it doesn't belong; and it revives the problem of how to condemn the head-crushing operation.

I am not commenting on the view that each operation might be morally permissible, or on the view that each should be categorically condemned as a killing of an innocent human being. My topic is the middle position which condemns the head-crushing but not the hysterectomy. A prohibition of intentional killing condemns neither operation; a prohibition of killing *simpliciter* condemns both. I can find no unconfused way of driving a moral wedge between them.

That is enough about that. I want now to consider how someone might try to force the death of a child into the scope of what is intended by the surgeon who crushes its head; and I shan't say any more about the confusion which may lie behind this attempt.

Philippa Foot suggests that the moralists in question might say that the child's death is 'too close' to the intended crushing of its head to fall outside the intention, the idea being that whatever is very 'close' to what you intend is itself intended. She rightly says that someone who takes this line may 'have considerable difficulty in saying where the line is to be drawn' around what is 'too close'; but that is minor compared with the difficulty of explaining what 'too close' means in this context, and why closeness in this sense, whatever it is, should have moral significance. In the absence of any help with this, I shall spend no longer on this proposal.

The only other move I have seen relies on first shifting from whether the surgeon intends to bring about the child's death to whether he intends to kill the child. That shift may well be legitimate, and I shall not challenge it. It prepares the way for an argument which I do want to challenge, namely one which says that if the surgeon intends his crushing of the child's head he must intend his killing of the child because the crushing *is* the killing. That is Charles Fried's line of thought, as applied not to killing but to harming, when he writes: 'It is inadmissible to say that one intends to put a bullet through a man, stab him, crush him, or blow him to atoms but does not intend to harm him. All of these things just *are* harming him.' * The crucial word 'are' is not explained. Let us consider what it could mean when used in this sort of way — as it is by other writers as well. Someone who says this could be aiming to express a necessary truth about concept-inclusion: putting a bullet through someone is harming him, it might be said, in the way that suing someone is making use of the procedures of the law, and adding up numbers is doing arithmetic. But that cannot be what is meant here; for it is too obviously false that crushing and stabbing *conceptually* or *essentially* involve harming or killing. So the claim must be a contingent one about the nature of particular actions: this head-crushing (the claim must be) is a killing, this stabbing is a harming. Some theorists of action do imply such things. Anscombe and Davidson, for instance, hold that if you do X *by* doing Y then your X-ing is identical with your Y-ing; and since the surgeon kills the child *by* crushing its head, these philosophers would say that the crushing of the head is identical with the killing of the child. That is a tenable view, but it cannot be used to bring the killing of the child

* Charles Fried, *Right and Wrong* (Cambridge: Harvard University Press, 1978).

within the ambit of the surgeon's intention; for on this coarse-grained account of action identity, it is shiningly clear that you can intend to do X without intending to do Y even if your X-ing is your Y-ing. His pulling of the trigger was his killing of his wife; he intended to pull the trigger; he did not intend to kill his wife. Given the failure of these moves, and the apparent success of the test question, I conclude that the surgeon need not intend the death of the child whose head he crushes. Those who want to condemn the head-crushing had better find some other reason for doing so; but then I have shown that they had better do that anyway.

But we are not out of the wood. I can cheerfully accept that the surgeon does not intend the death of the child; but the principles which led to that result also produce others which make a mockery of the whole idea of what is intended as a means. I shall explain how.

First, I must bring into the open something I have mainly left implicit. Because what someone intends to bring about is limited by what he believes, the only items that can be intended are ones about which one can have beliefs. Now, there are powerful reasons — stemming mainly from work of Kripke's, I think — for saying that you cannot have a belief about a particular future event. A thought about a concrete particular must be an *effect* of that particular or of some event of which it is the subject; and if causation always runs from past to future, no thought can be an effect of an event which has not yet occurred. Therefore, there are no *de re* thoughts about future events. If someone loses his temper and I say 'I knew that was going to happen', I ought not to mean that I expected *that* outburst of temper, but only that I expected *an outburst of temper* pretty much like that one. And in putting the test question to one of the bombers, we are not asking how he would have behaved if he had not expected those deaths, but only how he would have behaved if he had not expected deaths.

It follows that intentions, also, are aimed at kinds of event rather than at particular events. He didn't pull the trigger intending to bring about *that* flight of the bullet, but only intending to bring about *a* flight of the bullet. The terror bomber could not possibly have intended to produce *those* deaths. He may have intended to bring about deaths, or deaths of civilians, or deaths of those civilians, or deaths by fire of those civilians, and so on. The intention could be aimed at a kind which is as specific as you like, but it could not be aimed at a particular event.

Now, consider the following innocent example. A political leader takes action against a trade union, intending to bring about a month-long state of disintegration in which the various locals break off from the parent body and severally fall into further disunity. This is his intended means to the end of the union's being unable to call a strike during December. He is rightly sure that if the union falls apart for that long it will never be reconstituted, but all he cares about or intends is the one-month dissolution: if he were sure that the union would recover during January and flourish for many years, that would not reduce his motivation for moving against it. Looked at intuitively, the case is a possible one, and the test question yields an acceptable description of it — one-month dissolution intended, subsequent dissolution expected but not intended.

This politician has killed the union, knowing that he was doing so. But he did not intend to kill it — if killing involves its being permanently inoperative. He intended to produce an event with a certain feature (union inoperative through December), and expected it to have a further feature (union inoperative from January first onwards); but since he didn't intend the latter, he didn't intend the conjunction of the two; and so, as I said, he did not intend to kill the union.

I am assuming that if feature F is a conjunction of features G and H, you don't intend to produce an F unless you intend to produce a G and intend to produce an H. That amounts to saying that in delimiting what someone intends, we should shave it as close as possible. I say this because it is implied by the only account of intentions which I can make sense of. If there is a way around it — I mean one which goes deeper than an unexplained use of the phrase 'too close' — I shall listen to it with interest.

That was about the killing of a union. Now re-apply it to some killings of people — for instance the civilians in the terror raid. I said that the intention was to kill them so as to lower morale. But now that turns out to be too crude an account of the matter. All that was intended was that the people's bodies should be inoperative for long enough to cause a general belief that they were dead, this belief lasting long enough to speed the end of the war: there is nothing in that which requires, through a causally downstream inference, that the inoperativeness be permanent; and so there is nothing requiring that the people actually become dead. Of course the terror bomber knew that the people would become not merely inoperative for a while but downright dead — he had no hope of achieving the lesser thing without achieving the greater. But the greater thing is complex, and only one constituent in it was intended as a means.

There are other cases too, and not all involving death though they do all involve irreversible change: for instance, the arsonist does not intend the building to be permanently destroyed, just that it be reduced to cinders for long enough for the insurance company to pay up; and so on.

The scope of the problem can be somewhat reduced through a move suggested by Gilbert Harman. He has pointed out that the test question for delimiting intentions may make them look more fine-grained than they really are. Suppose that someone expects his behaviour to produce an F and a G, and that his only thought about this is a coarse-grained one about F-and-G-in-a-lump, with nothing in his mind corresponding to the notion of 'producing F and not producing G' — that being a mental refinement which he has not achieved. There could still be true counterfactuals about

how he would have behaved *if he had* expected to produce an F
and not a G, and one of these might be that *if he had* had that
expectation he would still have behaved as he did in actuality. But
if his actual state of mind involves nothing of the form 'F and
not G', we ought not to say that he intends to produce F and does
not intend to produce G.

We could argue about what it is for a distinction to be actually
registered in a mind, but let's not. It is presumably sufficient for
this that the person should consciously, episodically think of the
distinction — e.g., that the arsonist should play with the idea of
the world's running normally to the point where the insurance
company pays off, and then events in the vicinity of the building
running in reverse like a film played backwards. He need not
think of it as naturally possible, let alone probable. All he needs
is some thought of it, sparked by fancy or whimsy or being asked
the relevant test question; and similarly with the terror bomber.

So even if we give Harman's idea full force, that arsonist and
that terror bomber do not intend the destruction of the building
or the killing of the people. The scope of the absurdity has not
been reduced much. How is the absurdity to be got rid of?

It does not help to point out that there is absolutely no chance
that a disintegrated human body or incinerated building will ever
be restored to full health. If that, or the terror bomber's knowledge of it, implied that he intends not only the disintegration but
also its permanence, then this whole inquiry has got off on the
wrong foot, as have the moralists whose views I have been exploring. They think, in my opinion rightly, that we have the notion
of what is not intended but is foreseen as an *inevitable* by-
product of one's means. If that is wrong, and everything which
is certain to ensue from one's conduct is intended, then all we
have left is the contrast between what you intend as your required
means and what you foresee as a *probable* by-product of your
means; and that is not something I want to discuss.

It may occur to you that when the bomber kills someone, there is a particular, temporally circumscribed event which is the person's becoming dead: that happens at one minute past noon — it doesn't drag on forever. That is true, but it doesn't help with our problem. It would be relevant only if *that event* were what the bomber intended to produce; but that would be an intention aimed at a particular event, which is impossible. And if you shift over to the claim that he intended to produce *a* becoming-dead, you are saying precisely what I have given reason for denying: for I have argued — cogently, I hope — that the bomber intends to produce a dismantling and does not intend to produce a dying, though he is sure that the dismantling he produces will be a dying.

One might seek help from the fact that this difficulty arises only with irreversible change. Perhaps there are reasons for treating that in some special manner which protects it from my destructive argument — for example, reasons for not allowing ourselves, when delimiting intentions, to resolve a feature of the form 'F forever' into ones of the form 'F for a while' and 'F thereafter'. The trouble with that is that it would disqualify not only the absurd results with the reflective arsonist and terror bomber, but also the unabsurd treatment of the thoughtful politician's moves against the trade union.

Those are three failed attempts to neutralize the absurd results which I have reached. I can think of no others and am inclined to infer that the concept of what is 'intended as a means' cannot be given a firm, clear, theoretic grounding which implies what we think true and not what we think false regarding what people intend.

That could in turn have a bearing on the moral issue discussed in the middle part of this lecture. Someone who uses the concept of 'intended as a means' as a load-bearing part of his moral system is prima facie in trouble if the best available account of this concept leads to results which are clearly not intuitively acceptable. This is not the familiar problem about borderline cases, mentioned by Foot and dismissed as 'sophistical' by Anscombe on the grounds that 'the fact of twilight does not mean that you cannot tell day from night.' The difficulty I have uncovered is less like twilight than like a blazing sun in a black, star-studded sky.

Let us consider what options are open to someone who thinks that there is nothing wrong with my derivation of the absurd results, and who nevertheless rests moral weight on the difference between what one intends as a means and what one foresees as a by-product.

One option would be to let the term 'intend' be guided by a rigorously close-shaving use of the test question, to accept the implication that my absurd results are true, and yet still to rest moral weight on the concept of 'intended as a means'. Cases like that of the two bombers could be coped with in either of two ways: by backing away from them, saying that there is no moral line to be drawn there; or by re-describing them, saying that the bad kind of event which one bomber intends to produce and the other doesn't is a lengthy disintegration of the bodies of civilians.

I would be charmed if any of the moralists in question did in that way embrace my absurd results. I would also be astonished. Anyway, it is an option about which I have nothing useful to say.

Another possibility is to argue that my treatment of the concept of intention can be replaced by a better one which does not yield absurd results in cases of irreversible change. I cannot discuss that possibility, of course, until the rival account is produced.

There appears to remain only one other possible response for someone who holds that the concept of 'intended as a means' has moral significance. It goes as follows.

'Your absurd results *are* absurd and should be rejected. Perhaps there is no rival analysis of intention which avoids them, but what of that? When it comes to determining what a person intends as his means to his end, we can settle this case by case, confident of mutual agreement (at least so far as the irreversible-change problem is concerned) and with no perturbation or difficulty. We agree that the good cases are perfectly good, the bad ones perfectly absurd. What more could you want?'

Of course that is enough to entitle the notion of 'intended as a means' to a place in our thought and language, but it doesn't entitle it to a place in our basic moral thinking — or anyway not in mine. This is a respect in which people differ: the difference came up early in my first lecture, and in the middle of my second, and now in conclusion I allude to it once more.

One form of dissent from it is easy to understand. It is the dissent of someone who holds that the source of moral truth is the utterances of some person (e.g., God) or some group of people (e.g., the society of which he is a member). If a person thinks that he must abide by somebody's judgment that it is wrong (say) to *kill* people, expressed with the use of the verb 'to kill', then for him that is a moral datum whose edges are as obscure to him as is the precise meaning of 'kill', as that word is used by his moral authority. And he might similarly have to take it from his authority that it is bad for civilian deaths to be 'intended as a means', regarding this as a fundamental moral truth although he can only interpret it through his informal idea of what a person can reasonably be said to intend.

It is not my purpose to mock this approach to morals, and I wish I had not once allowed myself to describe it as reducing morality to 'mere obedience'. Still, it does involve something like obedience, and that gives it its reason for admitting word-meanings into the foundations of morality. Perhaps other reasons are available to people with other views about the source of moral truth, though I don't know of any. Anyway, I invite attention to the split between those who will and those who won't conduct their basic moral thinking in terms which are apparently not controllable by clear, objective, deeply grounded conceptual principles. In these lectures I have presented some results which I have come to on one side of that split, but I have not argued for being on that side and not on the other. Rather, I have simply adopted certain standards for what makes a distinction fit to bear moral weight, and have argued that by those standards there is no positive/negative difference, and no intended/foreseen difference which belongs in the load-bearing part of a moral structure. I am defenceless against anyone who would run the arguments in the contrapositive direction, saying that standards of fitness which lead to those conclusions should be rejected. Even you do think that, I hope you will also think that the issue has been worth bringing into the open.

Children as Moral Observers

ROBERT COLES

THE TANNER LECTURES ON HUMAN VALUES

Delivered at
The University of Michigan

April 9, 1980

ROBERT COLES is Professor of Psychiatry and Medical Humanities at Harvard University. He was educated at that school as well as Columbia University and the University of Chicago. Among his many books are literary as well as scientific explorations of the human mind. His multi-volume *Children of Crisis* has received a number of awards, including the Ralph Waldo Emerson Award of Phi Beta Kappa, the Weatherford Prize, the Lillian Smith Award, the McAlpin Medal, and the Pulitzer Prize. Among his most recent books are *A Festering Sweetness*, a volume of poetry, and *Women of Crisis: Lives of Struggle and Hope*. Professor Coles received the Family Life Book Award of the Child Study Association of America in 1967 and the Hefheimer prize for research of the American Psychiatric Association in 1968. He is a *New Republic* contributing editor and serves on the boards of *Contemporary Psychoanalysis*, *Child Psychiatry and Human Development*, the *American Poetry Review*, and *Aperture*.

In this century of the child, there is little left, it seems, to say about what does or does not happen to the young. If we are to believe some of the more resolutely theoretical child psychoanalysts (and how can anyone ever actually prove them right or wrong?) a baby of six months or eight months has a good chance of being, from time to time, in the midst of a depression, of experiencing envy, or, less ominously, knowing gratitude. There is, Melanie Klein tells us, a "paranoid position" for infants — a spell of strenuous distrust with regard to the world. Psycho-analytic critics of that (mostly English) school of child analysis have wondered why their colleagues have been so willing to connect infantile life with words such as "envy" or "gratitude" or "depression," in the absence of the kind of scientific effort Anna Freud has so shrewdly and so tactfully called "direct observation." But even if a group of intensely speculative psychoanalysts have let themselves get carried away; have resorted to nothing less than a series of wild or exuberant flights of fancy; have imposed their theoretical will, so to speak, upon babies not yet able to speak or understand words, hence tell what is on their minds or compre-hend what is on the minds of those around them — still, it will surely be of some significance for those future social historians who will be trying to figure out this age, that such a line of con-jecture could not resist the youngest of the young, and could be offered to the world in the name of science itself.

There is little, in fact, that we haven't allowed children to be quite congenial with, psychologically. We are proud, these days, that we know how many-sided our boys and girls are — how lusty and truculent, how competitive and jealous, how cunning and devious. Their eyes miss little, we tell ourselves; their ears are always open — at night, even, when the slightest noise in the house might well get connected to this or that notion of a given child's. There are not only Oedipal complexes, but pre-Oedipal "issues" — again, backward the clock, so far as our sense of what matters psychologically. And we are by no means confined to the house with respect to those old Greek triangles of passion, once somewhat aristocratic with respect to antagonists, but now updated for each and every household, no matter the region, race, culture, language, historical or social experience — or so some psychological theorists would have it. The nursery, the neighborhood, and, not least, the schools are also full of psychological nuance and subtlety, a constant, everyday psychodrama only waiting to be interpreted by those who are "trained," those who have what is called the "theoretical equipment" believed necessary to do descriptive and analytic justice to an extraordinary psychological complexity — what, in sum, used to be passed off as "childhood," or as the first years in someone's "life."

No child simply "plays" anymore, or just happens to get into a fight, or develops an innocent crush or an occasional grudge that gets chalked up to the consequences of childish games — not if some of us who get called "experts," and many of us who are anxious indeed to get called "psychologically sophisticated" are to be heeded. And the same goes for boys who end up on athletic fields or in gangs or for that matter with a hobby, a consuming interest, or for girls who do or don't (it makes no difference!) end up on those same fields, or who manage to find one or another kind of company, or involvement of the mind. We are sure, those of us who claim to know so much about the mental life of children, that there is a lot going on; and it is a life that is only partially apparent. Underneath, deep down, below the surface (so the imagery goes) there are — what? The answer is an astonishing richness of emotional experience: angers and resentments, hopes and fears, attachments and losses, dozens and dozens of anticipations, and one dread after another. Even the healthiest of boys and girls (a description fewer and fewer of us dare assert

for our children, because we are mere laymen, mere mothers or
fathers or schoolteachers) are, surely, in possession of that famous
"seething cauldron" of instinctive energy. Does not our very
humanity offer it to us? It is an energy which presses relentlessly
upon us; an energy which we learn to resist, to shape and mold, to
allow furtive or guarded or only limited expression; an energy we
end up, even before we go to kindergarten, censoring, or feeling
ashamed to have; an energy which haunts us at night, as if determined, in weird or violent or tempestuously erotic dreams or
nightmares, that we be reminded (again, at eight or nine, never
mind eighteen or nineteen, or through all the decades that follow)
how vulnerable we are to a powerfully assertive and complicated
emotional life referred to abstractly (and these days, altogether
commonly) as "unconscious" in nature.

Put differently, twentieth-century children (that is, ours who
live in the Western democracies, and especially, the United States)
are regarded as extremely knowing; as rather subtle observers of
the adult world, not to mention their own generation; as quick to
spot any number of attitudes, emotions, preferences or outright
prejudices in other people, large or small. Those same children
are considered continually resourceful in their acquisition and use
of psychological knowledge. They cultivate allies, plot against
enemies, cling to attachments, harbor resentments, and constantly,
no matter what, keep trying to figure out where they stand vis-à-vis
just about everyone they meet.

There is a distinct sense in which they may be regarded as
social and political observers; their minds have every intention of
maintaining a certain emotional *status quo*, or of fixing up a
(perceived) injury to a former balance of forces, or of achieving,
finally and for good, what hasn't up to now been, but what ought
be, so the child believes — and such aspirations are the result of
taking stock of things, judging who is friendly or not so friendly,
or, indeed, quite unfriendly, and how so-and-so rates in someone
else's eyes, and on and on. True, we are talking about not the

manipulations of our Congress or the U.N., but the politics of the nursery, the playground, the classroom or the schoolyard, not to mention the family dining room or living room or bedrooms. But the central thrust of today's psychology acknowledges every subjective and more than a few objective elements of so-called adult political life to be at work among children.

Who, these days, after all, would be surprised at the notion of children as quite able to bargain, threaten, cajole, beg, calculate, join with others for various reasons, bear grudges, even plot, lie, resort to violence? Every schoolteacher who has taken his or her fair share (if not dose) of "educational psychology" courses, every parent who has read one or another of the books that claim to give us a splendid view of "child growth and development," knows full well the intricate texture of a boy's or girl's mental life — so much so that even "experts" claim to be puzzled as they tell us of the many kinds of fantasies entertained, the puzzling variety of behavior demonstrated, all in response to problems or issues which themselves seem frustrating if not impenetrable in their diversity and complexity to the adults who study them, write about them, never mind treat them.

As for anyone who wants to come along and say that life, even psychological life, can't be all that complicated, and especially since it is *small children* whose thoughts are in question — well, there are sufficient resources in the contemporary language of psychiatry, or in the common expressions of our particular culture, to slap a wrist or two, if not send the pitiable individual to a corner of some room. *Naïve* would be one banishing word; others might be *old-fashioned*, or *simple-minded*, or, God forbid, *unsophisticated*. If necessary, there always are the big guns — phrases resonant with Calvinist condemnation, but a Vienna rather than Geneva version of the saved and damned: the person in question has "resistance" to seeing the obvious, is "blocked" in so doing by "conflicts," needs "help" to do so, is "working out" one or another "problem" by not recognizing and acknowledging the perfectly obvious.

An entire essay could be written on that last line of thinking, if not judgment — the ways not a few of us have put psychology and psychiatry to moral use: a means of applauding or roundly condemning those we happen to like or dislike. All too many don't even admit (at least to others, and, incredible to say, not even, maybe, to ourselves) that we do, indeed, have what used to be considered the common human inclination to gather gradually, in this life, a number of preferences, one way or another, with regard to people, places, things, or ideas, ideals, viewpoints. Instead, we talk about "value-free" social science or psychology. We insist that we want to understand, only understand. We claim that we have rid ourselves of our "hang-ups," and so are in a position to see those of others, everywhere in evidence. But we do not get excited; do not show ourselves to be "emotional" or "over-involved," not to mention angry at or passionate about something. The point is to be cool; to be warily noncommittal; to nod knowingly, get the other person to talk; to listen to him or her or them (in one of those countless "groups" that cover certain areas of America's human landscape); and only after a respectable length of time, to come up with a pointed interpretation: you seem to be saying *this*, or I hear you saying *that*, or you've got "work" to do on one or another score. And Lord, if the person takes issue with the remarks or even (the poor lost soul) dares strenuously disagree: he or she is "upset," is obviously having "trouble," and needs, of course, what we have: our way of looking at things, our way of talking, our way of deporting ourselves.

It is not new, naturally, for some people to set themselves apart from others, even do so smugly and stupidly; and do so by using a particular language, resorting incessantly to code words and phrases, and assigning blame to others for a certain manner or posture. But now our American children, in large numbers, are caught up in such a development — and we tend to regard those children as, again, not unlike us adults who are so commonly told we have "problems," and ought go "talk with someone." That is to say, young people are not only felt to be full of dozens and dozens of attitudes and insights with respect to the way people behave, and why; those same boys and girls (how strange the jeopardy that goes with such complex awareness!) are declared to be in a constantly changing, even escalating struggle. Each year or two, we remind ourselves, there are new hurdles, new sources of anxiety and apprehension to overcome. One cannot take for granted "emotional growth," or something called "human development." It is best that we be ever alert, and, under optimum circumstances, ready to intervene, if not devise (what else?) various "preventative measures."

Here is Anna Freud, in *Normality and Pathology in Childhood* (1965), writing about what became called, by the 1930's, a "psychoanalytic education" for children:

At the time when psychoanalysis laid great emphasis on the seductive influence of sharing the parents' bed and the traumatic consequences of witnessing parental intercourse, parents were warned against bodily intimacy with their children and against performing the sexual act in the presence of even their youngest infants. When it was proved in the analyses of adults that the withholding of sexual knowledge was responsible for many intellectual inhibitions, full sexual enlightenment at an early age was advocated. When hysterical symptoms, frigidity, impotence, etc., were traced back to prohibitions and the subsequent repressions of sex in childhood, psychoanalytic upbringing put on its program a lenient and permissive attitude toward the manifestations of infantile, pregenital sexuality. When the new instinct theory gave aggression the status of a basic drive, tolerance was extended also to the child's early and violent hostilities, his death wishes against parents and siblings, etc. When anxiety was recognized as playing a central part in symptom formation, every effort was made to lessen the children's fear of parental authority. When guilt was shown to correspond to the tension between the inner agencies, this was followed by the ban on all educational measures likely to produce a severe super-ego. When the new structural view of the personality placed the onus for maintaining an inner equilibrium on the ego, this was translated into the need to foster in the child

the development of ego forces strong enough to hold their own
against the pressure of the drives. Finally, in our time, when
analytic investigations have turned to earliest events in the first
year of life and highlighted their importance, these specific insights are being translated into new and in some respects revolutionary techniques of infant care.

When she is through with that important summary of one
segment of our recent social history, she hastens to add this
pointed comment: "In the unceasing search for pathogenic agents
and preventive measures, it seemed always the latest analytic discovery which promised a better and more final solution to the
problem."

And she does not shirk a candid appraisal of what did not,
finally, prove to be possible:

Above all, to rid the child of anxiety proved an impossible
task. Parents did their best to reduce the children's fear of them,
merely to find that they were increasing guilt feelings, i.e., fears
of the child's own conscience. Where in its turn, the severity of
the super-ego was reduced, children produced the deepest of all
anxieties, i.e., the fear of human beings who feel unprotected
against the pressure of their drives.

Moreover, she offers an almost Sisyphean comment — as if it
were, alas, a bit of the folk wisdom we ought, by now, have
thoroughly absorbed into our heads: "It is true that the children
who grew up under its influence [that of a "psychoanalytic education"] were in some respects different from earlier generations;
but they were not freer from anxiety or from conflicts, and therefore not less exposed to neurotic and other mental illnesses."

After her last card gets played, the hope is, no doubt, that we
will walk away properly chastened: "This [result] need not have
come as a surprise if optimism and enthusiasm for preventive
work had not triumphed with some authors over the strict application of psychoanalytic tenets."

Miss Freud, one presumes, is not operating or writing out of the netherworld of neurosis, negative transference, and resistance. She has spent a lifetime with children, and given them credit for a good deal of feisty shrewdness; a never-say-die capacity, in most cases, given any chance at all, to respond intelligently and with great agility to whatever stress comes their way. In the book from which the above quotes are drawn, she is not by any means turning on her own profession, or offering a counsel of despair. She is, indeed, cautioning her particular audience (mostly child psychoanalysts) that they have, eagerly or reluctantly, become foils in a given era's messianic hopes, if not fantasies. And she is, too, at other points in her book, quite honorably willing, in a most forthcoming way, to acknowledge that one never does, really, know — not even if one is Anna Freud — how any child will turn out. A lad who seems exceedingly troubled, at age A, may end up rather well off, psychologically, at age B. And vice versa — since it is no rarity to find children certified by "experts" as "normal" or "well adjusted" who end up, later in life, a holy mess, or, at best, dull and dreary members of "the human race."

Such ironies of life, the unpredictability of things, the continual complexity of childhood, the inconsistencies and contradictions and paradoxes and ambiguities that plague the young and their all-too-attentive elders — in all that one finds the stuff of a grand novel: *Middlemarch*, say, or *War and Peace*, whose creators knew better than letting the life of any character, or any statement about this world, be presented as *the* truth, as an unqualified approximation of *everything*. Still, with respect to children, and that abstraction about their time as such — namely, "childhood"— one wonders whether Anna Freud's recital of illusions spun and illusions rent, expectations raised, then dashed, only to give way to new ones, will prompt the kind of detached, wry, self-critical scrutiny she may have had in mind for herself, for all of us caught up with theoretical ambitiousness, and, not least, with a desire to lend ourselves to the priestly as well as the intellectual purposes of a certain kind of society — highly industrial, given to intense consumerism, all taken up with science, skeptical about religion, and preoccupied with the here and now, not to mention the self.

Since our children are credited with such enormous emotional depth, since they are known to us as sharply perceptive, insistently questioning, extremely artful, if not sly and cunning, when it comes to sizing up people, their motives and hang-ups, their lusts and hates and worries, then why ought we not wonder whether these young ones, too, may have been noticing some of the things Miss Freud has asked us to realize? And whether they, too, may even be capable of the kind of self-distance she has managed and asked us to begin trying to achieve? Moreover, speaking of ironies, psychological and historical, it is rather a strange turn of affairs that has us, today, least inclined — disinclined, really — to allow children the very attributes another, earlier age freely granted them: the ability (the *responsibility*) to make moral distinctions, to assume moral burdens, to ready themselves for moral initiatives.

By now it is a commonplace, courtesy of Philippe Ariès, in *Centuries of Childhood* (1965), that a while back (in the Middle Ages, say, and well into the Renaissance) children were generally treated as young adults. They were so dressed, so addressed. They began work around the time we think of sending our sons and daughters to elementary school! In this century, right now, if one wants to get a bit of a reminder of that "distant past," one can visit the camps where migrant farm families work. There, one will often enough, too often by far, I regret to say, see children of seven or eight not attending school, and working hard, sunup to sundown, as harvesters. They are certainly treated as adults, albeit not the most favored ones, by any number of men and women around them — not only parents, but growers, foremen, county officials, and so on. In any event, Ariès makes it quite clear that the issue is psychological as well as cultural, material, economic — a notion, in other times, that a *person* who is eight or nine is quite able to fend for himself or herself when it comes to matters of the mind and heart and soul. To be sure, infants require what we know or should know they do — loving care, and no small amount of discipline. But "the age of reason" was set at seven back then, and that meant a conviction on the part of bigger and older human beings about the psychological competence, in many respects, of smaller and younger ones. By seven and beyond, one was supposed to know not to lie and cheat, not to disobey, not to get carried away with one's own whims and fancies to such an extent that one neglects one's obligations and duties, which have been handed down, and which therefore will be, it is assumed, self-evident.

Nor need we retire to the past, call upon earlier generations, for testimony about a particular point of view. It is a paradox — our contemporary estimate of the moral intelligence of children. On the one hand, we declare them wise almost beyond belief; on the other hand, we grant them scant tendency for ethical reflection, emphasize the animal-like, instinct-ridden, impulsive side of their lives. And don't pay as much attention as we might, for all our widely proclaimed preoccupation with their lives, to what they might let us know, indeed what they have already told us. In the face of my persistent *psychiatric* curiosity (how were those black children caught up in the severe stress of Southern school desegregation managing during the early 1960's?) boy after boy and girl after girl had another kind of story to tell me, as in this instance — New Orleans, 1961:

I don't know why they say all those bad words. They tell me they're going to kill me, every day they say so. There's one lady, she's big, real big, who swears and swears. She gets red in the face. She might be getting sick, the way she looks. There's a man, and he calls me nigger, nigger, nigger; he just keeps repeating the word. Every once in a while, he says nigger *girl*, nigger *girl*! When I look at him, he starts swearing, like the fat lady. When I don't look at him, he doesn't swear too much. I saw him once drive up; he was "late." He started shouting at me: "Why are you so early?" I wanted to turn and tell him that I wasn't early;

he was just late. But you can't say a word. People like him, people like her — they're not good people. They're bad people. They're looking for some poor colored person — like me! — to put all the blame on, the blame for what they've done.

I don't know what to think about those people in the crowd. All I know is that the minister is right, when he says there is a Devil, and he's around, and you have to stand up and say you're on God's side and not on the Devil's side. When I walk by the crowd, and they say all the swears to me, I try to smile, and think of Jesus. Didn't He hear people say a lot of bad words? My mother has told us to think of Jesus, and I do. My father gets mad; he'd fight them back, the white folks. But I can't do that. I'm only one person. The federal marshals they have with me, guarding me — they're white, and they would probably leave me and join the mob, if there was a big fight.

I don't want to fight, anyway. We're told in Sunday School to "turn the other cheek," and I know how: you pay no attention to the rotten apples in the barrel, and you keep reminding yourself that there are lots of good apples. My grandmother says that's what to think, and I try my best. I told her once that maybe there are a lot more rotten apples than good ones. She asked me how *I* knew! I said I wasn't sure, but I thought the people who show up every morning weren't so "special." My grandmother says they *are* "special," but they look to me like the people we see on the bus, and downtown in the stores. You make a wrong move on the bus or in the stores, or *anywhere*, and you're in trouble. It was my grandmother who used to tell me that, before they decided to pick me for the desegregation — to go to that white school. When I reminded her once, she said hush. She said I have to be strong, and I should believe there are *good* white folks. But where are they?

If you ask me, we're here so God can find out how strong we are. If we pass, if we prove ourselves, then He'll open up the door; and when we die, we'll live all the time. That's something I think about, too — God and His smile. The minister says Jesus smiled at a lot of children. I've wondered at times if He is watching, when they take me to school, and all those people say I'll die, I'll be killed, pretty soon, so I'd better watch out! I dreamed once, and in the dream God was there, and He told me He *was* watching, and not to worry. I felt better then. I was sure He'd do something, if the mob got real bad. Even the federal marshals are afraid it will get worse. They've got a lot of plans, about what to do, if "they" try this, and if "they" try something else. The marshals have a list of what to do, and they have a map, and they have a lot of phone numbers, and they have their guns — you can't forget the pistols! I guess only Jesus Christ, our Lord, didn't need the police protecting Him; but like my daddy says, even He had a lot of trouble, and they did get Him, or they tried to, and that was the worst day, *ever*.

As one listens to such remarks, made over a day or two of conversations, in the context of discussions obviously generated by the press of a traumatic and continuing "social reality" (not to mention a "racial reality" of a rather long-lived nature) one finds it rather too easy for sympathetic pieties to come forth: that lovely, frightened, brave girl, experiencing each and every morning, each and every afternoon, the persisting, nasty, brutish venom of a vicious and stupid mob — and one undeterred for longer than was either necessary or just by a complacent, a blind, an outrageously short-sighted, narrow-minded political authority, that of the city of New Orleans, that of the state of Louisiana. Now it is different — and one hastens to add, to insist, that today's mobs are mostly northern; and not a few have appeared in the city of Boston, which has, for generations, sent finger-pointing social critics south.

Still, the question here is not regional self-righteousness, or the ironies of history, but rather the nature of childhood thinking. We had best listen to that seven-year-old black girl, born of parents who had no formal education to speak of — and these days, alas, they'd be called "culturally deprived" and "culturally disadvantaged." And as we do so, we'd best keep in mind this: her comments are by no means the special insights of a remarkably gifted child, a one-in-a-million bequest of "nature" to this world of ours. Do we really need a so-called "expert," parading his years of "research" with various American children of different sorts (with respect to age, racial or social or regional background) to tell us what has been appreciated over and over again by parents and grandparents and older brothers and sisters and schoolteachers and scout leaders and athletic coaches and ministers and doctors and nurses — by anyone who has occasion to have a talk or two with a child, to watch and listen while a child looks and hears and speaks with statements and questions, with comments and asides, with speculations and affirmations and refusals and objections and hard words and sneers and occasionally a hue and cry or a catcall? Do we really need, more precisely, yet another of our secular "authorities" to tell us that children, young children indeed, definitely do possess a moral sensibility, an increasingly well-muscled notion of right and wrong, and, yes, a yearning that justice be done?

The nods may be forthcoming to that question, but with them, soon enough, one can anticipate the demurrers. We are told, repeatedly, that children aren't really "moral" or "ethical" in their thinking; they are moralistic, rigidly intent on obeying perceived rules and regulations, responsive to their own literal-mindedness, and, not least, to a "primitive" kind of conscience, the demands of a "super-ego" fiercely intent on dealing with those purely instinctual forces which threaten to overwhelm all of us, whatever our age. For years, as a resident in psychiatry and child psychiatry, and later, while attending psychoanalytic seminars in New Orleans (where I was also watching children such as the one just quoted go through the hurdles of extreme social disruption and historical change) I heard about the "archaic" super-ego or the "inflexible" one. And later, by theorists such as Lawrence Kohlberg, essentially the same point would be made: true, children of seven or eight, for instance, may mind their p's and q's, may demonstrate at almost all times a fastidious intention of being found on the "right" side of just about any contest, and may let everyone in sight know how submissive they are to adult authority. But there is, in such behavior, no real critical thought, no effort to weigh and sift matters, judge them on their merits with care and concern. "Not to reason why, but to do and die" — a child's "charge of the light brigade," we have been told, under the aegis of that greatest of personal tyrants, the negative aspects of the so-called "internalized objects," or, collectively, the super-ego, whose stern, unqualified, ever-demanding voices become for each child a mandate.

Now, there is no doubt that children certainly do show them-selves, time and again, to be as compliant as can be — sticklers for what a parent says, what a teacher requires, rather than human beings anxious to scan a particular scene with notions like "jus-tice" or "equity" or the Bill of Rights in mind. But so do the rest of us, at various moments in our lives — even those men and women we all tend to consider moral giants. Gandhi, for instance, could at once be a leading ethical protagonist of this century, yet also be cranky, teasing, even mean-spirited, as his followers and sympathetic observers, no less, have reported. Only an idolatrous fool would want to deny anyone, however impressive and singular his or her life, a good quota of "neurosis" (Freud) or "finitude" (Tillich) or flawed humanity (Tolstoy), or maybe just plain old sinfulness (the Bible).

Twentieth-century psychology has told us nothing if not the universality of mental conflict, of qualities such as "aggression," "narcissism," "ambivalence," and to mention a trait referred to earlier, an "envy" which the English psychoanalyst Melanie Klein has speculated to be present almost at the very beginning of our lives. Is anyone to be excepted from such a generalization? Not Freud, I fear, and not Einstein and not Dr. Schweitzer and not Dorothy Day, and not any of the Old Testament prophets, and not the Christian saints and martyrs, and yes, not even Jesus Christ himself, whose willingly assumed humanity made him, too, heir to the flesh, so to speak. Is not that the lesson of the Cross — Christ's last moments of loneliness, of radical doubt, of profound and terribly anguished distrust? He had been "forsaken" — or so he believed, for those awful moments. Those of us who read the Bible are surely meant to be reminded that if no less than the Messiah, God's "only begotten son," should not be able to contain a piercing cry of abandonment, then the rest of us are going to come up, inevitably, with our fair share of apprehensive, suspicious, quite mistrustful responses.

The issue, finally, is one of proportion, of balance. How significantly, how frequently, do children get to the moral heart of things, as compared to adults? I suspect the answer is that the texture of a person's moral life is not by any means necessarily a function of his or her age. I have to ask that the young witness summoned earlier be given her day in court, and I have to insist, again, that she is not at all alone, so far as her "morality" goes. There she was, after all: vulnerable and harassed without letup. There she was, black and poor and living in the deep South at an unfavorable moment in that region's history — a moment the brunt of which she took on the chin every day for a whole school year. If one examines the record of her various observations, as her parents and neighbors and relatives and friends and teachers heard them, as I happened by extreme good luck to do likewise, one realizes the extent and depth of her moral vision, her moral analysis. She was, without a question, able to understand the pain and hurt and consequent blindness and malice in her tormentors. Understand, but not excuse; she witnessed evil and called it that. She could, that is, transcend her own predicament, connect what she was experiencing to what others all over the world, and in other times, have had to go through.

A Christian child, she remembered Christ's travail. A black child, she was able to remember and keep on noticing the injustices historical fate has visited upon her people. She did not become a prima donna, for all the cameras that dwelt upon her, for all the police and marshals who had to escort and guard her. She was able, against high odds, to do a bit of demonstrating herself; she became a moral match for the segregationist demonstrators who paid her such fierce mind. She was modest, quiet, unassuming, not without a sense of humor about the reason for her celebrity or notoriety. She even understood the different ways various New Orleans people viewed her. She was, in other words, sociologically as well as ethically astute. I don't know who holds the keys to the cabinet which contains scrolls that are handed down to the morally reflective, the morally "mature," and I rather suspect that the issue, as so often is the case, turns out to be one of power — the theorist's desire to decide who deserves his or her approval, accolade: a given psychological designation. But any scheme or hierarchy that leaves this child out, or arbitrarily or with condescension consigns her to a moral "lower depth" or an ethical embryo, a state of early "development" in such matters, ought be itself scrutinized very closely, to say the least.

In twenty years of so-called "fieldwork" with American children of all backgrounds, I have heard ethical reflection put into questions — endlessly, it seems, questions. And to ask one myself: why not? Here is a Louisiana white child, a boy of nine, talking about the same racial conflict that bore down so cruelly on the black child quoted above:

How did all this happen? I asked my daddy, and he said he didn't know. Why don't they settle the fight, and let us go back to school? At first I liked being home, but now I'd rather be back in school. I wonder sometimes: what did God mean, when He made the colored, and He made us? He must have had a reason, I'm sure. You wonder what's fair. That's what the minister asks about everything, and when he asks it, I ask, too — what's fair for the white and fair for the colored? I asked our Sunday School teacher and she said it beats her, and I asked my daddy, and he said the only fairness you'll get is in Heaven, and my mother, she said you have to be as good as you know how, and I guess she's right. I asked her how you know if you're being good, and she said you just know. I hope so.

A mother with a Kantian perspective! A child grappling with the rights and wrongs of society, and with his own mind's various moral perceptions. I don't see why that child's questions have to be "explained" as a "reaction formation" against "aggression," as a "displacement" or "sublimation" connected to one or another Oedipal difficulty. I wonder, too, whether that child's cognitive faculties will be any sharper when he is forty than they already were when he was yet to be ten. Nor is any college psychology professor or psychiatrist likely to do much better than this boy, of a working-class segregationist family, all too easily categorized and dismissed by my ilk as "redneck." Who will ask to be called that child's superior when it comes to reflecting about the nature of injustice, or dealing with the tension between a political reality and a Christian ethic, or considering the matter of ethical standards — how we get them, realize their character, hold on to them?

Sometimes I wonder whether the course of moral development in childhood and adolescence isn't precisely the opposite of that outlined for us by many of our psychological theorists. I do *not* mean that children are born "good" or "pure" or splendidly responsive to *any* social or cultural mandate. I do *not* mean, in the tradition of Rousseau's *Émile*, or maybe, the tradition of his interpreters, that infants, toddlers, schoolchildren are *only* demonstrating that they have been victimized if they show signs of being mean or nasty or self-centered or pushy or grabby. It is *not* a matter of innocence and purity being gradually, during childhood, defiled; nor is it a matter of almost infinite possibilities being slowly curbed, undercut. Whether one subscribes to the biblical story of Original Sin, or sees that account as a metaphor of sorts, or insists upon "aggression" and "narcissism" as inevitable elements in the makeup of anyone and everyone, the issue for every child and every parent remains the same: how to come to terms with each other, and together, how to make the inevitable accommodations that "life" in one way or another requires?

As mothers and fathers know, as doctors know, and as infants and older babies get to know rather quickly, there are limits to this world, flaws in it; there is, too, fate and chance, good luck and bad luck, and always, mystery. One can eat only so much without getting sick. One can scream only so much without getting hoarse. One can flail about only so long without getting weary or exhausted. Day is followed by night. Health is interrupted, even under the best of circumstances, by illness. Accidents happen, even to the most circumspect or cautious. Day after day children learn all that, and sometimes know it better than those of us who get so wrapped up in our various determinisms (culture as against drives, society as against the individual, the id as against the ego, the child as a flexible innocent and the child as an untamed animal or as yet another of God's budding sinners) that we overlook the body's givens and the world's as well, the mix of determinate and indeterminate — and how the proportion varies! — that each of us lives with, starting when we're born.

It is in the nature of human beings, through language, to take stock of things, to look around and ask, to come up with answers. We are the self-conscious ones, the creatures who know that there has to be a last breath and live under the shadow of that knowledge. Such an existential banality is never, it seems, connected with the lives of children — not (in contrast) the case with many other banalities, derived from economic materialism, psychoanalytic speculation, social meliorism, behaviorism, utopianisms of all sorts, as well as theological interpretation. Well before children go to school, they know how to speak; indeed, the linguistic capacities of the young child are astonishing — and one would think, reason to stop some of us in our tracks as we spell out all that children don't know, can't comprehend, aren't able ethically to mull over and ask about. Can there be any "morality" without language? I don't know, but that is a reasonable subject for discussion; we get close indeed, doing so, to an important issue in child development and moral development both. And we don't need any new and expensive studies to tell us that language is the great acquisition (its precise biological and psychological origins still a mystery to us, for all the theories) of *pre*school children.

Have we watched closely enough how that language is used in those childhood years, or have too many of us been interested in other matters: the emotions that exert themselves upon children, or the habits they learn, or the games, the gadgets, the things they can manipulate — their so-called skills? Even those of us interested in the "reasoning" of children often show our interest in such a way that the child is pushed into a corner of sorts; we present the boy or girl with "problems" to solve, or we take note of responses to certain questions we have asked, and from our tests decide that a child of such-and-such an age is, or is not, capable of dealing with this or that moral problem, not to mention challenge to his or her reasoning ability. I have no wish to dispute the value of accurate cognitive assessment of children; or for that matter, careful (and restrained and tactful) emotional assessment, as done with special distinction, over these past decades, by Anna Freud and her coworkers at London's Hampstead Clinic. But no series of tests or interviews were meant fully to circumscribe the particulars of this life we live, whether it be that of an adult or a child.

As every psychiatrist knows (or ought know) the entire apparatus of diagnostic tests and evaluations and interviews gives only some sense, at best, of certain clinical issues in a person's life. Similarly, with cognitive appraisals — of intellectual function, of reasoning ability, and so on: an individual's manner and competence in that regard are *somewhat* appraised. When moral questions are connected to intellectual ones — by intellectuals who have devised modes of testing for what they are looking for — then we are, again, faced with a series of intellectual (and maybe, moral) questions *ourselves*: what precisely are we *trying* to find out, and what *are* we finding out, and what are we *not* finding out, and what may we well *not* be in a position to find out — that is, by administering tests to children?

Even as a street-smart ghetto child, or a child from a culture not our own (that of the psychological observer) may challenge us to devise new ways of responding as observers, as analytic researchers, and, one hopes, as human beings, so any child's moral *life* may require us to have a few thoughts about the all too convenient, and perhaps arbitrary or categorical manner in which we define and assert a young person's (or an adult's) powers of moral analysis, let alone the way he or she is spending time on this earth — to the good or to the bad. When one hears, day in and day out, children all over the world trying to understand the rights and wrongs of the world, speaking of what ought be allowable or seemly, referring to what is unfair, mean-spirited, unbecoming — then one wonders whether a new frontier of the super-ego needs exploration, a frontier of territory not so harsh, forbidding, or reflexively punitive; and whether, also, a few more (a lot more, actually) studies of what children do, *in fact,* manage to say and achieve for themselves ethically ought also be launched, and, perhaps, carried out, though in situations not of our (the researcher's) manufacture, but rather in situations which are determined by life itself.

In the summer of 1979 my two sons, both teenagers, and I happened to be in Soweto, South Africa. We were talking with the black children there, in schools and in homes. We also talked with white children, of both Afrikaner and English ancestry. Here is part of what one black child of eleven told us:

One day, I'm ready to go die for my people. It's that bad. We are treated like dogs. My mother says no, but I say yes, that is how they treat us, the white people. The next day, I feel sorry for them. When I go to Joburg [Johannesburg] I look at the white people, and there is fear in their faces. They can't see us, but we see them. They don't want to see us, but we have to see them! I hope, some day, God helps us settle this; He will have to come down here again, and open a lot of eyes! I believe He might get hung up on the cross again!

I don't know how to label this child psychiatrically or cognitively; he is an "adequate" student, his teachers told us, and no one in Soweto, including his parents, has complained of his "behavior." While others discuss what is and is not possible with respect to "moral development" for him and the many children like him all over the world, one can only sit and wonder about his remarks — the patience, the thoughtfulness, the righteousness, the good and clean anger, the indignation, and, too, the sadness: a spirit, already, of resignation which is not unlike that shown us by someone believed by many, over the generations, to have been our Savior. And across town, so to speak, in the important, modern, thriving city that boy mentioned, a white boy only a half year older speaks:

A lot of people worry. They ask: will there be more trouble in Soweto? I hope not. We should give the people there something. I don't know all they need, but they need a lot. Our maid is a good person. She says not to worry; there won't be more trouble. My father says there *will*. My mother says she hopes and prays there won't be. It's too bad when people don't trust each other. I can understand why there's trouble in Soweto; they are poor there, very poor. If I was a poor person, I'd want to get more for myself and my family — my people. But you don't go and rob. There are a lot of burglaries. I would never steal. Maybe, if I was very poor, I might — if I was hungry; if I was a father, and my son was hungry, or my daughter. I would still feel bad, though, if I had to do it.

A child caught in a terrible historical tragedy, and not unaware, by any means, of its true nature. He muses, moves back and forth in his loyalties, shows compassion, fear, a high regard for his own fortunes, a decent sense of how ill it fares for others, a respect for laws, and an uneasy sense that they are, for many, almost beside the point, because a brutish and "separate" existence compels obedience to one law only, that of survival, hence the thievery, and hence the distinction between one person's ordinary temptation to steal and another person's desperate belief that there is little choice *but* to do so. I don't believe that such a "mere child," as some might have him, is all that far removed, in his moral sensibility, from his great countryman Alan Paton.

There is no use rescuing children from one set of unqualified generalizations (with respect to their limitations), only to strait-jacket them with another absolute or two. I am not suggesting that children are born sages. I know that they aren't what Words-worth occasionally heralded them to be: wonderfully spirited souls with scarcely a mean bone in their bodies. Children can be callous, spiteful, utterly (for moments and longer) wrapped up in themselves, and unresponsive, it seems, to anyone's code of honor — the case even for very well brought up and quite "nor-mal," intelligent children. Those same children, however, can also be thoughtful, kind, sensitive, and sensible — earnestly anxious to do right, to be fair, to give (and give of themselves) liberally, even altruistically. And *some* children (please don't ask for a per-centage; I'm not sure whether we'll ever know how to find out an exact number) are rather often as just described — fine, fine human beings a lot of the time, in the way they think of and get on with others.

What, then, is one to conclude, if anything? If children are not angels and not devils, they sometimes are — again, what? Well, they are like their parents and teachers and other adults; they are a mixture of things — including, emphatically, as one ele-ment, the ability and willingness to be attentive observers of the human scene, and subsequently as well as consequently, moralists. Henry James gave us in *What Maisie Knew* precisely that, a child who was energetically prepared to watch, to take continual notice, to surmise, and, finally, to conclude — as to facts, yes, but also as to the moral dimensions of a particular situation. So too with the haunting adolescent Portia Quayne, in *The Death of the Heart* — Elizabeth Bowen's attempt to show us that a child dropped into a moral vacuum will, in time, drift and roam and equivocate as the rest of the (London, haute bourgeoisie) crowd manages to do. And those children Dickens gives us — their wickedness laced with gentleness, or vice versa! They are children abused (*Oliver Twist*), children awaiting their destiny (*Great Expectations*), children caught in the crazy turmoil of a law that does its fair share of generating crime (*Bleak House*); they are, in sum, evidence of a Victorian novelist's determination to give us nothing less than a shrewd, tentative, *balanced* judgment on the matter of what obtains, morally, in the minds of children.

It is a balance, a sense of proportion, we ought strive to attain for ourselves as we think about our sons and daughters — our future of sorts. For Dickens the boy Jo stood for something in all of us, young as well as old — a moral possibility that takes the form of, again, attentiveness:

And there he sits, munching and gnawing, and looking up at the great Cross on the summit of St. Paul's Cathedral, glittering above a red and violet-tinted cloud of smoke. From the boy's face one might suppose that sacred emblem to be, in his eyes, the crowning confusion of the great, confused city; so golden, so high up, so far out of reach. There he sits, the sun going down, the river running fast, the crowd flowing by him in two streams — everything moving on to some purpose and to one end — until he is stirred up, and told to "move on" too.

So it went for a child over a century ago; and so it goes for countless children today. They are not only told to "move on" by policemen; parents, teachers, guidance counselors, child psychiatrists — they all, too, tell children to do that: tell the young to "grow up," to stop worrying about our Sowetos, about the many injustices of this world. Or worry *a bit* — and again, "move on." And then *we* decide that only a few of *us*, the much older, can see as Jo did, and respond to what is seen as he did. Unquestionably Jo was no moral philosopher; nor are most of us, including without a doubt our children. But there is within many of them, as within many of us, a redemptive side: eyes that can sustain a spell of moral vision, ears that can pick up the ethical heart of a given matter. Of that we can be sure; and, therefore, be both hopeful, because of the moral possibilities in this world, and full of sadness, because so often those possibilities are wasted, or, more forcibly, crushed outright.

Economics or Ethics?

GEORGE J. STIGLER

THE TANNER LECTURES ON HUMAN VALUES

Delivered at
Harvard University

April 24, 25, and 28, 1980

GEORGE J. STIGLER was educated at the University of Washington, Northwestern University, and the University of Chicago. He has taught at a number of institutions, among them the University of Minnesota, Brown University, and Columbia University, and he has lectured at the London School of Economics. He has served in many capacities as a public policy advisor and is presently Director of the University of Chicago's Center for the Study of the Economy and the State. Professor Stigler has been a Guggenheim Fellow and a Fellow of the Center for Advanced Study in the Behavioral Sciences. He is author of a number of books in the areas of economic theory, industrial organization, public regulation, and the history of economics, and serves as editor of the *Journal of Political Economy*. Since 1958 he has been Charles R. Walgreen Distinguished Service Professor of American Institutions at the University of Chicago.

I. THE ECONOMIST AS PREACHER

I wish to express my gratitude to Gary Becker, Richard Posner, and Stephen Stigler for important assistance, and acknowledge my immense debt to Aaron Director for discussions of these issues both during the preparation of the lectures and in the many years of our friendship. Most of the writing was done while I was a visiting scholar at the Hoover Institution at Stanford University, and I thank Glenn Campbell for providing this attractive setting.

*   *   *

Economists seldom address ethical questions as they impinge on economic theory or economic behavior. They (and I) find this subject complex and elusive in comparison with the relative precision and objectivity of economic analysis. Of course the ethical questions are inescapable: one must have goals in judging policies, and these goals will certainly have ethical content, however well concealed it may be. These lectures will explore some of the problems raised by ethical questions, using the history of economics as an important vehicle in the exploration.

In this first lecture I propose to discuss how economists — primarily great English economists in the main line of development of economics — have advised men and societies on proper conduct. My interest on this occasion is not so much in the advice they have given as in the ethical basis on which this advice has been grounded. Economists have no special professional knowledge of that which is virtuous or just, and the question naturally arises as to how they are able to deliver confident and distinctive advice to a society that is already well supplied with that commodity.

1. How Much Preaching?

The first, probably the most important, and possibly the most surprising thing to say about the economist–preachers is that they have done very little preaching. I suppose that it is essential to state what I mean by preaching. I mean simply a clear and reasoned recommendation (or, more often, denunciation) of a policy or form of behavior by men or societies of men. It is hardly desirable to label every non-neutral word as preaching — indeed our language is rather short of words that cannot be used in such a way as to hint of approval or disapproval. During a recent war one economist remarked that he was against "business as usual," and a second was moved to ask whether the speaker was against "business, comma, as usual."

I shall illustrate my loose definition of preaching and many subsequent points by quotations from famous economists, and I digress for a moment to explain their authority to any non-economists who are present. All but one of the economists I quote were highly intelligent, disciplined men whose views on subjects related to economics deserve your attention and thoughtful consideration, but no more. One, Adam Smith, is differently placed: if on first hearing a passage of his you are inclined to disagree, you are reacting inefficiently; the correct response is to say to yourself: I wonder where I went amiss?

When Adam Smith speaks of the debasement of the currency — which of course proceeds at a much more rapid pace today than it did during his lifetime — he says, "By means of those operations the princes and sovereign states which performed them were enabled, in appearance, to pay their debts and to fulfill their engagements with a smaller quantity of silver than would otherwise have been requisite. It was indeed in appearance only; for their creditors were really defrauded of a part of what was due to them." [1] I consider this to be preaching since "fraud" is not

[1] *The Wealth of Nations*, Glasgow ed. (Oxford: Clarendon Press, 1976), I, 43–44.

merely a descriptive word. On this mild and I hope reasonable definition of a moral judgment, I have just quoted the only clear example of preaching in the first hundred pages of the *Wealth of Nations*. The preaching becomes more frequent in Smith's latter pages, but it is almost nonexistent in Ricardo's *Principles*, quite sparse in Mill's *Principles*, and virtually nonexistent in Marshall's *Principles*. Of course these admirable men expressed approval or disapproval of many things with every degree of literary subtlety. It would be easy to compile many remarks like Jevons's that the Morrill Tariff Act of 1861 was "the most retrograde piece of legislation that this [nineteenth] century has witnessed," in which disapproval is at least hinted at.[2] But these dicta are noteworthy for their scarcity rather than their frequency in the professional works of the economists.

The proposition that economists are not addicted to taking frequent and disputatious policy positions will appear incredible to most non-economists, and implausible to many economists. The reason, I believe, for this opinion is that in talking to a non-economist, there is hardly anything in economics except policy for the economist to talk about. The layman is unequipped to discuss with an economist the problems that concern professional economics at any time: he would find that in their professional writing the well-known columnists of *Newsweek* are quite incomprehensible. The typical article in a professional journal is unrelated to public policy — and often apparently unrelated to this world. Whether the amount of policy-advising activity of economists is rising or falling I do not know, but it is not what professional economics is about.

The great economists, then, have not been preoccupied with preaching. Indeed, none has become great because of his preaching — but perhaps I should make an exception for Marx, whom some people rank as a great economist and I rank as an immensely influential one. The fact that the world at large thinks of us as

[2] *The Coal Question* (London: Macmillan, 1865), p. 326.

ardent enthusiasts for a hundred policies is not pure error, but it tells more about what the world likes to talk about than what economics is about. The main task of economics has always been to explain real economic phenomena in general terms, and throughout the last two centuries we have adhered to this task with considerable faithfulness, if not always with considerable success.

2. Preaching to Whom?

It is my impression that the clergy of former times devoted their finest efforts to mending the behavior of individuals, but that in recent times they have sought rather to mend social policy. Whether this impression be right or wrong, economists have seldom spent much time exhorting individuals to higher motives or more exemplary conduct.

Again I return to Mr. Smith. The servants of great joint stock companies such as the East India Company, Smith avers, were concerned only with their own personal fortunes.

Nothing could be more compleatly foolish than to expect that the clerks of a great counting-house at ten thousand miles distance, and consequently almost quite out of sight, should, upon a simple order from their masters, give up at once doing any sort of business upon their own account, abandon for ever all hopes of making a fortune, of which they have the means in their hands, and content themselves with the moderate salaries which those masters allow them, and which, moderate as they are, can seldom be augmented, being commonly as large as the real profits of the company trade can afford. . . . They will employ the whole authority of government, and pervert the administration of justice, in order to harass and ruin those who interfere with them in any branch of commerce which, by means of agents, either concealed, or at least not publickly avowed, they may publickly chuse to carry on.[3]

After having described these wretchedly venal servants, who exploit both their masters and their victims, Smith hurries on to

[3] *Wealth of Nations*, II, 638–39.

say, "I mean not, however, by any thing which I have here said, to throw any odious imputation upon the general character of the servants of the East India company, and much less upon that of any particular persons. It is the system of government, the situation in which they are placed, that I mean to censure; not the character of those who have acted in it."[4] So it is social institutions that one should castigate: men respond to these situations in predictable, and probably unchangeable, ways. This is not to approve or disapprove of the principle of self-interest that guides men, although Smith might well have agreed with the remark of Frank H. Knight, whom we shall later meet more intimately, that anything which is inevitable is ideal!

Smith's general practice of addressing little preaching to individuals in their private behavior has continued to this day to be the practice of economists. Of course mortal man cannot wholly abstain from all instruction to the young, the inferior, and the great, and an enumeration of these acts would be amusing to you and embarrassing to me. Malthus complained that the lower classes were excessively attentive to what he termed "the passion between the sexes," and even John Stuart Mill shared with him a propensity to propose Draconian methods of dealing with the popular implementation of this passion. Alfred Marshall pointed out the unwisdom of gambling with the aid of the law of diminishing marginal utility, but later, fortunately, Milton Friedman and Jimmie Savage were able to excuse this activity with the aid of a law of increasing marginal utility. A vast number of economists have believed that the sin of myopia with respect to future needs is pervasive. We were once told that a corporation has no soul to damn or body to kick — a statement that has been emphatically and prosperously refuted by many politicians to this day. Yet surely a devil embodied in a person is a much more satisfying object of dislike and disapproval than some impersonal institution. These lapses of economists from concern with social rather

---

[4] Ibid., II, 641.

than individual behavior are forgivable — a concession to their
membership in the human race.

But the lapses are not defensible. Social policies and institutions, not individual behavior, are the proper object of the
economist–preacher's solicitude. This orientation is demanded by
the very logic of economic theory: we deal with people who maximize their utility, and it would be both inconsistent and idle for
us to urge people not to do so. If we could persuade a monopolist
not to maximize profits, then other reformers could persuade resources not to flow to their most remunerative uses, and our theory
would become irrelevant.

3. PREACHING EFFICIENCY

In the economists' sermons the dominant theme has been that
good policy favors, and bad policy interferes with, the maximizing
of income of a society. We shall find other themes, but over the
last two hundred years efficiency in the sense of fuller achievement
of uncontroversial goals has been the main prescription of normative economists. Let us first look at a major example before turning to an examination of the content and authority of this primary
rule of good conduct.

The most sustained application of this principle by Adam
Smith was in the attack on interferences with free trade and on
mercantilism generally; he devoted one-fourth of his large treatise
to this cause. Smith thus asserted that:

The natural effort of every individual to better his own condition,
when suffered to exert itself with freedom and security, is so
powerful a principle, that it is alone, and without any assistance,
not only capable of carrying on the society to wealth and prosperity, but of surmounting a hundred impertinent obstructions
with which the folly of human laws too often incumbers its operations; though the effect of these obstructions is always more or less
either to encroach upon its freedom, or to diminish its security.[5]

[5] Ibid., I, 540.

The argument for free trade was deepened some forty years later by the theory of comparative costs, but the central policy conclusion remained, in Ricardo's words, that "under a system of perfectly free commerce, each country naturally devotes its capital and labour to such employments as are most beneficial to each." [6] This position has been almost universally accepted by economists to this day.

Many other examples, but none more important, of the economists' use of efficiency as the criterion for desirable economic policy could be given. The central element of the criticism of monopoly is that it reduces the efficiency of the use of resources. The central element of the criticism of labor market interferences, such as minimum wage laws or barriers to geographical or occupational mobility, has been their effect on the allocation of resources. An economist is a person who, reading of the confinement of Edmond Dantès in a small cell, laments his lost alternative product.

In Smith's time and for a few decades thereafter the argument for efficiency was embellished with a rhetoric of sacred and inviolable rights of natural liberty. But if the concern with natural liberty was ever strong,[7] it had disappeared by the mid-Victorian age.

The attack on the efficiency of public policies will only be appropriate and convincing when achievement of the goals and costs of the policies are undisputed. If one policy will achieve more of a given goal than a second policy with the same cost in resources, the former policy is clearly superior, and there is no room for argument over ethics. This has indeed been the essential nature of the great majority of the economists' preachings on public policy.

[6] David Ricardo, *Principles of Political Economy and Taxation*, P. Sraffa ed. (Cambridge: Cambridge University Press, 1951), p. 133.

[7] Of which I have some doubts. Thus Smith declares that prohibiting banks from issuing small bank notes is of course a violation of natural liberty, and yet it should be undertaken for the greater good of society; see *Wealth of Nations*, I, 324.

On this reading, the economist–preacher has simply helped to straighten out the issues for a frequently muddled nation. John Stuart Mill explained the misunderstandings that supported mercantilism with his customary lucidity: how common discourse confused money and wealth; how a trader does not consider his venture successful until he has converted his goods into money; how money is *par excellence* the command over goods in general, ready on the instant to serve any desire as no other commodity can; how the state "derives comparatively little advantage from taxes unless it can collect them in money," and so on.

> "All these causes conspire to make both individuals and government, in estimating their means, attach almost exclusive importance to money. . . ."

But mark well the conclusion:

> "An absurdity, however, does not cease to be an absurdity when we have discovered what are the appearances which made it plausible . . . ." [8]

And there we have the answer to the question of how the economist can operate so extensively and so easily as a critic of policy when he is not in possession of a persuasive ethical system. The answer is that he needs no ethical system to criticize error: he is simply a well-trained political arithmetician. He lives in a world of social *mistakes*, ancient and modern, subtle and simple, and since he is simply pointing out to the society that what it seeks, it is seeking inefficiently, he need not quarrel with what it seeks.

A world full of mistakes, and capable of producing new mistakes quite as rapidly as the economists can correct the old mistakes! Such well-meaning, incompetent societies need their economic efficiency experts, and we are their self-chosen saviors.

[8] *Principles of Political Economy* (Toronto: University of Toronto Press, 1965), I, 67.

Take away the linen of sophistication in which economists are nowadays dressed, and I believe that this is still the fundamental belief that underlies the large majority of the policy recommendations of our profession. There have indeed been grave income redistribution questions which are receiving increasing attention, but day in and day out for the economist the society's problems are usually problems of efficiency. We live in a mistake-prone world.

I believe that this view of society as a community with acceptable, if not always admirable, goals but possessing only a feeble understanding of efficient methods of achieving them was and is profoundly mistaken.

The mistake in this view should have been evident simply because throughout the period I am discussing there were vigorous controversies over the goals of policy. Indeed, in every literate society, even the most dictatorial, there are critics of the goals of the society. In Ricardo's day, for example, Godwin forcefully argued that the institutions of government and property were among the main causes of social misery. Perhaps Godwin is not an apposite illustration; I suppose that an anarchist is a free trader. Consider, then, Malthus, the first professor of political economy in the history of England, who was a supporter of the very protection of agriculture which was the target of Ricardo's attack.

Malthus argued that a nation specializing in manufactures and trade could easily find that its advantages were eroded by foreign or domestic competition, and in any event could be strongly dependent upon the prosperity of its trading partners. An exclusively agricultural nation could find itself locked into a stagnant feudal social system, or alternatively it could find itself unable to employ capital efficiently once its agricultural plant ceased to grow. Hence Malthus wished a mixed agricultural–commercial system.

I shall not conceal my doubt that Malthus actually demonstrated the superiority of this mixed agricultural–commercial system, but it is surely true that he raised a cloud of complications which were only slowly dealt with by later generations of free traders. Some of these complications concern the determinants of the long-term growth and stability of economies, on which to this day economists have not found confident understanding.

There is a second, and even stronger, reason why the economist — of all people — should be reluctant to characterize a large fraction of political activity as mistaken. The discipline that assumes man to be a reasonably efficient utility maximizer is singularly ill-suited to assuming that the political activity of men bears little relationship to their desires. I have argued the theme of intelligent political behavior often enough that I must here limit myself to the barest of remarks.[9] The failure to analyze the political process — to leave it as a curious mixture of benevolent public interest and unintentional blunders—is most unsatisfactory.

Whether one accepts or rejects the high hopes that some of us now entertain for the economic theory of politics, the assumption that public policy has often been inefficient because it was based upon mistaken views has little to commend it. To believe, year after year, decade after decade, that the protective tariffs or usury laws to be found in most lands are due to confusion rather than purposeful action is singularly obfuscatory. Mistakes are indeed made by the best of men and the best of nations, but after a century are we not entitled to question whether the so-called "mistakes" produce only unintended results?

Alternately stated, a theory that says that a large set of persistent policies are mistaken is profoundly anti-intellectual unless it is joined to a theory of mistakes. It is the most vacuous of "explanatory" principles to dismiss inexplicable phenomena as mistakes — everything under the sun, or above the sun, can be disposed of with this label, without yielding an atom of understanding.

---

[9] See, however, "Smith's Travels on the Ship of State," *History of Political Economy* 3, no. 2 (Fall 1971), and "The Theory of Economic Regulation," *The Bell Journal of Economics and Management Science* 2, no. 1 (Spring 1971), as well as the underlying literature of Anthony Downs, James Buchanan, and Gordon Tullock, and the public choice field.

We economists have traditionally made innumerable criticisms of the inefficiency of various policies, criticisms which have often been to their own (and my own) utter satisfaction. The meager success of these criticisms in changing these policies, I am convinced, stems from the fact that more than narrow efficiency has been involved in almost every case — that inexplicit or incomprehensible goals were served by these policies and served tolerably efficiently. Tariffs were redistributing income to groups with substantial political power, not simply expressing the deficient public understanding of the theory of comparative costs. We live in a world that is full of mistaken policies, but they are not mistaken for their supporters.

I wish to recur for a moment to the policy of mercantilism, which Smith attributed to the clever machinations of the merchants and traders against the simple, honorable landowners who still constituted the governing class of Great Britain in his time. Smith and his followers should have asked themselves whether simple error could persist, to the large and centuries-long cost of a class intelligent enough to hire the likes of Edmund Burke. I say, with great fear and trembling, that it is more probable that Smith, not the nobility of England, was mistaken as to the cost and benefits of the mercantile system. I say this for his sake: a world of great and permanent error would be a poor place for economics to live.

4. PREACHING EQUITY

There is one large set of policies which cannot easily be judged merely as to efficiency in reaching widely accepted, comparatively uncontroversial goals: I refer to those which seek to redistribute income. If Nelson and Jones have equal incomes, and a policy takes half of Nelson's income and gives it to Jones, a question of equity will inevitably arise in the minds of everyone except Jones.

For the century from Smith to Jevons, economists were correspondingly discreet in their discussions of income distribution. It may be supposed that Smith thought income distribution was a matter for markets to determine when he said, "To hurt in any degree the interest of any one order of citizens, for no other purpose but to promote that of some other, is evidently contrary to that justice and equality of treatment which the sovereign owes to all the different orders of his subjects." [10] I am inclined to accept this view even though one can find occasional departures such as his proposal to tax the "indolence and vanity of the rich" by having disproportionately heavy tolls on carriages of luxury (II, 246), for these departures are few and casual.[11]

The classical school did not depart far from Smith's practice. The evil effects of equality were held to be two: a decrease in incentives to thrift and work; and an increase in the population on Malthus' principles. Ricardo would deny the suffrage to those who would not respect the rights of property.[12] Mill, although he was the author of the comforting thesis that the distribution of wealth, unlike its production, was socially malleable, was unprepared to support a progressive income tax — in his case, because of a fear of the effects of leveling income upon the growth of population as well as because such a tax would be insufferably inquisitorial in administration. Bentham's flirtation with notions

[10] *Wealth of Nations*, II, 654.

[11] We find complaints at window taxes as being regressive (II, 373) and at tithes for not being proportional to rents (II, 358).

[12] "So essential does it appear to me, to the cause of good government, that the rights of property should be held sacred, that I would agree to deprive those of the elective franchise against whom it could justly be alleged that they considered it their own interest to invade them. But in fact it can be only amongst the most needy in the community that such an opinion can be entertained. The man of a small income must be aware how little his share would be if all the large fortunes in the kingdom were equally divided among the people. He must know that the little he would obtain by such a division could be no adequate compensation for the overturning of a principle which renders the produce of his industry secure. . . . The quantity of employment in the country must depend, not only on the quantity of capital, but upon its advantageous distribution, and, above all, on the conviction of each capitalist that he will be allowed to enjoy unmolested the fruits of his capital, his skill, and his enterprise. To take from him this conviction is at once to annihilate half the productive industry of the country . . . ." *Observations on Parliamentary Reform*, in *Works and Correspondence* 500–1.

of equality flowing from the utilitarian calculus left no imprint on friends, disciples, or tenants.

There was one interesting near-exception to this rule of near-silence on the redistribution of income. The rent of land, the payment for the use of its "original and indestructible" properties, was by definition a nonfunctional income, so that social control over rent would not affect the use of land. Hence Mill was the ardent supporter of the nationalization of future increments of land values. But even here Mill wished to compensate present landowners fully.[13]

All this was to change when, but not because, the theory of utility became a centerpiece of economics. In 1881 Edgeworth published *Mathematical Psychics*, in which the utilitarian calculus was presented with magnificent subtlety, imagery, and fruitfulness. A marriage was performed between utility and natural selection, culminating in proposals such as that people below a certain level of capacity should not be allowed to have children,[14] and that the possible correlation of capacity to produce with capacity to enjoy might lead even to the superiority of aristocracy. This effusion was in due time replaced by the classic formulation of the utilitarian rule of taxation, minimum sacrifice. The state should tax the rich *before* the poor, not simply more heavily than the poor, subject to the unexplored dangers of the effects of aggressively progressive taxation on production.[15] Progression followed from the twin assumptions that the marginal utility of income falls as income rises, and there is no systematic relationship between the amount of income a person possesses and his efficiency in converting income into utility.

---

[13] Mill was mistaken only in believing that present values did not include unbiased estimates of future increments in rents. A similar problem lurks behind his support of progressive taxation of estates. The posthumous *Chapters on Socialism* pays no attention to inequality (aside from that implicit in the discussion of poverty), even in discussing Blanc, Fourier, and Owen.

[14] Those denied "a share of domestic pleasures" might be consoled by emigration!

[15] See Francis Edgeworth, "The Pure Theory of Taxation," in *Collected Works Relating to Political Economy* (London: Macmillan, 1925), I, 111–42.

By 1912 Pigou was prepared to assert as an axiom of welfare economics that "economic welfare is likely to be augmented by anything that, leaving other things unaltered, renders the distribution of the national dividend less unequal." [16] He was still reluctant to engage in extensive direct redistribution, on the ground — so characteristic of this eccentric man — that the poor would not use the funds intelligently: "Women, who cook badly or feed their children on pickles, are not bankrupted out of the profession of motherhood; fathers who invest their sons' activities unremuneratively are not expelled from fatherhood. . . . What has been said, however, . . . should suffice to establish the thesis . . . that the poor, as entrepreneurs of investment in themselves and their children, are abnormally incompetent." [17] Fortunately the intelligence of the poor was rising at a powerful rate, so a few years later Pigou was able to write that "To charge the whole body of the poorer classes with ignorance and lack of capacity for management would, indeed, be to utter a gross libel." [18] Or was Pigou getting in step with society?

I shall assert what I believe I could document, a steadily rising concern with the distribution of income among economist–preachers during the last one hundred years. Today the consequences of any policy on the distribution of income is the early subject of every appraisal, and egalitarianism is an almost uncontroverted goal of social policy. Two broad statements can be made about the ascendancy of income distribution as the subject of ethical judgments on economic policy.

The first is that the expanding concern of economists with income distribution did not come from within economics. Until recently, the professional literature on income distribution has been sparse, relatively iconoclastic (especially with reference to the possibility of interpersonal comparisons of utility), and non-

[16] *Wealth and Welfare* (London: Macmillan, 1912), p. 24.

[17] Ibid., pp. 356–57, 358.

[18] *Economics of Welfare* (London: Macmillan, 1924), p. 709.

cumulative. It cannot be doubted that the economists have imported egalitarian values into economics from the prevailing ethos of the societies in which they live, and they have not been important contributors to the formation of that ethos. In the English tradition from which I have been drawing my examples, the Fabian socialists were immensely more influential and outspoken supporters of egalitarianism than the neoclassical economists.

The second generalization is that the wide acceptance of the ethical desirability of extensive income redistribution has inhibited the development of a positive theory of income distribution. Such a positive theory would explain how the size distribution of income affected, and was affected by, developments such as rising wealth and education, the roles of taxation and other forms of political action, the institutions of inheritance, and the changing nature of the family. Just such a positive theory is beginning to emerge, and I predict that it will have important effects upon the attitudes of economists toward policies of redistribution. The remarkable circumstance, however, that professional study of income distribution up to recent times was small and noncumulative is attributable to the fact that economists viewed the subject as primarily ethical.

5. CONCLUSION

I must bring this sermon on economic sermons to a close. The main lesson I draw from our experience as preachers is that we are well received in the measure that we preach what the society wishes to hear. Perhaps all preachers achieve popularity by this route.

The degree of popularity of a preacher does not necessarily measure his influence as a preacher, let alone as a scholar. In fact one could perhaps argue that unpopular sermons are the more influential — certainly if the opposite is true, and preachers simply confirm their listeners' beliefs, pulpits should be at the rear of congregations, to make clearer who is leading. Whether economic preachers lead or follow, they need an ethical system to guide their recommendations. I shall address the nature and sources of their ethics in the next lecture.

II. THE ETHICS OF COMPETITION: THE FRIENDLY ECONOMISTS

The system of organization of an economy by private decisions on the allocation of resources and the private determination of the composition and distribution of final outputs is variously known as the market system, the enterprise system, competition, laissez-faire, and by the Marxian word, monopoly-capitalism. This system has been the main method of control of economic life in the last two hundred years in the Western world, but the extent of governmental intervention has increased enormously in both its scope and depth of detail.

In this lecture I plan first to discuss the attitudes of the main-stream of English economists toward this system — the measure and content of their approval and disapproval of the enterprise system. I shall dwell only briefly on the pre-modern evolution of their attitudes and treat primarily with the modern attitudes toward the market. Thereafter, I shall address the questions of where the economists get their ethics and the effects of these ethical values on their work.

1. TO 1900: THE GROWTH OF CAUTION IN THE ECONOMISTS' DEFENSE

Until the mid-nineteenth century, the virtues of the enterprise system were as widely accepted as the belief in its efficiency. Private property turned sand into gold, and no one complained at the loss of the sand or the presence of the gold. The "natural system of liberty" was extended widely. It is true that considerable lists have been compiled of the public tasks which the classical economists assigned to the state to correct or reinforce private actions, but they were not widespread or systematic *programs*, rather a spattering of Band-Aids to be put on the body economic. Malthus denounced systems of equality as part of his population essay and Ricardo ridiculed Robert Owen's parallelograms.[1]

John Stuart Mill was much more ambivalent on the comparative merits of private enterprise and various forms of socialism. The ambivalence was attributable to three sources: his remarkable propensity to understand and state fairly almost any view; the influence of Harriet, the *femme fatale* of the history of economics; and the astonishing and absurd deficiencies which he assigned to private enterprise. He asserted that perhaps nine-tenths of the labor force had compensation which at best was loosely related to exertion and achievement — indeed so loosely that he expressed indignation that the "produce of labour should be apportioned as we now see it, almost in an inverse ratio to the labour." [2] He felt able to assert that a competitive market could not achieve a shortening of hours of work, even if all the laborers wished it.[3] It has been said that only a highly educated man can be highly mistaken. Mill is no refutation.

Nevertheless, while stating in explicit and implicit ways that political economy did not imply laissez-faire, he initiated a practice that was soon to become widely imitated. After listing several reasons for preferring laissez-faire — chiefly grounded on a desire for individual freedom and development, but grounded also on efficiency — Mill concludes, "few will dispute the more than sufficiency of these reasons, to throw, in every instance, the

---

[1] For those who are more familiar with the parallelograms of Euclid than those of Owen, the latter proposed a utopia composed of communities of 500 to 2,000 people, each located in a village "arranged in the form of a large Square, or Parallelogram," with a balanced agricultural and manufacturing economy in which "a full and complete equality will prevail"; see "Constitution, Laws, and Regulations of a Community," in *A New View of Society*, 1st American ed. (New York: Bliss and White, 1825), pp. 162–63.

[2] *Principles of Political Economy* (Toronto: University of Toronto Press, 1965), I, 207.

[3] Ibid., II, 956–57.

burthen of making out a strong case, not on those who resist, but on those who recommend, government interference. *Laissez-faire*, in short, should be the general practice: every departure from it, unless required by some great good, a certain evil." [4] The practice of denying laissez-faire as a theorem but asserting its expediency as a general rule soon became, and to this day (I shall later argue) has remained, the set-lecture of the economist. Soon Cairnes, Jevons, Sidgwick, Marshall, and J. M. Keynes confirmed the tradition.[5] Monopoly, externalities, ignorance, and other reasons for departing from laissez-faire accumulated, but as individual exceptions to a general rule.

This compromise, in which Pure Science was silent but Heavy Presumption favored laissez-faire, troubles me more than it has most economists. A science is successful in the measure that it explains in general terms the behavior of the phenomena within its self-imposed boundaries. Let me give an example: the science should be able to tell us the effects of a minimum wage law on the employment and compensation of all workers, the effects on consumers through price changes, and so on. The standard analysis, to be specific, predicts that a minimum wage law reduces the incomes of the least capable workers and of the community at large, and various other effects.

One could say that the theory does not lead to an unambiguous rejection of minimum wage laws because of limitations imposed by the economist's framework: for example, monopsony in the labor market or ignorance of workers leads to inefficient market results. Then, however, the economist should analyze the effects

---

[4] Ibid., II, 944–45. The argument is presented fully in book V, chapter XI.

[5] J. E. Cairnes, "Political Economy and Laissez-Faire," in *Essays in Political Economy* (London: Macmillan, 1873): "Economic science has no more connection with our present industrial system than the science of mechanics has with our present system of railways" (p. 257); W. S. Jevons, *The State in Relations to Labour* (London: Macmillan, 1882); H. Sidgwick, *Principles of Political Economy*, 3d ed. (London: Macmillan, 1901), bk. III, ch. II; A. Marshall, "Social Possibilities of Economic Chivalry," in *Memorials of Alfred Marshall*, ed. A. C. Pigou (London: Macmillan, 1925); and J. M. Keynes, *Scope and Method of Political Economy*, 4th ed. (London: Macmillan, 1930), ch. II.

reached under (say) minimum wage laws and laissez-faire with monopsony, and reach a definite result or no result. In either event, no *presumption* is established.

Alternatively, the theory may be deemed inconclusive for reasons lying outside the economists' domain; in particular, social values not recognized by the theory may reverse the conclusion.[6] For example, a desired income redistribution (or some other social value) may be achieved by the minimum wage law. Thus the apparent beneficiaries of a minimum wage law are the workers above the minimum wage, and indeed that is the reason the AFL-CIO supports the law. Or the workers in a high-wage area may be protected from the competition of a low-wage area, preserving a desired distribution of population.

Very well, let these or other reasons be sufficient to explain the informed passage and continuance of the minimum wage law by the community. Is it not then a fair request of economic theory that it include these results in its study of the minimum wage law? Why shouldn't the full range of consequences important to the society be important to the economist? Unless we invoke consequences outside the scope of rational inquiry — say, that the law favors believers in the true God, without further identification — it is not easy to live with both a pure science of economic phenomena and a set of nonderivative presumptions about practice. Of course the neglect of values other than efficiency may be defended on grounds of scientific division of labor, even though no other science seems inclined to study the neglected share. In any event, one wonders again where the presumption comes from.

I suspect the answer to these questions is that the economists have decided, possibly implicitly and silently, that the other values that might overcome the efficiency presumption are usually weak or conflicting, or even reinforce the conclusion based upon the studied effects. I am in no position to quarrel with this as a work-

[6] In Mill's view, the freedom from compulsion was the chief value justifying the presumption of laissez-faire; book V, chapter XI of the *Principles* is a preview of *On Liberty*.

ing philosophy: no matter how full the explanation of why we have minimum wages — and it is a study we should broaden — I predict that we economists will not like the law. But the working philosophy should not parade as science.

2. Marginal Productivity Ethics

The decline in open, unconditional praise of the enterprise system by economists suffered one important interruption at the end of the nineteenth century. The occasion was the discovery and widespread adoption of the marginal productivity theory.

The marginal productivity theory states that in competitive equilibrium each productive factor receives a rate of compensation equal to the value of its marginal or additional contribution to the enterprise that employs it. If the productive factor is a laborer, and he works as (say) a service worker with negligible capital equipment, in equilibrium his wage will equal simply the amount of revenue his services add to the enterprise. If, as is usually the case, the product of all factors is commingled, the marginal product may be manifested as a slightly larger crop or a more reliable machine or some other salable attribute.

If you declare to a layman that a certain individual is paid his marginal product, after explaining perhaps more clearly than I have what a marginal product is, and then add, "Isn't that simply outrageous?," I predict that this layman will be amazed by your comment. In any event, several economists who were among the founders and disseminators of the marginal productivity theory did take exactly the view that the value of the marginal product of a person was the just rate of his remuneration.

The most famous exponent of this view was John Bates Clark. In his magnum opus, *The Distribution of Wealth* (1899), he stated:

The welfare of the laboring classes depends on whether they get much or little; but their attitude toward other classes — and therefore the stability of the social state — depends chiefly on the question, whether the amount they get, be it large or small, is what they produce. If they create a small amount of wealth and get the whole of it, they may not seek to revolutionize society; but if it were to appear that they produce an ample amount and get only a part of it, many of them would become revolutionists, and all would have the right to do so. . . .

Having first tested the honesty of the social state, by determining whether it gives to every man his own [product], we have next to test its beneficence, by ascertaining whether that which is his own is becoming greater or smaller.[7]

T. N. Carver of Harvard was also an exponent of productivity ethics:

But if the number of a particular kind of laborers is so small and the other factors are so abundant that one more laborer of this particular kind would add greatly to the product of the combination, then it is not inaccurate to say that his physical product is very high. That being the case, his value is very high. This, therefore, is the principle which determines how much a man is worth, and consequently, according to our criterion of justice, how much he ought to have as a reward for his work.[8]

I have not sought to discover how many economists joined in this ethical justification of competition. I believe that many economists did so, not so often by explicit avowal as by the implicit acceptance of the propriety of marginal productivity as the basis for remuneration. Pigou, for example, wished to define an exploitive wage, and he chose as his definition a wage which fell below the value of the marginal product of the worker.[9]

This literature is usually referred to as "naïve productivity ethics," with the adjective serving not to distinguish it from some other more sophisticated ethical system but to express disapproval.

[7] (New York: Macmillan Co., 1899), pp. 4–5.

[8] *Essays in Social Justice* (Cambridge: Harvard University Press, 1915), p. 201.

[9] *The Economics of Welfare*, 2d ed. (London: Macmillan, 1924), p. 754.

The classic statement of this disapproval is the famous essay by Frank Knight, "The Ethics of Competition" (1923).[10] Four charges are made against the claims of the competitive system to be just:

1. An economic system molds the tastes of its members, so the system cannot be defended on the ground that it satisfies demands efficiently.[11]

2. The economic system is not *perfectly* efficient: there are indivisibilities, imperfect knowledge, monopoly, externalities, etc.[12]

3. The paramount defect of the competitive system is that it distributes income largely on the basis of inheritance and luck (with some minor influence of effort). The inequality of income increases cumulatively under competition.[13]

4. Viewed (alternatively) as a game, competition is poorly fashioned to meet acceptable standards of fairness, such as giving everyone an even start and allowing a diversity of types of rivalries.

When I first read this essay a vast number of years ago, as a student writing his dissertation under Professor Knight's supervision, you should not be surprised to hear that I thought his was a conclusive refutation of "productivity ethics." When I reread

[10] *Quarterly Journal of Economics*; reprinted in *The Ethics of Competition* (Chicago: University of Chicago Press, 1976).

[11] ". . . the social order largely forms as well as gratifies the wants of its members, and the natural consequence [is] that it must be judged ethically rather by the wants which it generates . . ." (ibid., p. 51).

[12] Hence, "in conditions of real life no possible social order based upon a *laissez-faire* policy can justify the familiar ethical conclusions of apologetic economics" (ibid., p. 49).

[13] "The ownership of personal or material productive capacity is based upon a complex mixture of inheritance, luck, and effort, probably in that order of relative importance" (ibid., p. 56). "The luck element is so large . . . that capacity and effort may count for nothing [in business]. And this luck element works cumulatively, as in gambling games generally" (ibid., p. 64).

it a year or so ago, I was shocked by the argumentation. Knight made a series of the most sweeping and confident empirical judgments (such as those underlying the first and third charges) for which he could not have even a cupful of supporting evidence. Moreover, why was it even relevant, with respect to his second charge, that real-world markets are not perfectly competitive in his special sense: one can define a perfect standard to judge imperfect performance, and assuredly real-world performance under any form of economic organization will be less than perfect by any general criterion. Knight kept referring to the objections to competitive results under any "acceptable ethical system" but never told us what such a system contained in the way of ethical content. His own specific judgments do not seem compelling, as when he asserted that "no one contends that a bottle of old wine is ethically worth as much as a barrel of flour." Dear Professor Knight, please forgive your renegade student, but I do so contend, if it was a splendid year for claret.

I shall have more to say about acceptable ethical positions shortly, but for the moment I wish only to assert that the appeal of productivity ethics for income distribution commands wide support not only from the public but also from the economists when they are watching their sentiments rather than their words. Ethical values cannot be counted by a secret ballot referendum, but the support for a productivity ethic is indeed widespread. Even Marx, like Pigou, defined surplus value as the part of a worker's product that he was not paid. The fact that more than skill and effort go into remuneration — that in Knight's example bearded women get good circus jobs simply by not shaving — is not enough to dismiss productivity ethics.

3. THE ETHICS OF ECONOMISTS

I have postponed as long as possible the question: where do economists get their ethical systems? My answer is: wherever they can find one.

One occasional source has been a widely acceptable philosophical system. The most important such system in the history of economics has been utilitarianism, which was strongly influential on Bentham's circle, Sidgwick, Marshall, Pigou, and above all Edgeworth. I have already referred to Edgeworth's *Mathematical Psychics* (1881), which is in good part a reproduction of his earlier monograph, *New and Old Methods of Ethics* (1877). Edgeworth presents the utilitarian ethic in full grandeur:

'Mécanique Sociale' may one day take her place along with 'Mécanique Celeste,' throned each upon the double-sided height of one maximum principle, the supreme pinnacle of moral as of physical science. As the movements of each particle, constrained or loose, in a material cosmos are continually subordinated to one maximum sum-total of accumulated energy, so the movements of each soul, whether selfishly isolated or linked sympathetically, may continually be realizing the maximum energy of pleasure, the Divine love of the universe.[14]

Edgeworth's calculus and Sidgwick's *Methods of Ethics* represent the high point of the utilitarian ethics in neoclassical economics.

It proved to be a major obstacle to the explicit use of the utilitarian ethic that it required additional information, particularly about the efficiency of different persons in producing utility, that admitted of no objective determination. Recall that Edgeworth was led to recognize the possibility that an aristocracy might be the best of all societies.

Even when the difficulty of comparing utilities could be overcome, and it was generally overcome by consensus rather than by argument or evidence, the systematic ethic led to an embarrassing consequence. Let me explain by example.

When one traces out the applications of a general ethical system one encounters problems such as one that Alfred Marshall faced. He examined the properties of good excise taxes in a chapter suitably entitled "Theories of Changes in Normal De-

[14] *Mathematical Psychics*, p. 12.

mand and Supply in Relation to the Doctrine of Maximum Satisfaction."[15] According to the utilitarian theory, it is more desirable, Marshall stated, to tax necessaries rather than luxuries because the demand for necessaries is less elastic and therefore an excise tax will occasion a smaller loss of consumer utility (surplus).[16] Of course he rejected this recommendation of regressive taxation because it ignored ability to pay taxes.

It might be argued that if Marshall had properly weighted the marginal utility of income of the poor as greater than that of the rich, he would be freed of embarrassment. Possibly, although he would then have needed to compare the magnitudes of utilities with taxation of luxuries and taxation of necessaries. In any event, other embarrassing implications are readily found, for example, that the utilitarian goal would imply cosmopolitan income redistribution.

And that is the trouble with a comprehensive ethical system: it leads to conclusions which are unpopular with the community and therefore unpopular with the economists. I believe, although I have not undertaken the substantial task of verifying, the proposition that wherever an ethical system has clashed with widespread social values, the economists have abandoned the implications of the ethical system. If that is indeed the case, it strongly argues for the acceptance of the community's values with whatever inconsistencies they contain.

John Rawls once proposed a way out of this impasse — a method of deriving general ethical values that were both inductive and capable of consistent application. His proposal was as follows. Select a set of competent judges and ask them to decide many and varied specific conflicts that arise between individuals in the society. Given their decisions, seek an explication or principle that correctly predicts these decisions on average and call that principle the ethical principle. Any implicit ethical principles

15 *Principles of Economics* (1920), bk. V, ch. XIII.
16 Ibid., p. 467 n.

that had been followed by the competent judges would be recovered by this procedure. One might complain at the elitist nature of the procedure, and a fundamental question is of course whether any principles would be found to exist.[17] Rawls's later and influential presentation of a modified utilitarian theory of justice has no such inductive basis, which suggests that he also found an inductive ethics difficult to systematize, and possibly difficult to accept.[18]

If economists have been content to base their goals upon the ruling views of the educated classes, as I believe to be the case, that is not quite the same thing as saying that they have simply taken an implicit opinion poll on ethical values and either accepted the majority view or distributed themselves in proportion to the frequencies of views held by these classes. Their own discipline has had its own influence.

Members of other social sciences often remark, in fact I must say complain, at the peculiar fascination that the logic of rational decision-making exerts upon economists. It is such an interesting logic: it has answers to so many and varied questions, often answers that are simultaneously reasonable to economists and absurd to others. The paradoxes are not diminished by the delight with which economists present them. How pleased Longfield must have been when he showed that if, in periods of acute shortage, the rich bought grain and sold it at half price to the poor, the poor were not helped. How annoyed the ecclesiastical readers of Smith must have been to learn that the heavy subsidization of clerical training served only to lower the income of curates. How outraged even some economists are with Becker's "rotten kid theorem," which demonstrates that altruistic treatment of a selfish person forces him to behave as an unselfish person would.

Economic logic centers on utility-maximizing behavior by

[17] See "Outline of a Decision Procedure for Ethics," *The Philosophical Review* 60 (1951): 177–97.

[18] See *A Theory of Justice* (Cambridge: Harvard University Press, 1971).

individuals. Such behavior may be found in every area of human behavior — and my just-mentioned colleague, Gary Becker, has analyzed it with striking results in areas such as crime, marriage and divorce, fertility, and altruistic behavior — but the central application of economic theory has been in explicit markets. The power of self-interest, and its almost unbelievable delicacy and subtlety in complex decision areas, has led economists to seek a large role for explicit or implicit prices in the solution of many social problems.

As a result, in a period of rapid and extensive movement away from reliance on competitive markets to allocate resources and to distribute income, economists have not led the trend but rather followed it at substantial distance. They have sought persistently to employ prices to abate pollution or to ration energy or to incite safety conditions. They have been at the forefront of what presently appears to be a modest policy of deregulation of certain areas of economic behavior.

It would take a wiser person than I to determine which shares of this market orientation of economists are due to professional training, to attachment to a demonstrably efficient machinery for allocating resources that is largely (but not completely) independent of the goals being sought, and to ethical values in the market organization of economic activity. But this last component, the ethical attractiveness of voluntary exchange, plays at least some part in our attitudes, and I shall give an example of its role.

Market transactions are voluntary and repetitive. These traits are much less marked in political transactions, or military transactions, although perhaps not in religious transactions. Because the market transactions are voluntary, they must benefit at least one party and not injure the other. Because they are repetitive, they (usually) make deceit and nonfulfillment of promises unprofitable. A reputation for candor and responsibility is a commercial asset — on the enterprise's balance sheet it may be called good will.

Nothing in rational behavior precludes the formation of habits which economize on decision-making costs. One such habit according to Marshall is probity: "The opportunities for knavery are certainly more numerous than they were; but there is no reason for thinking that men avail themselves of a larger proportion of such opportunities than they used to do. On the contrary, modern methods of trade imply habits of trustfulness on the one side and power of resisting temptation to dishonesty on the other, which do not exist among a backward people." [19] A still stronger, and much earlier, extension of the same argument was made by Smith:

Whenever commerce is introduced into any country, probity and punctuality always accompany it. These virtues in a rude and barbarous country are almost unknown. Of all the nations in Europe, the Dutch, the most commercial, are the most faithful to their word. The English are more so than the Scotch, but much inferiour to the Dutch, and in the remote parts of this country they (are) far less so than in the commercial parts of it. This is not at all to be imputed to national character, as some pretend. There is no natural reason why an Englishman or a Scotchman should not be as punctual in performing agreements as a Dutchman. It is far more reduceable to self interest, that general principle which regulates the actions of every man, and which leads men to act in a certain manner from views of advantage, and is as deeply implanted in an Englishman as a Dutchman. A dealer is afraid of losing his character, and is scrupulous in observing every engagement. When a person makes perhaps 20 contracts in a day, he cannot gain so much by endeavouring to impose on his neighbours, as the very appearance of a cheat would make him lose. Where people seldom deal with one another, we find that they are somewhat disposed to cheat, because they can gain more by a smart trick than they can lose by the injury which it does their character. They whom we call politicians are not the most remarkable men in the world for probity and punctuality. Ambassadors from different nations are still less so: they are praised for any little

[19] *Principles of Economics*, 8th ed. (London: Macmillan, 1920), p. 7.

advantage they can take, and pique themselves a good deal on this degree of refinement. The reason of this is that nations treat with one another not above twice or thrice in a century, and they may gain more by one piece of fraud than (lose) by having a bad character. France has had this character with us ever since the reign of Lewis XIVth, yet it has never in the least hurt either its interest or splendour.[20]

I do not know whether in actual fact the participants in economic transactions behave more honestly than those in diplomatic exchanges or in primitive barter, and I am reasonably confident that Marshall and Smith also did not know when they wrote these passages, whatever they have learned since. But I do believe that they, and most modern economists, accept the substance of their position on commercial morality.

This belief is based not upon some poll of opinion but on our daily practice. Modern economists almost invariably postulate transactions free of fraud or coercion. This postulate is partially presented in mathematical versions as the budget equation, which states that for each economic agent the sum of values received equals the sum of values given up. No transaction therefore leaves anyone worse off, ex ante, than he was before he entered it — almost a definition of a noncoercive transaction.

There is no inherent reason for us to make this assumption, and two good reasons for not doing so. The first reason for including fraud and coercion in economics is that they are probably impossible to distinguish from honorable dealing. Assume that I take a shortcut home through a park each night, and once a week on average I am robbed of my trousers — I have learned not to carry money. Is this not a voluntary transaction in which I pay a toll of one-fifth of a pair of trousers per day for access to the shortcut? Assume that I sell to you a plot of land which you erroneously believe to cover an oil pool, and I know the truth.

[20] *Lectures on Jurisprudence* (Cambridge: Cambridge University Press, 1978), pp. 538–39.

Am I being fraudulent? If so, modify the circumstances so that you know there is oil and I don't. Clearly we can find situations in which the presence of fraud is rejected by half the population.

Second, even when fraud or coercion is unambiguous in the eyes of the society, that is no reason to believe that ordinary economic analysis is inapplicable. Fraudulent securities will be supplied in such quantity that their marginal costs, including selling costs, equal their marginal revenue. One would not expect criminals to earn more than they could obtain in legitimate callings, proper allowance being made for all costs of doing business. The ordinary propositions of economics hold for crime.

I conclude that we economists have customarily excluded fraud and coercion because we have thought that they are not empirically significant elements in the ordinary economic transactions of an enterprise economy.

Although economists have displayed a larger affection for the system of private enterprise than has the remainder of the educated public, this is not to say that prevalent social views have no influence on technical economic writing. Consider the enormous attention that is devoted to monopoly in modern economic theory, an attention so vast that it has virtually taken possession of the literature on industrial organization. The evidence that monopoly is important is negligible, and the evidence that it is a quite minor influence on the workings of the economy is large. I have slowly been approaching the view of Schumpeter, that the eminent role of monopoly in economic literature is due to the influence of general social views.[21]

4. WHAT IS ETHICS?

Economists, I have just said, believe that economic transactions are usually conducted on a high level of candor and responsibility,

[21] The recent attention economists have paid to conservation of resources and to all varieties of pollution also represents a response to popular discussion of these matters rather than the result of autonomous professional economic research.

because it is in the interest of the parties to behave honorably in repetitive transactions. Hence honesty pays.

Against this view we may set that of Archbishop Richard Whately, himself something of an economist as well as a noted logician and divine. The man who acts on the principle that honesty is the best policy, said his Grace, is a man who is not honest.[22] He did not elaborate, but the meaning is clear: he who behaves honestly because it is remunerative is simply an amoral calculator; an honest man is one whose principles of right conduct are adopted independently of their consequences for him.

If every person in a society shared the utilitarian goal of maximum utility for the society, all would presumably behave honestly because there is a large deadweight loss to society in erecting defenses against dishonesty and punishing its manifestations. If even one person did not share this ethic, it might well pay him to engage in acts of dishonesty — indeed it would hardly pay the society to take defensive steps against him or her. One may therefore conclude that honesty would be a utilitarian ethic for the society as a whole, even though honesty did not pay (was not utilitarian) for an individual.

Do people possess ethical beliefs which influence their behavior in ways not dictated by, and hence in conflict with, their own long-run utility-maximizing behavior? This question is not free of ambiguity: if we allow unlimited altruism in the individual's utility function, we are back to social utilitarianism. Less to avoid this result than to attain a position that seems empirically defensible, I shall assume that the altruism is strong within the family and toward close friends and diminishes with the social distance of the person — very much the position Adam Smith advanced in his *Moral Sentiments*.[23] This interpretation does not determine the answer to the question whether people act

[22] Nassau W. Senior, *Journals, Conversations and Essays Relating to Ireland* (London: Longmans Green, 1868), II, 271.

[23] See Ronald H. Coase, "Adam Smith's View of Man," *Journal of Law and Economics* 19 (1976): 529–46.

on ethical principles. Indeed it eliminates the easy answer, "of course, they give to charity."

The question of the existence of effective ethical values is of course an empirical question, and in principle it should be directly testable. I recall reading of an experiment in which stamped and addressed but unsealed envelopes with small sums of money were scattered in the streets, and records were compiled of which envelopes were mailed to the designated recipient. My faint recollection is that more envelopes were mailed when the designated recipient was a charity, but that most sums were appropriated by the finders.

One could quarrel at the design of this test, as I recall it, for it gave no information on the finders: perhaps those who were conversing with their clergymen when the envelope was found behaved differently from those who were conversing with their bookies. Still, it is an interesting line of inquiry, one that would be a better employment of the recent doctorates in philosophy than the employments which are reported.

Let me predict the outcome of the systematic and comprehensive testing of behavior in situations where self-interest and ethical values with wide verbal allegiance are in conflict. Much of the time, most of the time in fact, the self-interest theory (as I interpreted it on Smithian lines) will win. In a set of cases that is not negligible and perhaps not random with respect to social characteristics of the actors, the self-interest hypothesis will fail — at least without a subtle and unpredictable interpretation of self-interest.

I predict this result because it is the prevalent one found by economists not only within a wide variety of economic phenomena, but in their investigations of marital, child-bearing, criminal, religious, and other social behavior as well. We believe that man is a utility-maximizing animal — apparently pigeons and rats are also — and to date we have not found it informative to carve out a section of his life in which he invokes a different goal of behavior.

In fact, the test I have just proposed has very little potential scope, I shall argue, because most ethical values do not conflict with individual utility-maximizing behavior.

I pursue this dangerous line of thought in my final lecture.

III. THE ETHICS OF COMPETITION:
THE UNFRIENDLY CRITICS

In the century following the appearance of the *Wealth of Nations*, the pace of economic progress accelerated to levels never before achieved on so continuous and comprehensive a scale. The technology, the economy, the lives, and even the politics of the Western world underwent profound and lasting changes. The standard of living reached continually higher levels, longevity increased, and education spread over the entire society.

It was to be expected that the radical changes accompanying this astonishing economic development would arouse deep opposition and bitter criticism from some groups. Important figures in the cultural circles of Great Britain were soon nostalgic for a romantic past. Robert Southey, the poet laureate, viewed the earlier cottage system and the factory system through bifocal spectacles with rose and black tints, respectively:

. . . we remained awhile in silence, looking upon the assemblage of dwellings below. Here, and in the adjoining hamlet of Mill-beck, the effects of manufactures and of agriculture may be seen and compared. The old cottages are such as the poet and the painter equally delight in beholding. Substantially built of the native stone without mortar, dirtied with no white-lime, and their long low roofs covered with slate, if they had been raised by the magic of some indigenous Amphion's music, the materials could not have adjusted themselves more beautifully in accord with the surrounding scene; and time has still further harmonized them with weather-stains, lichens and moss, short grasses and short fern, and stone-plants of various kinds. The ornamented chimneys, round or square, less adorned than those which, like little turrets, crest the houses of the Portuguese peasantry; and yet not less happily suited to their place, the hedge of clipt box beneath the windows, the rose bushes beside the door, the little patch of flower ground, with its tall holly-hocks in front; the garden beside, the beehives, and the orchard with its bank of daffodils and snow-drops (the earliest and the profusest in these parts), indicate in the owners some portion of ease and leisure, some regard to neat-ness and comfort, some sense of natural and innocent and health-ful enjoyment. The new cottages of the manufacturers are . . . upon the manufacturing pattern . . . naked, and in a row.

How is it, said I, that everything which is connected with manufactures presents such features of unqualified deformity? From the largest of Mammon's temples down to the poorest hovel in which his helotry are stalled, these edifices have all one char-acter. Time cannot mellow them; nature will neither clothe nor conceal them; and they remain always as offensive to the eye as to the mind![1]

Of the innumerable voices that joined in this swelling chorus, I shall briefly notice two.

Thomas Carlyle, who gave the dismal science this name, wrote with his customary passion:

And yet I will venture to believe that in no time, since the beginnings of Society, was the lot of those same dumb millions of toilers so entirely unbearable as it is even in the days now passing over us. It is not to die, or even to die of hunger, that makes a man wretched; many men have died; all men must die, — the last exit of us all is in a Fire-Chariot of Pain. But it is to live miserable we know not why; to work sore and yet gain nothing; to be heart-worn, weary, yet isolated, unrelated, girt in with a cold universal Laissez-faire: it is to die slowly all our life long, imprisoned in a deaf, dead, Infinite Injustice, as in the accursed iron belly of a Phalaris' Bull! This is and remains forever intolerable to all men whom God has made. Do we wonder at French Revolutions,

---

[1] *Sir Thomas More; Or Colloquies on the Progress and Prospects of Society* (Lon-don: John Murray, 1829), I, 173–74.

Chartisms, Revolts of Three Days? The Times, if we will consider them, are really unexampled.[2]

Finally, John Ruskin's immense Victorian audience was repeatedly instructed in the vices of industrialism. He was prepared to sum up his entire message in the declaration: "Government and cooperation are in all things the Laws of Life; Anarchy and competition the Laws of Death."[3] A more explicit version runs: "It being the privilege of the fishes as it is of rats and wolves, to live by the laws of demand and supply; but the distinction of humanity, to live by those of right."[4]

A full tour through the modern critics of the competitive organization of society would be a truly exhausting trip. It would include the drama, the novel, the churches, the academies, the lesser intellectual establishments, the socialists and communists and Fabians and a swarm of other dissenters. One is reminded of Schumpeter's remark that the Japanese earthquake of 1924 had a remarkable aspect: it was not blamed on capitalism. Suddenly one realizes how impoverished our society would be in its indignation, as well as in its food, without capitalism.

It is no part of my present purpose to sketch this opposition, and still less to attempt to refute it. Many excellent replies have been penned: Southey's passage with which I began called forth the full scorn — and that is truly a vast scorn — of Macaulay:

Mr. Southey has found out a way, he tells us, in which the effects of manufactures and agriculture may be compared. And what is this way? To stand on a hill, to look at a cottage and a factory, and to see which is the prettier. Does Mr. Southey think that the body of the English peasantry live, or ever lived, in substantial or ornamented cottages, with box-hedges, flower-gardens,

[2] *Past and Present* (Chicago: Henneberry, n.d.), p. 296.

[3] *The Complete Works of John Ruskin* (New York: Thomas Crowell, n.d.).

[4] *The Communism of John Ruskin* (New York: Humboldt, 1891), edited by W. P. B. Bliss, p. 52 n.

beehives, and orchards? If not, what is his parallel worth? We despise those mock philosophers who think that they serve the cause of science by depreciating literature and the fine arts. But if anything could excuse their narrowness of mind, it would be such a book as this.[5]

Macaulay in fact would give Southey credit for only "two faculties which were never, we believe, vouchsafed in measure so copious to any human being — the faculty of believing without a reason, and the faculty of hating without a provocation." [6]

Later, and usually lesser, defenders of laissez-faire have proved that the critics behaved as critics usually do: inventing some abuses in the system they attacked; denouncing some of its virtues as abuses; exaggerating the real shortcomings; and being singularly blind to the difficulties of any alternative economic system, when they faced this problem at all. But these characteristics are not unique to the critics of private enterprise and may well be inherent in criticisms of any existing order.

I begin with this smattering of early critics only to suggest that important leaders of public opinion have long been opposed to a competitive economic system. There is a natural temptation to credit to them and their numerous present-day progeny the decline that has occurred in the public esteem for private enterprise and the large expansion of state control over economic life. I urge you to resist that temptation. After a preliminary look at the so-called followers of opinion, I shall return to the leaders and seek to explain their attitudes and to question their importance. If my interpretation is correct, it raises interesting questions on the future of private enterprise.

1. HAVE ATTITUDES CHANGED?: THE LOWER CLASSES

History is written by and for the educated classes. We know

---

[5] "Southey's Colloquies on Society," in Thomas Babington Macaulay, *Critical, Historical, and Miscellaneous Essays* (New York: Mason, Baker & Pratt, 1873), II, 148–49.

[6] Ibid., p. 132.

more about the thoughts and actions of an eighteenth-century lord than about 100,000 members of the classes which were at or near the bottom of the income and educational scales. No one can deduce, from documentary evidence, the attitudes of these lower classes toward economic philosophies, whereas the noble lord's words are enshrined in Hansard and several fat volumes of published correspondence. Hence we cannot determine from direct documentary sources what the attitudes toward laissez-faire of these lower classes have been.

Nevertheless, it is an hypothesis that is plausible to me and I hope tenable to you that these lower classes — who have increased immensely in wealth and formal education in the last several hundred years — have been strongly attracted to the economic regime of laissez-faire capitalism. One highly persuasive evidence of this is the major spontaneous migrations of modern history: the armies of Europeans that came to the United States, until barriers were created at both ends; the millions of Chinese who have sought entrance to Hong Kong, Shanghai, and other open Asian economies; the millions of Mexicans who these days defy American laws designed to keep them home. These have not been simply migrations from poorer to richer societies, although even that would carry its message, but primarily migrations of lower classes of the home populations. An open, decentralized economy is still the land of opportunity for the lower classes.

The stake of the lower classes in the system of competition is based upon the fact that a competitive productive system is remarkably indifferent to status. An employer finds two unskilled workers receiving $3.00 per hour an excellent substitute for a semiskilled worker receiving $8.00 per hour. A merchant finds ten one-dollar purchases by the poor more profitable than a seven-dollar purchase by a prosperous buyer. This merchant is much less interested in the color of a customer than in the color of his money.

If it is true that a large share of the population of modern societies (and many other societies as well) eagerly migrates to competitive economies when given the opportunity, why have these people supported the vast expansion of governmental controls over economic life in the many democratic societies in which they constitute an important part of the electorate?

I shall postulate now, and argue the case later, that the lower classes have not supported regulatory policies and socialism because they were duped or led by intellectuals with different goals. Instead, these classes have shared the general propensity to vote their own interests. Once the unskilled workers enter an open society, they will oppose further free immigration. The most poorly paid workers are aware of the adverse effects of minimum wage laws, and their representatives vote against such laws.[7] It would be feasible to devise numerous tests of this rational interpretation of lower-class political behavior: as examples, have they been supporters of heavy governmental expenditures on higher education, or of the pollution control programs?

Studies such as I call for will demonstrate, I believe, that the lower classes have been quite selective and parsimonious in their desired interventions in the workings of the competitive economy, simply because not many regulatory policies work to their benefit. These classes will seek and accept all the transfer payments the political system allows, but they have little to gain from regulatory policies that reduce the income of society.

But these lower classes do not dominate our political system. In the long run they have more votes in the marketplace than they have at the ballot box, despite appearances to the contrary. They do not have in full measure the necessary or useful attributes of successful political coalitions, such as common economic and social origins and interests, nor are they localized in space or cohesive in age and social background. They have access to the press or the electromagnetic spectrum only as receivers. They do

---

[7] See J. B. Kau and P. H. Rubin, "Voting on Minimum Wages: A Time-Series Analysis," *Journal of Political Economy* 86 (1978): 337–42.

not directly control the flow of information. These characteristics do not imply that they are the victims of some conspiracy or that they have no influence on political events. It does mean that the marketplace measures their preferences more finely and more promptly than the literature or the politics of the society, even if that society is as democratic as Great Britain or the United States.

This premium placed by politics on certain educational and social characteristics of the voting population is, I believe, the first of two reasons for the failure of the lower classes to play a larger role in modern regulatory policy. The second and more fundamental reason is that the lower classes are by no means a majority: the very efficiency of the competitive economic system has depleted the ranks of the poor and the ill-educated! The productivity of the economy has moved the children of immigrants or poor farm families into the middle classes. A fair fraction of the best economists in the United States are one or two generations away from the garment trades.

When private enterprise elevates many of its lower-class supporters to the middle classes, they find a much larger agenda of desirable state action. The restrictions on entrance into skilled crafts and learned occupations will serve as an important example of the large number of profitable uses of political power that are open to the various groups in the middle classes. If Groucho Marx would not join a country club that would admit the likes of him, private enterprise has reversed the paradox and expells those who learned to play the game well.

2.   Have Attitudes Changed?: The Intellectuals

The intellectual has been contemptuous of commercial activity for several thousand years, so it is not surprising that he has made no exception for the competitive economy. Yet the larger part of the present-day class that lives by words and ideas rather than by commodity processing owes its existence to the productiveness of modern economic systems. Only economies that are highly productive by historical standards can send their populations to schools for twelve to eighteen years, thus providing employment to a large class of educators. Only such a rich society can have a vast communications industry and pervasive social services — other large areas of employment of the intellectual classes. So it is at least a superficial puzzle why these intellectuals maintain much of the traditional hostility of their class to business enterprise — contemptuous of its motives, critical of its achievements, supportive at least of extensive regulation and often of outright socialization.

An answer that many will give is that the competitiveness of economic relationships, the emphasis on profit as a measure of achievement, the difficulties encountered by those cultural activities that do not meet the market test — are precisely the source of opposition: materialism is hostile to the ethical values cherished by the intellectual classes.

A second, and almost opposite, explanation is that these upper classes find their chief patrons and their main employment in government and its activities. Even though the growth of government relative to private economic activity is conditional on the productivity of the private economy, the self-interest of the intellectuals is in the expansion of the government economy.

I believe that this is true in the short run, and the short run is at least a generation or two. The extensive regulatory activities of the modern state are, both directly and in their influence on the private sector, the source of much of the large demand for the intellectual classes. For example, if higher education in America were private, so its costs were paid directly by students rather than so largely by public subventions, the education sector would shrink substantially, not because of increases in efficiency, although such increases would surely occur, but because for large numbers of older students, school attendance would no longer be a sensible investment of their time. The state has greatly reduced the relative cost of higher education for the individual student, although it has raised the relative cost for society. Similarly, the immense panoply of regulatory policies has generated a public employment of perhaps half a million persons, with an even larger number of people occupied in complying with or evading the policies the first group are prescribing.

In short, the intellectuals are the beneficiaries of the expansion of the economic role of government. Their support is, on this reading, available to the highest bidder, just as other resources in our society are allocated. Have not the intellectuals always been respectful of their patrons?

I am not striving for paradox or righteousness, so I would emphasize, like Adam Smith, that no insinuations are intended as to the deficient integrity of the intellectuals, which I naturally believe to be as high as the market in ideas allows. No large number of intellectuals change positions after wetting a finger and holding it in the wind: they cultivate those of their ideas which find a market. Ideas without demands are simply as hard to sell as other products without demands. If anyone in this audience wishes to become an apostle of the single tax after the scripture of Henry George, for example, I recommend that he or she acquire and cherish a wealthy, indulgent spouse.

3. IDEOLOGY AND THE INTELLECTUALS

A self-interest theory of the support for and opposition to private enterprise will shock many people, and not simply because the theory I propose is so elementary and undeveloped (although these are admitted defects). Many and perhaps most intellectuals will assert that the opposition of intellectuals to private enterprise is based upon ethical and cultural values divorced from self-interest, and that the intellectuals' opposition has played an important leader role in forming the critical attitude of the society as a whole.

An invariably interesting scholar who urged the power-ful influence of the intellectuals on social trends was Joseph Schumpeter. Schumpeter's full argument for the prospective col-lapse of capitalism contains an elusive metaphysical view of the need for legitimacy of a social system, and a charismatic role for its leading classes, that was, he felt, incompatible with the rational calculus of the capitalist mind. The intellectuals were playing their customary role of critics of social order:

> On the one hand, freedom of public discussion involving free-dom to nibble at the foundations of capitalist society is inevitable in the long run. On the other hand, the intellectual group cannot help nibbling, because it lives on criticism and its whole position depends on criticism that stings; and criticism of persons and of current events will, in a situation in which nothing is sacrosanct, fatally issue in criticism of classes and institutions.[8]

The intellectuals are credited in particular with radicalizing the labor movement.

That intellectuals should believe that intellectuals are im-portant in determining the course of history is not difficult to understand. The position is less easy for even an intellectual economist to understand since it sets one class of laborers aside and attributes special motives to them. On the traditional eco-nomic theory of occupational choice, intellectuals distribute them-selves among occupations and among artistic, ethical, cultural, and political positions in such numbers as to maximize their in-comes, where incomes include amenities such as prestige and apparent influence. On the traditional economic view, a Galbraith could not do better working for Ronald Reagan and a Friedman could not do better working for Carter or Kennedy, and I could not do better telling you that intellectuals are terribly important.[9]

[8] *Capitalism, Socialism and Democracy*, 3d ed. (New York: Harper Torchbooks, 1950), p. 151.

[9] Please recall the statement that concludes the last section, that the allocation system works, usually *not* by individuals choosing merchantable ideas, but by only cer-tain of their ideas finding markets.

It is worth noticing that Schumpeter partially accepted this position in pointing out that the declining market prospects of the intellectual class were one basis for their criticism of the market.[10]

Please do not read into my low valuation of the importance of professional preaching a similarly low valuation of scientific work. Once a general relationship in economic phenomena is discovered and verified, it becomes a part of the working knowledge of everyone. A newly established scientific relationship shifts the arena of discourse and is fully adopted by all informed parties, whatever their policy stands. Whether a person likes the price system or dislikes it and prefers a form of non-price rationing of some good, he must accept the fact of a negatively sloping demand curve and take account of its workings. The most influential economist, even in the area of public policy, is the economist who makes the most important scientific contributions.

On the self-interest theory, applied not only to intellectuals but to all of the society, we should look for all to support rationally the positions that are compatible with their long-run interests. Often these interests are subtle or remote, and often the policies that advance these interests are complex and even experimental. For example, it would require a deeper and more comprehensive analysis than has yet been made of the effects of the vast paraphernalia of recent regulation of the energy field to identify and measure the costs and benefits of these policies. But at least in principle, and to a growing degree in practice, we can determine the effects of public policies and therefore whose interests they serve.

The case is rather different with respect to the role of ideology, if that ambiguous word is appropriated to denote a set of beliefs which are not directed to an enlarged, long-run view of self-interest. If an anti-market ideology is postulated, and postulated to be independent of self-interest, then what is its origin and what is its content? Do we not face an inherently arbitrary choice if we

10 *Capitalism, Socialism and Democracy*, pp. 152–53.

follow this route?: anti-market values are then some humanistic instinct for personal solidarity rather than arms-length dealings, or a search for simplicity and stability in a world where competitive technology is the sorcerer's apprentice, or a wish for a deliberately inefficient egalitarianism, or something else. Choices in this direction are surely as numerous and arbitrary as choices of ethical systems, and indeed that is what they are. Perhaps no one, and certainly no economist, has the right to disparage such non-utility-maximizing systems, but even an economist is entitled to express skepticism about the coherence and content, and above all the actual acceptance on a wide scale, of any such ideology.

In the event, ideology is beginning to make fugitive appearances in the quantitative studies of the origins of public policies. Thus, if one wishes to know why some states lean to income taxes and others to sales taxes, the most popular measure of the higher values (or of intellectual confusion?) entertained by a state is the percentage of its vote cast for McGovern in 1972! At this level, ideology is only a name for a bundle of undefined notions one refuses to discuss.

The simplest way to test the role of ideology as a nonutility-maximizing goal is to ascertain whether the supporters of such an ideology incur costs in supporting it. If on average and over substantial periods of time we find (say) that the proponents of "small is beautiful" earn less than comparable talents devoted to urging the National Association of Manufacturers to new glories, I will accept the evidence. But first let us see it.

4. The Calculus of Morals

I arrive by the devious route you observe at the thesis that flows naturally and even irresistibly from the theory of economics. Man is eternally a utility-maximizer, in his home, in his office — be it public or private — in his church, in his scientific work, in short, everywhere. He can and often does err: perhaps the calculation is too difficult, but more often his information is incomplete. He learns to correct these errors, although sometimes at heavy cost.

What we call ethics, on this approach, is a set of rules with respect to dealings with other persons, rules which in general prohibit behavior which is only myopically self-serving, or which imposes large costs on others with small gains to oneself. General observance of these rules makes not only for long-term gains to the actor but also yields some outside benefits ("externalities"), and the social approval of the ethics is a mild form of enforcement of the rules to achieve the general benefits.[11] Of course some people will gain by violating the rules. More precisely, everyone violates some rule or other occasionally, and a few people violate important rules often.

Two difficulties with enlarging and elaborating this approach to ethical codes are worth mentioning. The first is the constant temptation to define the utility of the individual in such a way that the hypothesis is tautological. That difficulty is serious because there is no accepted content to the utility function — I gave my interpretation at the end of the second lecture, and it made a person's utility depend upon the welfare of the actor, his family, plus a narrow circle of associates. Still, the difficulties in using utility theory can be exaggerated. A rational person learns from experience, so it is a contradiction of the utility-maximizing hypothesis if we observe systematically biased error in predictions: thus one cannot surreptitiously introduce the theory of mistakes. The development of a content-rich theory of utility-maximizing is a never-ending task.

A second difficulty with the utility-maximizing hypothesis is that it is difficult to test, less because of its own ambiguities than because there is no accepted body of ethical beliefs which can

---

[11] The expression of this social approval by an individual is itself enforced by the approval of other individuals and therefore constitutes a system of informal law. Clearly this line of argument takes us (as Michael McPherson pointed out) into political (i.e., not purely individualistic) theory.

be tested for consistency with the hypothesis. In the absence of such a well-defined set of beliefs, any ad hoc ethical value can be presented, and of course no respectable theory can cope with this degree of arbitrariness of test.

In particular, a system of ethics of individual behavior is all that one can ask a theory of individual utility-maximizing behavior to explain. Political values — values that the society compels its members to observe by recourse to political sanctions — include such popular contemporary policies as income redistribution and prohibition of the use of characteristics such as race and age and sex in certain areas of behavior (but not yet in other areas such as marriage). It requires a political theory rather than an individualistic ethical theory to account for policies and goals whose chief commendation to a substantial minority of people is that their acceptance spares them a term in jail.

With these disclaimers, I believe that it is a feasible and even an orthodox scientific problem to ascertain a set of widely and anciently accepted precepts of ethical personal behavior, and to test their concordance with utility-maximizing behavior for the preponderance of individuals. In fact Rawls's proposal of a method of constructing an inductive ethical system, which I briefly described earlier, is exactly the procedure that would show that the ethical system was based on utility-maximizing behavior. My confidence that the test would yield this result will be disputed by many people of distinction, and that argues all the more for making the test.

5. CONCLUSION

I have presented the hypothesis that we live in a world of reasonably well-informed people acting intelligently in pursuit of their self-interests. In this world leaders play only a modest role, acting much more as agents than as instructors or guides of the classes they appear to lead.

The main aspects of social development all have discoverable purposes and should run predictable courses. It is precisely the great virtue — and the great vulnerability — of a comprehensive theory of human behavior that it should account for all persistent and widespread phenomena within its wide domain.

If the hypothesis proves to be as fertile and prescient in political and social affairs as it has been in economic affairs, we can look forward to major advances in our understanding of issues as grave as the kinds of economic and political systems toward which we are evolving. Even if it does not achieve this imperial status, I am wholly confident that it will become a powerful theme guiding much work in the social sciences in the next generation. I would give much to learn what it will teach us of the prospects of my friend, the competitive economy.

The Twilight of Self-Reliance: Frontier Values and Contemporary America

WALLACE STEGNER

THE TANNER LECTURES ON HUMAN VALUES

Delivered at
The University of Utah

February 25, 1980

WALLACE STEGNER studied at the University of Utah and the University of Iowa, receiving his Ph.D. from the latter institution in 1935. He is the author of twelve novels and seven nonfiction works, as well as numerous articles and reviews. *His Angle of Repose* was awarded a Pulitzer Prize in 1971, and *The Spectator Bird* received a National Book Award in 1976. Dr. Stegner has been a Guggenheim Fellow, a Fellow of the Center for Advanced Study in the Behavioral Sciences, a Senior Fellow of the National Endowment for the Humanities, and Montgomery Fellow at Dartmouth College (1980), among others. He has taught at several universities, including the University of Utah, the University of Wisconsin, Harvard University, and Stanford University from 1945 to 1971, when he retired as Jackson E. Reynolds Professor of Humanities.

Henry David Thoreau was a philosopher not unwilling to criticize his country and his countrymen, but when he wrote the essay entitled "Walking" in 1862, at a time when his country was engaged in a desperate civil war, he wrote with what Mark Twain would have called the calm confidence of a Christian with four aces. He spoke America's stoutest self-confidence and most optimistic expectations. Eastward, he said, he walked only by force, but westward he walked free: he must walk toward Oregon and not toward Europe, and his trust in the future was total.

If the moon looks larger here than in Europe, probably the sun looks larger also. If the heavens of America appear infinitely higher, and the stars brighter, I trust that these facts are symbolical of the height to which the philosophy and poetry and religion of her inhabitants may one day soar. . . . I trust that we shall be more imaginative, that our thoughts will be clearer, fresher, and more ethereal, as our sky — our understanding more comprehensive and broader, like our plains — our intellect generally on a grander scale, like our thunder and lightning, our rivers and mountains and forests — and our hearts shall even correspond in breadth and depth and grandeur to our inland seas. Perchance there will appear to the traveler something, he knows not what, of *laeta* and *glabra*, of joyous and serene, in our very faces. Else to what end does the world go on, and why was America discovered?

The question was rhetorical; he knew the answer. To an American of his generation it was unthinkable that the greatest story in the history of civilized man — the finding and peopling of the New World — and the greatest opportunity since the Creation — the chance to remake men and their society into something cleansed of past mistakes, and closer to the heart's desire —

should end as one more betrayal of human credulity and hope.

Some moderns find that idea perfectly thinkable. Leslie Fiedler finds in the Montana Face, which whatever else it is is an authentically American one, not something joyous and serene, but the large vacuity of self-deluding myth. Popular books which attempt to come to grips with American values in these times walk neither toward Oregon nor toward Europe, but toward dead ends and jumping-off places. They bear such titles as *The Lonely Crowd*, *The Organization Man*, *Future Shock*, *The Culture of Narcissism*. This last, subtitled "American Life in an Age of Diminishing Expectations," reports "a way of life that is dying — the culture of competitive individualism, which in its decadence has carried the logic of individualism to the extreme of a war of all against all, the pursuit of happiness to the dead end of a narcissistic preoccupation with the self." It describes "a political system in which public lying has become endemic and routine," and a typical citizen who is haunted by anxiety and spends his time trying to find a meaning in his life. "His sexual attitudes are permissive rather than puritanical, even though his emancipation from ancient taboos brings him no sexual peace. . . . Acquisitive in the sense that his cravings have no limits, he does not accumulate goods and provisions against the future, in the manner of the acquisitive individualist of the nineteenth century political economy, but demands immediate gratification and lives in a state of restless, perpetually unsatisfied desire."

Assuming that Thoreau spoke for his time, as he surely did, and that Christopher Lasch speaks for at least elements and aspects of his, how did we get from there to here in little more than a century? Have the sturdiness of the American character and the faith in America's destiny that Thoreau took for granted been eroded entirely away? What happened to confidence, what happened to initiative and strenuousness and sobriety and responsibility, what happened to high purpose, what happened to hope? Are they gone, along with the Puritans' fear of pleasure? Was the American future, so clear in Thoreau's day, no more than a reflection of apparently unlimited resources, and does democracy dwindle along with the resources that begot it? Were we never really free, but only rich? In any event, if America was discovered only so that its citizens could pursue pleasure or grope for a meaning in their lives, then Thoreau and Lasch would be in agreement: Columbus should have stood at home.

Even if I knew answers, I could not detail them in an hour's lecture, or in a book. But since I believe that one of our most damaging American traits is our contempt for all history, including our own, I might spend an hour looking backward at what we were and how America changed us. A certain kind of modern American in the throes of an identity crisis is likely to ask, or bleat, "Who am I?" It might help him to find out who he started out to be, and having found that out, to ask himself if what he started out to be is still valid. And if most of what I touch on in this summary is sixth-grade American history, I do not apologize for that. History is not the proper midden for digging up novelties. Perhaps that is one reason why a nation bent on novelty ignores it. The obvious, especially the ignored obvious, is worth more than a Fourth of July or Bicentennial look.

2

Under many names — Atlantis, the Hesperides, Groenland, Brazillia, the Fortunate Isles — America was Europe's oldest dream. Found by Norsemen about the year 1000, it was lost again for half a millennium, and only emerged into reality at the beginning of the modern era, which we customarily date from the year 1500. There is even a theory, propounded by the historian Walter Webb in *The Great Frontier*, that the new world created the modern era — stimulated its birth, funded it, fueled it, fed it, gave it its impetus and direction and state of mind, formed its expectations and institutions, and provided it with a prosperity unexampled in history, a boom that lasted fully 400 years. If Professor Webb pushes his thesis a little hard, and if it has in it traces of the logical fallacy known as *post hoc, ergo propter hoc*, it still seems to me provocative and in some ways inescapable, and Webb seems entirely justified in beginning his discussion of America in medieval Europe. I shall do the same.

Pre-Columbian Europe, then. For 150 years it has been living close to the limit of its resources. It is always short of money, which means gold and silver, fiat money being still in the future. Its land is frozen in the structures of feudalism, owned by the crown, the church, and an aristocracy whose domains are shielded by laws of primogeniture and entail from sale or subdivision — from everything except the royal whim which gave, and can take away. Its food supply comes from sources that cannot be expanded, and its population, periodically reduced by the Black Death, is static or in decline. Peasants are bound to the soil, and both they and their masters are tied by feudal loyalties and obligations. Except among the powerful, individual freedom is not even a dream. Merchants, the guilds, and the middle class generally, struggle against the arrogance of the crown and an aristocracy dedicated to the anachronistic code of chivalry, which is often indistinguishable from brigandage. Faith is invested in a politicized, corrupt, but universal church just breaking up in the Reformation that will drown Europe in blood. Politics are a nest of snakes: ambitious nobles against ambitious kings, kings against pretenders and against each other, all of them trying to fill, by means of wars and strategic marriages, the periodic power vacuums created by the cracking of the Holy Roman Empire. The late Middle Ages still look on earthly life as a testing and preparation for the Hereafter. Fed on this opium, the little individual comes to expect his reward in heaven, or in the neck. Learning is just beginning to open out from scholastic rationalism into the empiricism of the Renaissance. Science, with all it will mean to men's lives and ways of thinking, has barely pipped its shell.

Out of this closed world Columbus sails in 1492 looking for

a new route to Asia, whose jewels and silks are coveted by Europe's elite, and whose spices are indispensable to nations with no means of preserving food except smoking and salting, and whose meat is often eaten high. The voyage of the three tiny ships is full of anxiety and hardship, but the end is miracle, one of those luminous moments in history: an after-midnight cry from the lookout on the *Pinta*, Columbus and his sailors crowding to the decks, and in the soft tropical night, by the light of a moon just past full, staring at a dark ambiguous shore and sniffing the perfumed breeze off an utterly new world.

Not Asia. Vasco da Gama will find one way to that, Magellan another. What Columbus has found is puzzling, of unknown size and unknown relation to anything. The imagination has difficulty taking it in. Though within ten years of Columbus' first voyage Vespucci will demonstrate that the Americas are clearly not Asia, Europe is a long time accepting the newness of the new world. Pedro de Castañeda, crossing the plains of New Mexico, Oklahoma, and Kansas with Coronado in 1541, is confident that they make one continuous land mass with China and Peru; and when Champlain sends Jean Nicolet to explore among the Nipissings on the way to Georgian Bay and the great interior lakes in 1635 — 133 years after Vespucci — Nicolet will take along in his bark canoe an embroidered mandarin robe, just in case, out on those wild rivers among those wild forests, he should come to the palace of the Great Khan and need ceremonial dress.

Understanding is a slow dawning, each exploration bringing a little more light. But when the dawn arrives, it is a blazing one. It finds its way through every door and illuminates every cellar and dungeon in Europe. Though the discovery of America is itself part of Europe's awakening, and results from purely European advances — foreshadowings of Copernican astronomy, a method for determining latitude, the development of the caravel and the lateen sail — the new world responds by accelerating every stir of curiosity, science, adventure, individualism, and hope in the old.

Because Europe has always dreamed westward, America, once realized, touches men's minds like fulfilled prophecy. It has lain out there in the gray wastes of the Atlantic, not only a continent waiting to be discovered, but a fable waiting to be agreed upon. It is not unrelated to the Hereafter. Beyond question, before it is half known, it will breed utopias and noble savages, fantasies of Perfection, New Jerusalems.

Professor Webb believes that to closed and limited Europe America came as a pure windfall, a once-in-the-history-of-the-world opportunity. Consider only one instance: the gold that Sir Francis Drake looted from Spanish galleons was the merest fragment of a tithe of what the Spaniards had looted from Mexico and Peru; and yet Queen Elizabeth out of her one-fifth royal share of the *Golden Hind's* plunder was able to pay off the entire national debt of England and have enough left to help found the East India Company.

Perhaps, as Milton Friedman would insist, increasing the money supply only raised prices. Certainly American gold didn't help Europe's poor. It made the rich richer and kings more powerful and wars more implacable. Nevertheless, trickling outward from Spain as gift or expenditure, or taken from its ships by piracy, that gold affected all of Europe, stimulating trade and discovery, science, invention, everything that we associate with the unfolding of the Renaissance. It surely helped take European eyes off the Hereafter, and it did a good deal toward legitimizing the profit motive. And as the French and English, and to a lesser extent the Dutch and Swedes, began raiding America, other and more substantial riches than gold flooded back: new food plants, especially Indian corn and the potato, which revolutionized eating habits and brought on a steep rise in population that lasted more than a century; furs; fish from the swarming Newfoundland banks, especially important to countries still largely Catholic; tobacco for the indulgence of a fashionable new habit; timber for ships and masts; sugar and rum from the West Indies.

Those spoils alone might have rejuvenated Europe. But there was something else, at first not valued or exploited, that eventually would lure Europeans across the Atlantic and transform them. The most revolutionary gift of the new world was land itself, and the independence and aggressiveness that land ownership meant. Land, unoccupied and unused except by savages who in European eyes did not count, land available to anyone with the initiative to take it, made America, Opportunity, and Freedom synonymous terms.

But only later. The early comers were raiders, not settlers. The first Spanish towns were beachheads from which to scour the country for treasure, the first French settlements on the St. Lawrence were beachheads of the fur trade. Even the English on Roanoke Island, and later at Jamestown, though authentic settlers, were hardly pioneers seeking the promised land. Many were bond servants and the scourings of debtors' prisons. They did not come, they were sent. Their hope of working off their bondage and starting new in a new country was not always rewarded, either. Bruce and William Catton estimate that eight out of ten indentured servants freed to make new lives in America failed — returned to pauperism, or became the founders of a poor-white class, or died of fevers trying to compete with black slaves on tobacco or sugar plantations, or turned outlaw.

Nevertheless, for the English who at Jamestown and Plymouth and the Massachusetts Bay Colony began to take ownership of American land in the early seventeenth century, land was the transfiguring gift. The historian who remarked that the entire history of the United States could be read in terms of real estate was not simply making words.

Here was an entire continent which, by the quaint assumptions of the raiders, was owned by certain absentee crowned heads whose subjects had made the first symbolic gesture of claiming it. They had rowed a boat into a rivermouth, sighted and named a cape, raised a cross on a beach, buried a brass plate, or harangued a crowd of bewildered Indians. Therefore Ferdinand and Isabella, or Elizabeth, or Louis owned from that point to the farthest boundary in every direction. But land without people was valueless. The Spaniards imported the *encomienda* system — that is, transplanted feudalism — and used the Indians as peons. The French built only forts at which to collect the wilderness wealth of furs. But the English were another kind, and they were the ones who created the American pattern.

"Are you ignorant of the difference between the king of England and the king of France?" Duquesne asked the Iroquois in the 1750's. "Go see the forts that our king has established and you will see that you can still hunt under their very walls . . . . The English, on the contrary, are no sooner in possession of a place than the game is driven away. The forest falls before them as they advance, and the soil is laid bare so that you can scarce find the wherewithal to erect a shelter for the night."

To be made valuable, land must be sold cheap or given away to people who would work it, and out of that necessity was born a persistent American expectation. The very word "claim" that we came to use for a parcel of land reflected our feeling that free or cheap land was a right, and that the land itself was a commodity. The Virginia Company and Lord Calvert both tried to encourage landed estates on the English pattern, and both failed because in America men would not work land unless they owned it, and would not be tied to a proprietor's acres when they could go off into the woods and have any land they wanted, simply for the taking. Their claim might not be strictly legal, but it often held: hence the development of what came to be known as squatters' rights. As Jefferson would later write in *Notes on Virginia*, Europe had an abundance of labor and a dearth of land, America an abundance of land and a dearth of labor. That made all the difference. The opportunity to own land not only freed men, it made labor honorable and opened up the future to hope and the possibility of independence, perhaps of a fortune.

The consequences inform every notion we have of ourselves. Admittedly there were all kinds of people in early America, as there are all kinds in our time — saints and criminals, dreamers and drudges, pushers and con men. But the new world did something similar to all of them. Of the most energetic ones it made ground-floor capitalists; out of nearly everyone it leached the last traces of servility. Cut off from control, ungoverned and virtually untaxed, people learned to resent the imposition of authority, even that which they had created for themselves. Dependent on their own strength and ingenuity in a strange land, they learned to dismiss tradition and old habit, or rather, simply forgot them. Up in Massachusetts the idea of the equality of souls before God probably helped promote the idea of earthly equality; the notion of a personal covenant with God made the way easier for social and political agreements such as the Plymouth Compact and eventually the Constitution of the United States. In the observed freedom of the Indian from formal government there may have been a dangerous example for people who had lived under governments notably unjust and oppressive. Freedom itself forced the creation not only of a capitalist economy based on land, but of new forms of social contract. When thirteen loosely-allied colonies made common cause against the mother country, the League of the Iroquois may well have provided one model of confederation.

"The rich stay in Europe," wrote Hector St. John de Crève-coeur before the Revolution. "It is only the middling and poor that emigrate." Middle class values emigrated with them, and middle class ambitions. Resentment of aristocrats and class distinctions accompanied the elevation of the work ethic. Hardship, equal opportunity to rise, the need for common defense against the Indians, and the necessity for all to postpone the rewards of labor brought the English colonists to nearly the same level and imbued all but the retarded and the most ne'er-do-well with the impulse of upward mobility. And if the practical need to hew a foothold out of the continent left many of them unlettered and ignorant, that deficiency, combined with pride, often led to the disparagement of cultivation and the cultivated as effete and European. Like work, barbarism and boorishness tended to acquire status, and in some parts of America still retain it.

Land was the base, freedom the consequence. Not even the little parochial tyranny of the Puritans in Massachusetts could be made to stick indefinitely. In fact, the Puritans' chief objection to Roger Williams, when they expelled him, was not his unorthodoxy but his declaration that the Colonists had no right to their lands, the king not having had the right to grant them in the first place. Williams also expressed an early pessimistic view of the American experiment that clashed with prevailing assumptions and forecast future disillusion. "The common trinity of the world — Profit, Preferment, and Pleasure — will be here the tria omnia, as in all the world besides . . . and God Land will be as great a God with us English as God Gold was with the Spaniard." A sour prophet indeed — altogether too American in his dissenting opinions and his challenging of authority. And right besides. No wonder they chased him off to Rhode Island.

Students of the Revolution have wondered whether it was really British tyranny that lit rebellion, or simply American outrage at the imposition of even the mildest imperial control after decades of benign neglect. Certainly one of George III's worst blunders was his 1763 decree forbidding settlement beyond the crest of the Alleghenies. That was worse than the Stamp Act or the Navigation Acts, for land speculators were already sniffing the western wind. When Daniel Boone took settlers over the Cumberland Gap in 1775 he was working for speculators. George Washington and Benjamin Franklin, who had a good deal to do with the Revolution, both had interests in western land. Only a very revisionist historian would call our revolution a real estate rebellion, a revolt of the subdividers, but it did have that aspect.

And very surely, as surely as the endless American forests put a curve in the helves of the axes that chopped them down, the continent worked on those who settled it. From the first frontiers in Virginia and Massachusetts through all the successive frontiers that, as Jefferson said, required Americans to start fresh every generation, America was in the process of creating a democratic, energetic, practical, profit-motivated society that resembled Europe less and less as it worked westward. At the same time, it was creating the complicated creature we spent our first century as a nation learning to recognize and trying to define: the American.

3

"Who then is the American, this new man?" asked Crèvecoeur, and answered his own question in a book published in 1782 as *Letters from an American Farmer*. We were, he said, a nation of cultivators; and it was the small farmer, the independent, frugal, hard-working, self-respecting freeholder, that he idealized — the same yeoman farmer that only a little later Jefferson would call the foundation of the republic. But out on the fringes of settlement Crèvecoeur recognized another type. Restless, migratory, they lived as much by hunting as by farming, for protecting their crops and stock against wild animals put the gun in their hands, and "once hunters, farewell to the plough. The chase renders them ferocious, gloomy, and unsocial"; they exhibit "a strange sort of lawless profligacy"; and their children, having no models except their parents, "grow up a mongrel breed, half civilized, half savage."

Crèvecoeur, familiar only with the eastern seaboard, thought the frontiersman already superseded almost everywhere by the more sober and industrious farmer. He could not know that on farther frontiers beyond the Appalachians, beyond the Mississippi, beyond the Missouri and the Rocky Mountains, the breed would renew itself for another hundred years, repeating over and over the experience that had created it in the first place. The Revolutionary War was only the climax of the American Revolution, which was the most radical revolution in history because it started from scratch, from wilderness, and repeated that beginning over and over.

The pioneer farmer has a respectable place in our tradition and an equally respectable place in our literature, from Cooper's *The Pioneers* to Rölvaag's *Giants in the Earth*. But it was the border hunter who captured our imaginations and became a myth. He was never a soft or necessarily attractive figure. Ferocious he always was, gloomy often, antisocial by definition. As D. H. Lawrence and a whole school of critics have pointed out, he was a loner, often symbolically an orphan, strangely sexless (though more in literature than in fact), and a killer. We know him not only from the Boones, Crocketts, Carsons, and Bridgers of history, but from Cooper's Leatherstocking and all his literary descendants. His most memorable recent portrait is Boone Caudill in A. B. Guthrie's *Big Sky*, who most appropriately heads for the mountains and a life of savage freedom after a murderous fight with his father. Most appropriately, for according to Lawrence's *Studies in Classic American Literature*, one essential symbolic act of the American is the murder of Father Europe, and another is rebaptism in the wilderness.

We may observe those symbolic acts throughout our tradition, in a hundred variations from the crude and barbarous to the highly sophisticated. Emerson was performing them in such essays as "Self-Reliance" ("Trust thyself: every heart vibrates to that iron string") and "The American Scholar" ("We have listened too long to the courtly muses of Europe"). Whitman sent them as a barbaric yawp over the rooftops of the world. Thoreau spoke them in the quotation with which I began this lecture, and put them into practice in his year on Walden Pond.

The virtues of the frontiersman, real or literary, are Indian virtues, warrior qualities of bravery, endurance, stoical indifference to pain and hardship, recklessness, contempt for law, a hawk-like need of freedom. Often in practice an outlaw, the frontiersman in literature is likely to display a certain noble savagery, a degree of natural goodness that has a more sophisticated parallel in the common American delusion, shared even by Jefferson, who should have known better, that untutored genius is more to be admired than genius schooled. In the variants of the frontiersman that Henry Nash Smith traces in *Virgin Land* — in flatboatman, logger, cowboy, miner, in literary and mythic figures from the Virginian to the Lone Ranger and Superman — the Indian qualities persist, no matter how overlaid with comedy or occupational detail. Malcolm Cowley has shown how they emerge in a quite different sort of literature in the stiff-upper-lip code hero of Ernest Hemingway.

We need not admire them wholeheartedly in order to recognize them in their modern forms. They put the Winchesters on the gunracks of pickups and the fury into the arguments of the gun lobby. They dictate the leather of Hell's Angels and the whanged buckskin of drugstore Carsons. Our most ruthless industrial, financial, and military buccaneers have displayed them. The Sagebrush Rebellion and those who would open Alaska to a final stage of American continent-busting adopt them as a platform. Without them there would have been no John Wayne movies. At least as much as the sobriety and self-reliant industry of the pioneer farmer, it is the restlessness and intractability of the frontiersman that drives our modern atavists away from civilization into the woods and deserts, there to build their yurts and geodesic domes and live self-reliant lives with no help except from trust funds, unemployment insurance, and food stamps.

This mythic figure lasts. He is a model of conduct of many kinds. He directs our fantasies. Curiously, in almost all his historic forms he is both landless and destructive, his kiss is the kiss of death. The hunter roams the wilderness but owns none of it. As Daniel Boone, he served the interests of speculators and capitalists; even as Henry David Thoreau he ended his life as a surveyor of town lots. As mountain man he was virtually a bond servant to the company, and his indefatigable labors all but eliminated the beaver and undid all the conservation work of beaver engineering. The logger achieved his roughhouse liberty within the constraints of a brutally punishing job whose result was the enrichment of great capitalist families such as the Weyerhausers and the destruction of most of the magnificent American forests. The cowboy, so mythically free in books and movies, was a hired man on horseback, a slave to cows and the deadliest enemy of the range he used to ride.

Do these figures represent our wistful dream of freedom from the shackles of family and property? Probably they do. It may be important to note that it is the mountain man, logger, and cowboy whom we have made into myths, not the Astors and General Ashleys, the Weyerhausers, or the cattle kings. The lowlier figures, besides being more democratic and so matching the folk image better, may incorporate a dream not only of freedom but of irresponsibility. In any case, any variety of the frontiersman is more attractive to modern Americans than is the responsible, pedestrian, hard-working pioneer farmer breaking his back in a furrow to achieve ownership of his claim and give his children a start in the world. The freedom of the frontiersman is a form of mortal risk and contains the seed of its own destruction. The shibboleth of this breed is prowess.

The pioneer farmer is another matter. He had his own forms of self-reliance; he was a mighty coper, but his freedom of movement was restricted by family and property, and his shibboleth was not prowess but growth. He put off the present in favor of the future. Travelers on the Midwestern frontier during the 1820's, 30's, and 40's were universally moved to amazement at how farms, villages, even cities, had risen magically where only a few years before bears had been measuring their reach on the trunks of trees. British travelers such as Mrs. Trollope found the pioneer farms primitive, the towns crude, and the brag of the townsmen offensive, but Americans such as Timothy Flint, Thomas Nuttall, and John James Audubon regarded the settlement of the Midwest with a pride that was close to awe. Mormons looking back on their communal miracles in Nauvoo and Salt Lake City feel that same pride. Progress we have always measured quantitatively, in terms of acres plowed, turnpikes graded, miles of railroad built, bridges and canals constructed. I heard former Governor Pat Brown of California chortle with delight when the word came that California had passed New York in the population race. All through our history we have had the faith that growth is good, and bigger is better.

And here we may observe a division, a fault-line, in American feeling. Cooper had it right in *The Pioneers* nearly 160 years ago. Leatherstocking owns Cooper's imagination, but the town builders own the future, and Leatherstocking has to give way. *The Pioneers* is at once ,an exuberant picture of the breaking of the wilderness and a lament for its passing; and it is as much the last of the frontiersmen as the last of the Mohicans that the Leatherstocking series mourns. Many of Cooper's successors have felt the same way — hence the elegiac tone of so many of our novels of the settlement and the land. We hear it in Willa Cather's *A Lost Lady*, where the railroad builder Captain Forrester is so much larger than anyone in the shrunken present. We hear it in Larry McMurtry's *Horseman, Pass By*, which before it was made into the movie *Hud* was a requiem for the old-time cattleman. A country virtually without history and with no regard for history — history is bunk, said Henry Ford — exhibits an odd mournfulness over the passing of its brief golden age.

The romantic figure of the frontiersman was doomed to pass with the wilderness that made him. He was essentially over by the 1840's, though in parts of the West he lingered on as an anachronism. His epitaph was read, as Frederick Jackson Turner noted in a famous historical essay, by the census of 1890, which found no continuous line of frontier existing anywhere in the United States. He was not the only one who died of that census report. The pioneer farmer died too, for without a frontier there was no more free land. But whether the qualities that the frontier had built into both frontiersman and farmer died when the line of settlement withered at the edge of the shortgrass plains — that is not so clear.

4

Not only was free land gone by 1890, or at least any free land capable of settlement, but by the second decade of the twentieth century the population of the United States, despite all the empty spaces in the arid West, had reached the density which historians estimate congested Europe had had in 1500. The growth that Jefferson had warned against had gone on with astounding speed. The urban poor of Europe whose immigration he would have discouraged had swamped the original nation of mainly-Protestant, mainly–North European origins, and together with the industrial revolution, accelerated by the Civil War, had created precisely the sort of manufacturing nation, complete with urban slums and urban discontents, that he had feared. We were just at the brink of changing over from the nation of cultivators that Crèvecoeur had described and Jefferson advocated into an industrial nation dominated by corporations and capitalistic buccaneers still unchecked by any social or political controls.

The typical American was not a self-reliant and independent landowner, but a wage earner; and the victory of the Union in the Civil War had released into the society millions of former slaves whose struggle to achieve full citizenship was sure to trouble the waters of national complacency for a century and perhaps much longer. The conditions that had given us freedom and opportunity and optimism were over, or seemed to be. We were entering the era of the muckrakers, and we gave them plenty of muck to rake. And even by 1890 the note of disenchantment, the gloomy Dostoyevskyan note that William Dean Howells said did not belong in American literature, which should deal with the more smiling aspects of life, had begun to make its way into our novels.

After 1890 we could ask ourselves in increasing anxiety the question that Thoreau had asked rhetorically in 1862. To what end *did* the world go on, and why *was* America discovered? Had the four hundred years of American experience created anything new, apart from some myths as remote as Romulus and Remus, or were we back in the unbreakable circle from which Columbus had sprung us?

From 1890 to the present there have been plenty of commentators, with plenty of evidence on their side, to say that indeed we have slipped back into that vicious circle; and when we examine the products of the Melting Pot we find lugubrious reminders that it has not melted everybody down into any sort of standard American. What we see instead is a warring melee of minority groups — racial, ethnic, economic, sexual, linguistic — all claiming their right to the American standard without surrendering the cultural identities that make them still unstandard. We seem to be less a nation than a collection of what current cant calls "communities": the Black Community, the Puerto Rican Community, the Chicano Community, the Chinese Community, the Gay Community, the Financial Community, the Academic Community, and a hundred others. We seem to approach not the standard product of the Melting Pot but the mosaic that Canadians look forward to, and that they think will save them from becoming the stereotypes they think we are.

With all respect to Canada, we are not a set of clones. We are the wildest mixture of colors, creeds, opinions, regional differences, occupations, and types. Nor is Canada the permanent mosaic it says it wants to be. Both nations, I am convinced, move with glacial slowness toward that unity in diversity, that *e pluribus unum* of a North American synthesis, that is inevitable, or nearly so, no matter which end it is approached from. When we arrive there, a century or two or three hence, darker of skin and more united in mind, the earlier kind of American who was shaped by the frontier will still be part of us — of each of us, even if our ancestors came to this continent after the frontier as a fact was gone.

For as Turner pointed out, the repeated experience of the frontier through more than two hundred and fifty years coalesced gradually into a package of beliefs, habits, faiths, assumptions, and values, and these values in turn gave birth to laws and institutions that have had a continuous shaping effect on every newer American who enters the society either by birth or immigration. These are the things that bind us together no matter how many other forces may be pushing us apart. Language is one thing. I believe it has to be English, for language is at the core of every culture and inseparable from its other manifestations. If we permit bilingualism or multilingualism more than temporarily as an aid to assimilation, we will be balkanized and undone, as Canada is in danger of being by the apparently irremediable division between the Anglophones and the Francophones. The Bill of Rights is another unifier. We rely on it daily — even our enemies rely on it. And the images of ourselves, including the variant myths, that we developed when we were a younger, simpler, and more hopeful nation are still another. The national character, diffuse or not, recognizable if not definable, admirable and otherwise, bends newcomers to its image and outlasts time, change, crowding, shrinking resources, and fashionable pessimism. It has bent those apparently untouched by the Melting Pot, bent them more than they may know. Thus James Baldwin, visiting Africa, discovered to his surprise that though black, he was no African: he was an American, and thought and felt like one.

Time makes slow changes in our images of ourselves, but at their best, the qualities our writers and mythmakers have perpetuated are worth our imitation. The untutored decency and mongrel smartness of Huckleberry Finn, as well as the dignity that the slave Jim salvaged out of an oppressed life, could only have been imagined in America. The innocent philistinism of Howells' Silas Lapham could have been imagined by a European observer, but the ethical worth that nearly ennobles Lapham in his financial crisis is — realistic or not — pure American. Henry James's American, significantly named Christopher Newman, has a magnanimity that matches his naïveté. And the literary archetypes of the pre-1890 period are not the only ones. We have had political leaders who have represented us in more than political ways, and two at least who have taught us at the highest level who we are and who we might be.

Washington I could never get next to; he is a noble impersonal obelisk on the Mall. But Jefferson and Lincoln are something else. Jefferson did more than any other man to shape this democracy: formulated its principles in the Declaration of Independence and insisted on the incorporation of the Bill of Rights into the Constitution; had a hand in preventing the establishment of a state church; created the monetary system; framed the rules for the government of the western territories; invented the pattern for the survey of the public domain; bought Louisiana; sent Lewis and Clark to the western ocean and back, thus fathering one of our most heroic legends and inventing Manifest Destiny. If he had a clouded love affair with the slave half-sister of his dead wife, that only winds him more tightly into the ambiguous history of his country. As for Lincoln, he gave eloquence and nobility to the homespun values of frontier democracy. He was native mind and native virtue at their highest reach, and he too, like Jefferson but more sternly, was mortally entangled in the slave question that threatened to break America apart before it came of age.

Historians in these anti-heroic times have sometimes scolded the folk mind for apotheosizing Jefferson and Lincoln; and certainly, from their temples on the Potomac, they do brood over our national life like demigods. But as Bernard DeVoto said in one of his stoutly American "Easy Chairs," the folk mind is often wiser than the intellectuals. It knows its heroes and clings to them stubbornly even when heroes are out of fashion. Unfortunately, it is about as unreliable in its choice of heroes as in its creation of myths. It has a dream of jackpots as well as a dream of moral nobility and political freedom; it can make a model for imitation out of Jim Fisk or a myth out of a psychopathic killer like Billy the Kid almost as readily as it makes them out of the Great Emancipator.

5

These days, young people do not stride into their future with the confidence their grandparents knew. Over and over, in recent years, I have heard the cold undertone of doubt and uncertainty when I talk with college students. The American Dream has suffered distortion and attrition; for many, it is a dream glumly awakened from.

Per Hansa, in *Giants in the Earth*, could homestead Dakota farmland, gamble his strength against nature, lose his life in the struggle, but win in the end by handing down a productive farm to his son, and insuring him a solid, self-respecting place in the world. Per Hansa's grandsons have no such chances. Only one of them can inherit the family farm, for it would not be an economic unit if divided (it barely is while still undivided), and so something like primogeniture must be invoked to protect it. The other sons cannot hope to buy farms of their own. Land is too high, money is too expensive, machinery is too costly. The products of a farm acquired on those terms could not even pay the interest on the debt. So the other sons have a choice between leaving the farm, which they know and like, and going into the job market; or hiring out as tenant farmers or hired hands to some factory in the field. All over the United States, for several decades, farms have become fewer, larger, and more mechanized, and family ownership has grown less. Though I have no statistics in the matter, I would not be surprised to hear before the end of the 1980's that investors from the Middle East, Hong Kong, and Japan own as much American farmland as independent American farmers do.

For the vast majority of American youth who are not farmers, the options of independence have likewise shrunk. What they have to consider, more likely than not, is a job — a good job, in a company with a good pay scale, preferably, and with guaranteed promotions and a sound retirement plan. The future is not a thing we want to risk; when possible, we insure against it. And for the economically disadvantaged, the core-city youth, the minorities ethnic or otherwise, the people with inferior capacities or bad training or no luck, it is as risky as it ever was in frontier times, but without the promise it used to hold, and with no safety valve such as free land used to provide.

So we return to the vision of Christopher Lasch in *The Culture of Narcissism*. With some of it, especially its glib Freudian analyses of straw men, I am not in sympathy. By some parts, even when I think accurate observations are being marshaled to a dubious conclusion, I have to be impressed. The vision is apocalyptic. Lasch sees our cities as bankrupt or ungovernable or both, our political life corrupt, our bureaucracies greedy and expanding, our great corporations pervaded by the dog-eat-dog individualism of managerial ambition, maximized profits, and "business ethics" — which bear the same relation to ethics that military intelligence bears to intelligence. He sees Americans degraded by selfishness, cynicism, and venality, religion giving way to therapy and lunatic cults, education diluted by the no-fail concept, high school graduates unable to sign their names, family life shattered and supervision of children increasingly passed on to courts, clinics, or the state. He sees sexuality rampant, love extinct, work avoided, instant pleasure pursued as the whole aim of life. He sees excellence disparaged because our expectations so far exceed our deserving that any real excellence is a threat. He sees the Horatio Alger hero replaced in the American Pantheon by the Happy Hooker, the upright sportsmanship of Frank Merriwell replaced by the sports manners of John McEnroe, and all the contradictory strains of American life beginning to focus in the struggle between a Far Right asserting frontier ruthlessness and unhampered free enterprise, and a welfare liberalism to which even the requirement of reading English in order to vote may seem like a violation of civil rights.

The culture hero of Lasch's America is no Jefferson or Lincoln, no Leatherstocking or Carson, no Huck Finn or Silas Lapham. He is no hero at all, but the limp, whining anti-hero of Joseph Heller's *Something Happened* — self-indulgent, sneaky, scared of his superiors, treacherous to his inferiors, held together only by clandestine sex and by a sticky sentiment for the children to whom he has given nothing, the wife whom he ignores and betrays, and the mother whom he filed away in a nursing home and forgot.

Not quite what Thoreau predicted. The question is — and it is a question forced by Lasch's implication that his generalizations, and Heller's character, speak for the whole culture — does the Lasch–Heller characteristic American match the Americans you know in Salt Lake City and I know in California and other people know in Omaha and Des Moines and Wichita and Dallas and Hartford and Bangor?

I doubt that we know many such limp dishrags as Heller's Bob Slocum, but we recognize elements of the world he lives in. We have watched the progress of the sexual revolution and the one-hoss-shay collapse of the family. We have observed how, in the mass media and hence in the popular imagination, celebrity has crowded out distinction. We have seen the gap widen between rich and poor, have seen crime push itself into high places and make itself all but impregnable, have watched the drug culture work outward from the ghettos into every level of American life. We are not unaware of how the Pleasure Principle, promoted about equally by prosperity, advertisers, and a certain kind of therapist, has eaten the pilings out from under dedication and accomplishment; how we have given up saving for the future and started spending for the present, because the Pleasure Principle preaches gratification, because the tax laws and inflation discourage saving and encourage borrowing. We have stood by uneasily while the Pleasure Principle invaded the schools, and teachers tried desperately to save something out of the wreck by pretending to be entertainers. Johnny can't read, but he expects his English class to be as entertaining as an X-rated movie. Increasingly he seems to be a vessel which dries out and deteriorates if it is not kept filled, and so for his leisure hours he must have a four-hundred-dollar stereo and/or a color TV, and when he walks around he carries a transistor radio, tuned loud. If he doesn't get a ski weekend during the winter term, he calls a school strike. He has never worn a tie, but he can vote, being eighteen.

We have lived through times when it has seemed that everything ran downhill, when great corporations were constantly being caught in bribery, price fixing, or the dumping of chemical wastes in the public's backyard — when corporate liberty, in other words, was indulged at the public expense. We have seen the proliferation of government bureaus, some of them designed to curb corporate abuses and some apparently designed only to inhibit the freedom of citizens. We have watched some of our greatest cities erupt in mindless violence. We have built ourselves a vast industrial trap in which, far from being the self-reliant individuals we once were, and still are in fantasy, we are absolutely helpless when the power fails.

Can any of the values left over from the frontier speak persuasively to the nation we have become? Some of the most antisocial of them still do, especially the ruthless go-getterism of an earlier phase of capitalism. Single-minded dedication, self-reliance, a willingness to work long and hard persist most visibly not in the average democratic individual but in the managers of exploitative industry and in spokesmen for the Far Right. Expressed in a modern context, they inspire not admiration but repulsion, they make us remember that some of the worst things we have done to our continent, our society, and our character have been done under their auspices. We remain a nation of real estate operators, trading increasingly small portions of the increasingly overburdened continent back and forth at increasingly inflated prices.

But I have a faith that, however obscured and overlooked, other tendencies remain from our frontier time. In spite of multiplying crises, galloping inflation, energy shortages, a declining dollar, shaken confidence, crumbling certainties, we cannot know many Americans without perceiving stubborn residues of toughness, ingenuity, and cheerfulness. The American is far less antisocial than he used to be; he has had to learn social values as he created them. Outside of business, where he still has a great deal to learn, he is very often such a human being as the future would be safe with.

I recognize Heller's Bob Slocum as one kind of contemporary American, but I do not commonly meet him in my own life. The kind I do meet may be luckier than most, but he seems to me far more representative than Bob Slocum, and I have met him all over the country and among most of the shifting grades of American life. He is likely to work reasonably hard, but not kill himself working; he doesn't have to, whether he is an electronics plant manager or a professor or a bricklayer. If he is still an individualist in many ways, he is also a belonger. If he belongs to a minority he is probably a civil rights activist, or at least sympathizer. If he belongs to that group of "middle Americans" about whom Robert Coles wrote a perceptive book, he may be confused and shaken by some equal-opportunity developments, but as often as not he understands the historical context and the necessity for increasing the access to opportunity, and if not supportive, is at least acquiescent.

He has not given up the future, as Lasch believes. He is often very generous. He gives to good causes, or causes he thinks good, and in a uniquely American way he associates himself with others in ad hoc organizations to fight for better schools, more parks, political reforms, social justice. That is the remote but unmistakable echo of the Plymouth Compact — government improvised for the occasion; government of, by, and for the people.

This American may be pinched, but he is not poor by any definition. He is lower middle, middle middle, upper middle. Whether he works for a corporation, a university, a hospital, a government bureau, whether he is a skilled laborer or a professional, he has a considerable stake in this society. He is always respectful of money, but he cannot be called money-crazy: money-craziness occurs much more commonly among the poor who have far too little or the rich who have far too much. Unless he is financially involved in growth, in which case he may be everything I have just said he is not, he is wary of uncontrolled growth and even opposed to it. Free enterprise in the matter of real estate speculation strikes him as more often fruitful of social ill than social good, just as industrialization strikes him not as the cure for our ills but the cause of many of them. He takes his pleasures and relaxations, and expects far more of them than his frontier grandparents did, but he can hardly be called a pleasure freak bent on instant gratification. He is capable, as many of us observed during a recent California drouth, of abstinence and economy and personal sacrifice in the public interest, and would be capable of much more of those if he had leaders who encouraged them.

This sort of American is either disregarded or disparaged in the alarming books that assay our culture. Lasch, though he would like him better than the kind he describes, seems to think him gone past retrieval. But Lasch, like some other commentators, is making a point and selects his evidence. To some extent also, he makes the New Yorker mistake of mistaking New York for the United States. To an even greater extent he reads a certain class as if it were a cross section of the entire population. He would honestly like to get us back onto the tracks he thinks we have left, or onto new tracks that lead somewhere, and he deplores what he sees as much as anyone would.

But in fact we may be more on the tracks than he believes we are. His book is rather like the books of captious British travelers in the first half of the nineteenth century. Not having experienced the potency of the dream of starting from scratch, he sees imperfections as failures, not as stages of a long slow effort. But there is something very American about *The Culture of Narcissism*, too. We have always had a habit, when we were not bragging, of accepting Father Europe's view that we are short on cultural finesse and that our fabled moral superiority is a delusion. It may *be* a delusion; that does not make an American a creature unworthy of study, or American society a dismal failure. We have never given up the habit we acquired while resisting George III: we knock government and authority, including our own; we bad-mouth ourselves; like Robert Frost's liberal, we won't take our own side in an argument.

It is time we did. In 1992, twelve years from now, it will be half a millennium since Columbus and his sailors poured out on deck to see the new world. In half a millennium we should have gone at least part way toward what we started out to be. In spite of becoming the dominant world power, the dominant industrial as well as agricultural nation, the dominant force for freedom in the world, in spite of the fact that historically our most significant article of export has been the principle of liberty, in spite of the fact that the persecuted and poor of the earth still look to the United States as their haven and their hope — ask a Mexican wet-back family, ask a family of Vietnamese boat people — many of us have never quite got it straight what it was we started out to be, and some of us have forgotten.

Habits change with time, but the principles have not changed. We remain a free and self-reliant people and a land of opportunity, and if our expectations are not quite what they once were, they are still greater expectations than any people in the world can indulge. A little less prosperity might be good for some of us, and I think we can confidently expect God to provide what we need. We could also do with a little less pleasure, learn to limit it in quantity and upgrade it in quality. Like money, pleasure is an admirable by-product and a contemptible goal. That lesson will still take some learning.

Give us time. Half a millennium is not enough. Give us time to wear out the worst of the selfishness and greed and turn our energy to humane and socially useful purposes. Give us a perennial few (a few is all any society can expect, and all any society really needs) who do not forget the high purpose that marked our beginnings, and Thoreau may yet be proved right in his prophecy.

Above all, let us not forget or mislay our optimism about the possible. In all our history we have never been more than a few years without a crisis, and some of those crises, the Civil War for one, and the whole problem of slavery, have been graver and more alarming than our present one. We have never stopped criticizing the performance of our elected leaders, and we have indeed had some bad ones and have survived them. The system was developed by accident and opportunity, but it is a system of extraordinary resilience. The United States has a ramshackle government, Robert Frost told Khrushchev in a notable conversation. The more you ram us, the harder we shackle. In the midst of our anxiety we should remember that this is the oldest and stablest republic in the world. Whatever its weaknesses and failures, we show no inclination to defect. The currents of defection flow the other way.

Let us not forget who we started out to be, or be surprised that we have not yet arrived. Robert Frost can again, as so often, be our spokesman. "The land was ours before we were the land's," he wrote. "Something we were withholding made us weak, until we found that it was ourselves we were withholding from our land of living." He was a complex, difficult, often malicious man, with grave faults. He was also one of our great poets, as much in the American grain as Lincoln or Thoreau. He contained within himself many of our most contradictory qualities, he never learned to subdue his selfish personal demon —

and he was never a favorite of the New York critics, who thought him a country bumpkin.

But like the folk mind, he was wiser than the intellectuals. No American was ever wiser. Listening to him, we can refresh ourselves with our own best image, and renew our vision of America: not as Perfection, not as Heaven on Earth, not as New Jerusalem, but as flawed glory and exhilarating task.

Omnes et Singulatim: Towards a Criticism of 'Political Reason'

MICHEL FOUCAULT

THE TANNER LECTURES ON HUMAN VALUES

Delivered at
Stanford University

October 10 and 16, 1979

I

The title sounds pretentious, I know. But the reason for that is precisely its own excuse. Since the nineteenth century, Western thought has never stopped labouring at the task of criticising the role of reason — or the lack of reason — in political structures. It's therefore perfectly unfitting to undertake such a vast project once again. However, so many previous attempts are a warrant that every new venture will be just about as successful as the former ones — and in any case, probably just as fortunate.

Under such a banner, mine is the embarrassment of one who has only sketches and uncompletable drafts to propose. Philosophy gave up trying to offset the impotence of scientific reason long ago; it no longer tries to complete its edifice.

One of the Enlightenment's tasks was to multiply reason's political powers. But the men of the nineteenth century soon started wondering whether reason weren't getting too powerful in our societies. They began to worry about a relationship they confusedly suspected between a rationalisation-prone society and certain threats to the individual and his liberties, to the species and its survival.

In other words, since Kant, the role of philosophy has been to prevent reason going beyond the limits of what is given in experience; but from the same moment — that is, from the development of modern states and political management of society — the role of philosophy has also been to keep watch over the excessive powers of political rationality — which is rather a promising life expectancy.

Everybody is aware of such banal facts. But that they are banal does not mean they don't exist. What we have to do with banal facts is to discover — or try to discover — which specific and perhaps original problems are connected with them.

The relationship between rationalisation and the excesses of political power is evident. And we should not need to wait for bureaucracy or concentration camps to recognize the existence of such relations. But the problem is: what to do with such an evident fact?

Shall we 'try' reason? To my mind, nothing would be more sterile. First, because the field has nothing to do with guilt or innocence. Second, because it's senseless to refer to 'reason' as the contrary entity to non-reason. Last, because such a trial would trap us into playing the arbitrary and boring part of either the rationalist or the irrationalist.

Shall we investigate this kind of rationalism which seems to be specific to our modern culture and which originates in Enlightenment? I think that that was the way of some of the members of the Frankfurter Schule. My purpose is not to begin a discussion of their works — they are most important and valuable. I would suggest another way of investigating the links between rationalisation and power:

1. It may be wise not to take as a whole the rationalisation of society or of culture, but to analyse this process in several fields, each of them grounded in a fundamental experience: madness, illness, death, crime, sexuality, etc.

2. I think that the word 'rationalisation' is a dangerous one. The main problem when people try to rationalise something is not to investigate whether or not they conform to principles of rationality, but to discover which kind of rationality they are using.

3. Even if the Enlightenment has been a very important phase in our history, and in the development of political technology, I think we have to refer to much more remote processes if we want to understand how we have been trapped in our own history.

This was my 'ligne de conduite' in my previous work: analyse the relations between experiences like madness, death, crime, sexuality, and several technologies of power. What I am working on now is the problem of individuality — or, I should say, self-identity as referred to the problem of 'individualising power'.

Everyone knows that in European societies political power has evolved towards more and more centralised forms. Historians have been studying this organisation of the state, with its administration and bureaucracy, for dozens of years.

I'd like to suggest in these two lectures the possibility of analysing another kind of transformation in such power relationships. This transformation is, perhaps, less celebrated. But I think that it is also important, mainly for modern societies. Apparently this evolution seems antagonistic to the evolution towards a centralised state. What I mean in fact is the development of power techniques oriented towards individuals and intended to rule them in a continuous and permanent way. If the state is the political form of a centralised and centralising power, let us call pastorship the individualising power.

My purpose this evening is to outline the origin of this pastoral modality of power, or at least some aspects of its ancient history. And in the next lecture, I'll try to show how this pastorship happened to combine with its opposite, the state.

The idea of the deity, or the king, or the leader, as a shepherd followed by a flock of sheep wasn't familiar to the Greeks and Romans. There were exceptions, I know — early ones in Homeric literature, later ones in certain texts of the Lower Empire. I'll come back to them later. Roughly speaking, we can say that the metaphor of the flock didn't occur in great Greek or Roman political literature.

This is not the case in ancient Oriental societies: Egypt, Assyria, Judaea. Pharaoh was an Egyptian shepherd. Indeed, he ritually received the herdsman's crook on his coronation day; and the term 'shepherd of men' was one of the Babylonian monarch's titles. But God was also a shepherd leading men to their grazing ground and ensuring them food. An Egyptian hymn invoked Ra this way: "O Ra that keepest watch when all men sleep, Thou who seekest what is good for thy cattle . . . ." The association between God and King is easily made, since both assume the same role: the flock they watch over is the same; the shepherd–king is entrusted with the great divine shepherd's creatures. An Assyrian invocation to the king ran like this: "Illustrious companion of pastures, Thou who carest for thy land and feedest it, shepherd of all abundance."

But, as we know, it was the Hebrews who developed and intensified the pastoral theme — with nevertheless a highly peculiar characteristic: God, and God only, is his people's shepherd. With just one positive exception: David, as the founder of the monarchy, is the only one to be referred to as a shepherd. God gave him the task of assembling a flock.

There are negative exceptions, too: wicked kings are consistently compared to bad shepherds; they disperse the flock, let it die of thirst, shear it solely for profit's sake. Jahweh is the one and only true shepherd. He guides his own people in person, aided only by his prophets. As the Psalms say: "Like a flock/hast Thou led Thy people, by Moses' and by Aaron's hand." Of course I can treat neither the historical problems pertaining to the origin of this comparison nor its evolution throughout Jewish thought. I just want to show a few themes typical of pastoral power. I'd like to point out the contrast with Greek political thought, and to show how important these themes became in Christian thought and institutions later on.

1. The shepherd wields power over a flock rather than over a land. It's probably much more complex than that, but, broadly speaking, the relation between the deity, the land, and men differs from that of the Greeks. Their gods owned the land, and this primary possession determined the relationship between men and gods. On the contrary, it's the Shepherd–God's relationship with his flock that is primary and fundamental here. God gives, or promises, his flock a land.

2. The shepherd gathers together, guides, and leads his flock. The idea that the political leader was to quiet any hostilities within the city and make unity reign over conflict is undoubtedly present in Greek thought. But what the shepherd gathers together is dispersed individuals. They gather together on hearing his voice: "I'll whistle and will gather them together." Conversely, the shepherd only has to disappear for the flock to be scattered. In other words, the shepherd's immediate presence and direct action cause the flock to exist. Once the good Greek lawgiver, like Solon, has resolved any conflicts, what he leaves behind him is a strong city with laws enabling it to endure without him.

3. The shepherd's role is to ensure the salvation of his flock. The Greeks said also that the deity saved the city; they never stopped declaring that the competent leader is a helmsman warding his ship away from the rocks. But the way the shepherd saves his flock is quite different. It's not only a matter of saving them all, all together, when danger comes nigh. It's a matter of constant, individualised, and final kindness. Constant kindness, for the shepherd ensures his flock's food; every day he attends to their thirst and hunger. The Greek god was asked to provide a fruitful land and abundant crops. He wasn't asked to foster a flock day by day. And individualised kindness, too, for the shepherd sees that all the sheep, each and every one of them, is fed and saved. Later Hebrew literature, especially, laid the emphasis on such individually kindly power: a rabbinical commentary on Exodus explains why Jahweh chose Moses to shepherd his people: he had left his flock to go and search for one lost sheep.

Last and not least, it's final kindness. The shepherd has a target for his flock. It must either be led to good grazing ground or brought back to the fold.

4. Yet another difference lies in the idea that wielding power is a 'duty'. The Greek leader had naturally to make decisions in the interest of all; he would have been a bad leader had he preferred his personal interest. But his duty was a glorious one:

even if in war he had to give up his life, such a sacrifice was offset by something extremely precious: immortality. He never lost. By way of contrast, shepherdly kindness is much closer to 'devotedness'. Everything the shepherd does is geared to the good of his flock. That's his constant concern. When they sleep, *he* keeps watch.

The theme of keeping watch is important. It brings out two aspects of the shepherd's devotedness. First, he acts, he works, he puts himself out, for those he nourishes and who are asleep. Second, he watches over them. He pays attention to them all and scans each one of them. He's got to know his flock as a whole, and in detail. Not only must he know where good pastures are, the seasons' laws and the order of things; he must also know each one's particular needs. Once again, a rabbinical commentary on Exodus describes Moses' qualities as a shepherd this way: he would send each sheep in turn to graze — first, the youngest, for them to browse on the tenderest sward; then the older ones; and last the oldest, who were capable of browsing on the roughest grass. The shepherd's power implies individual attention paid to each member of the flock.

These are just themes that Hebraic texts associate with the metaphors of the Shepherd–God and his flock of people. In no way do I claim that that is effectively how political power was wielded in Hebrew society before the fall of Jerusalem. I do not even claim that such a conception of political power is in any way coherent.

They're just themes. Paradoxical, even contradictory, ones. Christianity was to give them considerable importance, both in the Middle Ages and in modern times. Among all the societies in history, ours — I mean, those that came into being at the end of Antiquity on the Western side of the European continent — have perhaps been the most aggressive and the most conquering; they have been capable of the most stupefying violence, against themselves as well as against others. They invented a great many different political forms. They profoundly altered their legal structures several times. It must be kept in mind that they alone evolved a strange technology of power treating the vast majority of men as a flock with a few as shepherds. They thus established between them a series of complex, continuous, and paradoxical relationships.

This is undoubtedly something singular in the course of history. Clearly, the development of 'pastoral technology' in the management of men profoundly disrupted the structures of ancient society.

* * *

So as to better explain the importance of this disruption, I'd like to briefly return to what I was saying about the Greeks. I can see the objections liable to be made.

One is that the Homeric poems use the shepherd metaphor to refer to the kings. In the *Iliad* and the *Odyssey*, the expression ποιμὴν λαῶν crops up several times. It qualifies the leaders, highlighting the grandeur of their power. Moreover, it's a ritual title, common in even late Indo-European literature. In *Beowulf*, the king is still regarded as a shepherd. But there is nothing really surprising in the fact that the same title, as in the Assyrian texts, is to be found in archaic epic poems.

The problem arises rather as to Greek thought: There is at least one category of texts where references to shepherd models are made: the Pythagorean ones. The metaphor of the herdsman appears in the *Fragments* of Archytas, quoted by Stobeus. The word νόμος (the law) is connected with the word νομεύς (shepherd): the shepherd shares out, the law apportions. Then Zeus is called Νόμιος and Νέμειος because he gives his sheep food. And, finally, the magistrate must be φιλάνθρωπος, i.e., devoid of selfishness. He must be full of zeal and solicitude, like a shepherd.

Grube, the German editor of Archytas' *Fragments*, says that this proves a Hebrew influence unique in Greek literature. Other commentators, such as Delatte, say that the comparison between gods, magistrates, and shepherds was common in Greece. It is therefore not to be dwelt upon.

I shall restrict myself to political literature. The results of the enquiry are clear: the political metaphor of the shepherd occurs neither in Isocrates, nor in Demosthenes, nor in Aristotle. This is rather surprising when one reflects that in his *Areopagiticus*, Isocrates insists on the magistrates' duties; he stresses the need for them to be devoted and to show concern for young people. Yet not a word as to any shepherd.

By contrast, Plato often speaks of the shepherd–magistrate. He mentions the idea in *Critias*, *The Republic*, and *Laws*. He thrashes it out in *The Statesman*. In the former, the shepherd theme is rather subordinate. Sometimes, those happy days when mankind was governed directly by the gods and grazed on abundant pastures are evoked (*Critias*). Sometimes, the magistrates' necessary virtue — as contrasted with Thrasymachos' vice, is what is insisted upon (*The Republic*). And sometimes, the problem is to define the subordinate magistrates' role: indeed, they, just as the watchdogs, have to obey "those at the top of the scale" (*Laws*).

But in *The Statesman* pastoral power is the central problem and it is treated at length. Can the city's decision-maker, can the commander, be defined as a sort of shepherd?

Plato's analysis is well known. To solve this question he uses the division method. A distinction is drawn between the man who conveys orders to inanimate things (e.g., the architect), and the man who gives orders to animals; between the man who gives orders to isolated animals (like a yoke of oxen) and he who gives orders to flocks; and he who gives orders to animal flocks, and he who commands human flocks. And there we have the political leader: a shepherd of men.

But this first division remains unsatisfactory. It has to be pushed further. The method opposing *men* to all the other animals isn't a good one. And so the dialogue starts all over again. A whole series of distinctions is established: between wild animals and tame ones; those that live in water, and those that live on land; those with horns, and those without; between cleft- and plain-hoofed animals; between those capable and incapable of mutual reproduction. And the dialogue wanders astray with these never-ending subdivisions.

So, what do the initial development of the dialogue and its subsequent failure show? That the division method can prove nothing at all when it isn't managed correctly. It also shows that the idea of analysing political power as the relationship between a shepherd and his animals was probably rather a controversial one at the time. Indeed, it's the first assumption to cross the interlocutors' minds when seeking to discover the essence of the politician. Was it a commonplace at the time? Or was Plato rather discussing one of the Pythagorean themes? The absence of the shepherd metaphor in other contemporary political texts seems to tip the scale towards the second hypothesis. But we can probably leave the discussion open.

My personal enquiry bears upon how Plato impugns the theme in the rest of the dialogue. He does so first by means of methodological arguments and then by means of the celebrated myth of the world revolving round its spindle.

The methodological arguments are extremely interesting. Whether the king is a sort of shepherd or not can be told, not by deciding which different species can form a flock, but by analysing what the shepherd does.

What is characteristic of his task? First, the shepherd is alone at the head of his flock. Second, his job is to supply his cattle with food; to care for them when they are sick; to play them music to get them together, and guide them; to arrange their intercourse with a view to the finest offspring. So we *do* find the typical shepherd-metaphor themes of Oriental texts.

And what's the king's task in regard to all this? Like the shepherd, he is alone at the head of the city. But, for the rest, who provides mankind with food? The king? No. The farmer, the baker do. Who looks after men when they are sick? The king? No. The physician. And who guides them with music? The gymnast — not the king. And so, many citizens could quite legitimately claim the title 'shepherd of men'. Just as the human flock's shepherd has many rivals, so has the politician. Consequently, if we want to find out what the politician really and essentially is, we must sift it out from 'the surrounding flood', thereby demonstrating in what ways he *isn't* a shepherd.

Plato therefore resorts to the myth of the world revolving round its axis in two successive and contrary motions.

In a first phase, each animal species belonged to a flock led by a Genius–Shepherd. The human flock was led by the deity itself. It could lavishly avail itself of the fruits of the earth; it needed no abode; and after Death, men came back to life. A crucial sentence adds: "The deity being their shepherd, mankind needed no political constitution."

In a second phase, the world turned in the opposite direction. The gods were no longer men's shepherds; they had to look after themselves. For they had been given fire. What would the politician's role then be? Would *he* become the shepherd in the gods' stead? Not at all. His job was to weave a strong fabric for the city. Being a politician didn't mean feeding, nursing, and breeding offspring, but binding: binding different virtues; binding contrary temperaments (either impetuous or moderate), using the 'shuttle' of popular opinion. The royal art of ruling consisted in gathering lives together "into a community based upon concord and friendship,' and so he wove "the finest of fabrics." The entire population, "slaves and free men alike, were mantled in its folds."

The Statesman therefore seems to be classical antiquity's most systematic reflexion on the theme of the pastorate which was later to become so important in the Christian West. That we are discussing it seems to prove that a perhaps initially Oriental theme was important enough in Plato's day to deserve investigation, but we stress the fact that it was impugned.

Not impugned entirely, however. Plato did admit that the physician, the farmer, the gymnast, and the pedagogue acted as shepherds. But he refused to get them involved with the politician's activity. He said so explicitly: how would the politician ever find the time to come and sit by each person, feed him, give him concerts, and care for him when sick? Only a god in a Golden Age could ever act like that; or again, like a physician or pedagogue, be responsible for the lives and development of a few individuals. But, situated between the two — the gods and the swains — the men who hold political power are not to be shepherds. Their task doesn't consist in fostering the life of a group of individuals. It consists in forming and assuring the city's unity. In short, the political problem is that of the relation between the one and the many in the framework of the city and its citizens. The pastoral problem concerns the lives of individuals.

All this seems very remote, perhaps. The reason for my insisting on these ancient texts is that they show us how early this problem — or rather, this series of problems — arose. They span the entirety of Western history. They are still highly important for contemporary society. They deal with the relations between political power at work within the state as a legal framework of unity, and a power we can call 'pastoral', whose role is to constantly ensure, sustain, and improve the lives of each and every one.

The well-known 'welfare state problem' does not only bring the needs or the new governmental techniques of today's world to light. It must be recognised for what it is: one of the extremely numerous reappearances of the tricky adjustment between political power wielded over legal subjects and pastoral power wielded over live individuals.

I have obviously no intention whatsoever of recounting the

ution of pastoral power throughout Christianity. The immense problems this would raise can easily be imagined: from doctrinal problems, such as Christ's denomination as 'the good shepherd', right up to institutional ones, such as parochial organisation, or the way pastoral responsibilities were shared between priests and bishops.

All I want to do is bring to light two or three aspects I regard as important for the evolution of pastorship, i.e., the technology of power.

First of all, let us examine the theoretical elaboration of the theme in ancient Christian literature: Chrysostom, Cyprian, Ambrose, Jerome, and, for monastic life, Cassian or Benedict. The Hebrew themes are considerably altered in at least four ways:

1. First, with regard to responsibility. We saw that the shepherd was to assume responsibility for the destiny of the whole flock and of each and every sheep. In the Christian conception, the shepherd must render an account — not only of each sheep, but of all their actions, all the good or evil they are liable to do, all that happens to them.

Moreover, between each sheep and its shepherd Christianity conceives a complex exchange and circulation of sins and merits. The sheep's sin is also imputable to the shepherd. He'll have to render an account of it at the Last Judgement. Conversely, by helping his flock to find salvation, the shepherd will also find his own. But by saving his sheep, he lays himself open to getting lost; so if he wants to save himself, he must needs run the risk of losing himself for others. If he does get lost, it is the flock that will incur the greatest danger. But let's leave all these paradoxes aside. My aim was just to underline the force and complexity of the moral ties binding the shepherd to each member of his flock. And what I especially wanted to underline was that such ties not only concerned individuals' lives, but the details of their actions as well.

2. The second important alteration concerns the problem of

obedience. In the Hebrew conception, God being a shepherd, the flock following him complies to his will, to his law.

Christianity, on the other hand, conceived the shepherd–sheep relationship as one of individual and complete dependence. This is undoubtedly one of the points at which Christian pastorship radically diverged from Greek thought. If a Greek had to obey, he did so because it was the law, or the will of the city. If he did happen to follow the will of someone in particular (a physician, an orator, a pedagogue), then that person had rationally persuaded him to do so. And it had to be for a strictly determined aim: to be cured, to acquire a skill, to make the best choice.

In Christianity, the tie with the shepherd is an individual one. It is personal submission to him. His will is done, not because it is consistent with the law, and not just as far as it is consistent with it, but, principally, because it is his *will*. In Cassian's *Coenobitical Institutions*, there are many edifying anecdotes in which the monk finds salvation by carrying out the absurdest of his superior's orders. Obedience is a virtue. This means that it is not, as for the Greeks, a provisional means to an end, but rather an end in itself. It is a permanent state; the sheep must permanently submit to their pastors: *subditi*. As Saint Benedict says, monks do not live according to their own free will; their wish is to be under the abbot's command: *ambulantes alieno judicio et imperio*. Greek Christianity named this state of obedience ἀπάθεια. The evolution of the word's meaning is significant. In Greek philosophy, ἀπάθεια denotes the control that the individual, thanks to the exercise of reason, can exert over his passions. In Christian thought, πάθος is willpower exerted over oneself, for oneself. Ἀπάθεια delivers us from such wilfulness.

3. Christian pastorship implies a peculiar type of knowledge between the pastor and each of his sheep.

This knowledge is particular. It individualizes. It isn't enough to know the state of the flock. That of each sheep must also be known. The theme existed long before there was Christian pastorship, but it was considerably amplified in three different ways: the shepherd must be informed as to the material needs of each member of the flock and provide for them when necessary. He must know what is going on, what each of them does — his public sins. Last and not least, he must know what goes on in the soul of each one, that is, his secret sins, his progress on the road to sainthood.

In order to ensure this individual knowledge, Christianity appropriated two essential instruments at work in the Hellenistic world: self-examination and the guidance of conscience. It took them over, but not without altering them considerably.

It is well known that self-examination was widespread among the Pythagoreans, the Stoics, and the Epicureans as a means of daily taking stock of the good or evil performed in regard to one's duties. One's progress on the way to perfection, i.e., self-mastery and the domination of one's passions, could thus be measured. The guidance of conscience was also predominant in certain cultured circles, but as advice given — and sometimes paid for — in particularly difficult circumstances: in mourning, or when one was suffering a setback.

Christian pastorship closely associated these two practices. On one hand, conscience-guiding constituted a constant bind: the sheep didn't let itself be led only to come through any rough passage victoriously, it let itself be led every second. Being guided was a state and you were fatally lost if you tried to escape it. The ever-quoted phrase runs like this: he who suffers not guidance withers away like a dead leaf. As for self-examination, its aim was not to close self-awareness in upon itself, but to enable it to open up entirely to its director — to unveil to him the depths of the soul.

There are a great many first-century ascetic and monastic texts concerning the link between guidance and self-examination that show how crucial these techniques were for Christianity and how complex they had already become. What I would like to emphasise is that they delineate the emergence of a very strange phenomenon in Greco-Roman civilisation, that is, the organisation of a link between total obedience, knowledge of oneself, and confession to someone else.

4. There is another transformation — maybe the most important. All those Christian techniques of examination, confession, guidance, obedience, have an aim: to get individuals to work at their own 'mortification' in this world. Mortification is not death, of course, but it is a renunciation of this world and of oneself: a kind of everyday death. A death which is supposed to provide life in another world. This is not the first time we see the shepherd theme associated with death; but here it is other than in the Greek idea of political power. It is not a sacrifice for the city; Christian mortification is a kind of relation from oneself to oneself. It is a part, a constitutive part of the Christian self-identity.

We can say that Christian pastorship has introduced a game that neither the Greeks nor the Hebrews imagined. A strange game whose elements are life, death, truth, obedience, individuals, self-identity; a game which seems to have nothing to do with the game of the city surviving through the sacrifice of the citizens. Our societies proved to be really demonic since they happened to combine those two games — the city–citizen game and the shepherd–flock game — in what we call the modern states.

As you may notice, what I have been trying to do this evening is not to solve a problem but to suggest a way to approach a problem. This problem is similar to those I have been working on since my first book about insanity and mental illness. As I told you previously, this problem deals with the relations between experiences (like madness, illness, transgression of laws, sexuality, self-identity) knowledge (like psychiatry, medicine, criminology, sexology, psychology), and power (such as the power which is wielded in psychiatric and penal institutions, and in all other institutions which deal with individual control).

Our civilisation has developed the most complex system of

knowledge, the most sophisticated structures of power: what has this kind of knowledge, this type of power made of us? In what way are those fundamental experiences of madness, suffering, death, crime, desire, individuality connected, even if we are not aware of it, with knowledge and power? I am sure I'll never get the answer; but that does not mean that we don't have to ask the question.

II

I have tried to show how primitive Christianity shaped the idea of a pastoral influence continuously exerting itself on individuals and through the demonstration of their particular truth. And I have tried to show how this idea of pastoral power was foreign to Greek thought despite a certain number of borrowings such as practical self-examination and the guidance of conscience.

I would like at this time, leaping across many centuries, to describe another episode which has been in itself particularly important in the history of this government of individuals by their own verity.

This instance concerns the formation of the state in the modern sense of the word. If I make this historical connection it is obviously not in order to suggest that the aspect of pastoral power disappeared during the ten great centuries of Christian Europe, Catholic and Roman, but it seems to me that this period, contrary to what one might expect, has not been that of the triumphant pastorate. And that is true for several reasons: some are of an economic nature — the pastorate of souls is an especially urban experience, difficult to reconcile with the poor and extensive rural economy at the beginning of the Middle Ages. The other reasons are of a cultural nature: the pastorate is a complicated technique which demands a certain level of culture, not only on the part of the pastor but also among his flock. Other reasons relate to the sociopolitical structure. Feudality developed between individuals a tissue of personal bonds of an altogether different type than the pastorate.

I do not wish to say that the idea of a pastoral government of men disappeared entirely in the medieval church. It has, indeed, remained and one can even say that it has shown great vitality. Two series of facts tend to prove this. First, the reforms which had been made in the Church itself, especially in the monastic orders — the different reforms operating successively inside existing monasteries — had the goal of restoring the rigor of pastoral order among the monks themselves. As for the newly created orders — Dominican and Franciscan — essentially they proposed to perform pastoral work among the faithful. The Church tried ceaselessly during successive crises to regain its pastoral functions. But there is more. In the population itself one sees all during the Middle Ages the development of a long series of struggles whose object was pastoral power. Critics of the Church which fails in its obligations reject its hierarchical structure, look for the more or less spontaneous forms of community in which the flock could find the shepherd it needed. This search for pastoral expression took on numerous aspects, at times extremely violent struggles as was the case for the Vaudois, sometimes peaceful quests as among the Frères de la Vie community. Sometimes it stirred very extensive movements such as the Hussites, sometimes it fermented limited groups like the Amis de Dieu de l'Oberland. It happened that these movements were close to heresy, as among the Beghards, at times stirring orthodox movements which dwelt within the bosom of the Church (like that of the Italian Oratorians in the fifteenth century).

I raise all of this in a very allusive manner in order to emphasise that if the pastorate was not instituted as an effective, practical government of men during the Middle Ages, it has been a permanent concern and a stake in constant struggles. There was across the entire period of the Middle Ages a yearning to arrange pastoral relations among men and this aspiration affected both the mystical tide and the great millenarian dreams.

*   *   *

Of course, I don't intend to treat here the problem of how states are formed. Nor do I intend to go into the different economic, social, and political processes from which they stem. Neither do I want to analyse the different institutions or mechanisms with which states equipped themselves in order to ensure their survival. I'd just like to give some fragmentary indications as to something midway between the state as a type of political organisation and its mechanisms, viz., the type of rationality implemented in the exercise of state power.

I mentioned this in my first lecture. Rather than wonder whether aberrant state power is due to excessive rationalism or irrationalism, I think it would be more appropriate to pin down the specific type of political rationality the state produced.

After all, at least in this respect, political practices resemble scientific ones: it's not 'reason in general' that is implemented, but always a very specific type of rationality.

The striking thing is that the rationality of state power was reflective and perfectly aware of its specificity. It was not tucked away in spontaneous, blind practices. It was not brought to light by some retrospective analysis. It was formulated especially in two sets of doctrine: the *reason of state* and the *theory of police*. These two phrases soon acquired narrow and pejorative meanings, I know. But for the 150 or 200 years during which modern states were formed, their meaning was much broader than now.

The doctrine of reason of state attempted to define how the principles and methods of state government differed, say, from the way God governed the world, the father his family, or a superior his community.

The doctrine of the police defines the nature of the objects of the state's rational activity; it defines the nature of the aims it pursues, the general form of the instruments involved.

So, what I'd like to speak about today is the system of rationality. But first, there are two preliminaries: (1) Meinecke having published a most important book on reason of state, I'll speak mainly of the policing theory. (2) Germany and Italy underwent the greatest difficulties in getting established as states, and they produced the greatest number of reflexions on reason of state and the police. I'll often refer to the Italian and German texts.

*   *   *

Let's begin with *reason of state*. Here are a few definitions:

BOTERO: "A perfect knowledge of the means through which states form, strengthen themselves, endure, and grow."

PALAZZO (*Discourse on Government and True Reason of State*, 1606): "A rule or art enabling us to discover how to establish peace and order within the Republic."

CHEMNITZ (*De Ratione Status*, 1647): "A certain political consideration required for all public matters, councils, and projects, whose only aim is the state's preservation, expansion, and felicity; to which end, the easiest and promptest means are to be employed."

Let me consider certain features these definitions have in common.

1. Reason of state is regarded as an 'art', that is, a technique conforming to certain rules. These rules do not simply pertain to customs or traditions, but to knowledge — rational knowledge. Nowadays, the expression *reason of state* evokes 'arbitrariness' or 'violence'. But at the time, what people had in mind was a rationality specific to the art of governing states.

2. From where does this specific art of government draw its rationale? The answer to this question provokes the scandal of nascent political thought. And yet it's very simple: the art of governing is rational, if reflexion causes it to observe the nature of what is governed — here, the *state*.

Now, to state such a platitude is to break with a simultaneously Christian and judiciary tradition, a tradition which claimed that government was essentially just. It respected a whole system of laws: human laws; the law of nature; divine law.

There is a quite significant text by St. Thomas on these points. He recalls that "art, in its field, must imitate what nature carries out in its own"; it is only reasonable under that condition. The king's government of his kingdom must imitate God's government of nature; or again, the soul's government of the body. The king must found cities just as God created the world; just as the soul gives form to the body. The king must also lead men towards their finality, just as God does for natural beings, or as the soul does, when directing the body. And what is man's finality? What's good for the body? No; he'd need only a physician, not a king. Wealth? No; a steward would suffice. Truth? Not even that; for only a teacher would be needed. Man needs someone capable of opening up the way to heavenly bliss through his conformity, here on earth, to what is *honestum.*

As we can see, the model for the art of government is that of God imposing his laws upon his creatures. St. Thomas's model for rational government is not a political one, whereas what the sixteenth and seventeenth centuries seek under the denomination 'reason of state' are principles capable of guiding an actual government. They aren't concerned with nature and its laws in general. They're concerned with what the state is; what its exigencies are.

And so we can understand the religious scandal aroused by such a type of research. It explains why reason of state was assimilated to atheism. In France, in particular, the expression generated in a political context was commonly associated with 'atheist'.

3. Reason of state is also opposed to another tradition. In *The Prince*, Machiavelli's problem is to decide how a province or territory acquired through inheritance or by conquest can be held against its internal or external rivals. Machiavelli's entire analysis is aimed at defining what keeps up or reinforces the link between prince and state, whereas the problem posed by reason of state is that of the very existence and nature of the state itself. This is

why the theoreticians of reason of state tried to stay aloof from Machiavelli; he had a bad reputation and they couldn't recognize their own problem in his. Conversely, those opposed to reason of state tried to impair this new art of governing, denouncing it as Machiavelli's legacy. However, despite these confused quarrels a century after *The Prince* had been written, *reason of state* marks the emergence of an extremely — albeit only partly — different type of rationality from Machiavelli's.

The aim of such an art of governing is precisely not to reinforce the power a prince can wield over his domain. Its aim is to reinforce the state itself. This is one of the most characteristic features of all the definitions that the sixteenth and seventeenth centuries put forward. Rational government is this, so to speak: given the nature of the state, it can hold down its enemies for an indeterminate length of time. It can only do so if it increases its own strength. And its enemies do likewise. The state whose only concern would be to hold out would most certainly come to disaster. This idea is a very important one. It is bound up with a new historical outlook. Indeed, it implies that states are realities which must needs hold out for an indefinite length of historical time — and in a disputed geographical area.

4. Finally, we can see that reason of state, understood as rational government able to increase the state's strength in accordance with itself presupposes the constitution of a certain type of knowledge. Government is only possible if the strength of the state is known; it can thus be sustained. The state's capacity, and the means to enlarge it, must be known. The strength and capacities of the other states must also be known. Indeed, the governed state must hold out against the others. Government therefore entails more than just implementing general principles of reason, wisdom, and prudence. Knowledge is necessary; concrete, precise, and measured knowledge as to the state's strength. The art of governing, characteristic of reason of state, is intimately bound up with the development of what was then called either political

statistics, or *arithmetic*; that is, the knowledge of different states' respective forces. Such knowledge was indispensable for correct government.

Briefly speaking, then: reason of state is not an art of government according to divine, natural, or human laws. It doesn't have to respect the general order of the world. It's government in accordance with the state's strength. It's government whose aim is to increase this strength within an extensive and competitive framework.

*   *   *

So what the seventeenth- and eighteenth-century authors understand by 'the police' is very different from what we put under the term. It would be worth studying why these authors are mostly Italians and Germans, but whatever! What they understand by 'police' isn't an institution or mechanism functioning within the state, but a governmental technology peculiar to the state; domains, techniques, targets where the state intervenes.

To be clear and simple, I will exemplify what I'm saying with a text which is both utopian and a project. It's one of the first utopia-programmes for a policed state. Turquet de Mayenne drew it up and presented it in 1611 to the Dutch States General. In his book *Science in the Government of Louis XIV*, J. King draws attention to the importance of this strange work. Its title is *Aristo-Democratic Monarchy*; that's enough to show what is important in the author's eyes: not so much choosing between these different types of constitution as their mixture in view to a vital end, viz., the state. Turquet also calls it the City, the Republic, or yet again, the Police.

Here is the organisation Turquet proposes. Four grand officials rank beside the king. One is in charge of Justice; another, of the Army; the third, of the Exchecquer, i.e., the king's taxes and revenues; the fourth is in charge of the *police*. It seems that this officer's role was to have been mainly a moral one. According to Turquet, he was to foster among the people "modesty, charity, loyalty, industriousness, friendly cooperation, honesty." We recognize the traditional idea that the subject's virtue ensures the kingdom's good management. But, when we come down to the details, the outlook is somewhat different.

Turquet suggests that in each province, there should be boards keeping law and order. There should be two that see to people; the other two see to things. The first board, the one pertaining to people, was to see to the positive, active, productive aspects of life. In other words, it was concerned with education; determining each one's tastes and aptitudes; the choosing of occupations — useful ones: each person over the age of twenty-five had to be enrolled on a register noting his occupation. Those not usefully employed were regarded as the dregs of society.

The second board was to see to the negative aspects of life: the poor (widows, orphans, the aged) requiring help; the unemployed; those whose activities required financial aid (no interest was to be charged); public health: diseases, epidemics; and accidents such as fire and flood.

One of the boards concerned with things was to specialise in commodities and manufactured goods. It was to indicate what was to be produced, and how; it was also to control markets and trading. The fourth board would see to the 'demesne', i.e., the territory, space: private property, legacies, donations, sales were to be controlled; manorial rights were to be reformed; roads, rivers, public buildings, and forests would also be seen to.

In many features, the text is akin to the political utopias which were so numerous at the time. But it is also contemporary with the great theoretical discussions on reason of state and the administrative organisation of monarchies. It is highly representative of what the epoch considered a traditionally governed state's tasks to be.

What does this text demonstrate?

1. The 'police' appears as an administration heading the state, together with the judiciary, the army, and the exchecquer. True.

Yet in fact, it embraces everything else. Turquet says so: "It branches out into all of the people's conditions, everything they do or undertake. Its field comprises justice, finance, and the army."

2. The *police* includes everything. But from an extremely particular point of view. Men and things are envisioned as to their relationships: men's coexistence on a territory; their relationships as to property; what they produce; what is exchanged on the market. It also considers how they live, the diseases and accidents which can befall them. What the police sees to is a live, active, productive man. Turquet employs a remarkable expression: "The police's true object is man."

3. Such intervention in men's activities could well be qualified as totalitarian. What are the aims pursued? They fall into two categories. First, the police has to do with everything providing the city with adornment, form, and splendour. Splendour denotes not only the beauty of a state ordered to perfection; but also its strength, its vigour. The police therefore ensures and highlights the state's vigour. Second, the police's other purpose is to foster working and trading relations between men, as well as aid and mutual help. There again, the word Turquet uses is important: the police must ensure 'communication' among men, in the broad sense of the word. Otherwise, men wouldn't be able to live; or their lives would be precarious, poverty-stricken, and perpetually threatened.

And here, we can make out what is, I think, an important idea. As a form of rational intervention wielding political power over men, the role of the police is to supply them with a little extra life; and by so doing, supply the state with a little extra strength. This is done by controlling 'communication', i.e., the common activities of individuals (work, production, exchange, accommodation).

You'll object: but that's only the utopia of some obscure author. You can hardly deduce any significant consequences from it! But *I* say: Turquet's book is but one example of a huge literature circulating in most European countries of the day. The fact that it is over-simple and yet very detailed brings out all the better the characteristics that could be recognized elsewhere. Above all, I'd say that such ideas were not stillborn. They spread all through the seventeenth and eighteenth centuries, either as applied policies (such as cameralism or mercantilism), or as subjects to be taught (the German *Polizeiwissenschaft*; don't let's forget that this was the title under which the science of administration was taught in Germany).

These are the two perspectives that I'd like, not to study, but at least to suggest. First I'll refer to a French administrative compendium, then to a German textbook.

1. Every historian knows Delamare's *Compendium*. At the beginning of the eighteenth century, this administrator undertook the compilation of the whole kingdom's police regulations. It's an infinite source of highly valuable information. The general conception of the police that such a quantity of rules and regulations could convey to an administrator like Delamare is what I'd like to emphasise.

Delamare says that the police must see to eleven things within the state: (1) religion; (2) morals; (3) health; (4) supplies; (5) roads, highways, town buildings; (6) public safety; (7) the liberal arts (roughly speaking, arts and science); (8) trade; (9) factories; (10) manservants and labourers; (11) the poor.

The same classification features in every treatise concerning the police. As in Turquet's utopia programme, apart from the army, justice properly speaking, and direct taxes, the police apparently sees to everything. The same thing can be said differently: Royal power had asserted itself against feudalism thanks to the support of an armed force and by developing a judicial system and establishing a tax system. These were the ways in which royal power was traditionally wielded. Now, 'the police' is the term covering the whole new field in which centralised political and administrative power can intervene.

Now, what is the logic behind intervention in cultural rites, small-scale production techniques, intellectual life, and the road network?

Delamare's answer seems a bit hesitant. Now he says, "The police sees to everything pertaining to men's *happiness*"; now he says, "The police sees to everything regulating *'society'* (social relations) carried on between men." Now again, he says that the police sees to *living*. This is the definition I will dwell upon. It's the most original and it clarifies the other two; and Delamare himself dwells upon it. He makes the following remarks as to the police's eleven objects. The police deals with religion, not, of course, from the point of view of dogmatic truth, but from that of the moral quality of life. In seeing to health and supplies, it deals with the preservation of life; concerning trade, factories, workers, the poor and public order, it deals with the conveniences of life. In seeing to the theatre, literature, entertainment, its object is life's pleasures. In short, life is the object of the police: the indispensable, the useful, and the superfluous. That people survive, live, and even do better than just that, is what the police has to ensure.

And so we link up with the other definitions Delamare proposes: "The sole purpose of the police is to lead man to the utmost happiness to be enjoyed in this life." Or again, the police cares for the good of the soul (thanks to religion and morality), the good of the body (food, health, clothing, housing), wealth (industry, trade, labour). Or again, the police sees to the benefits that can be derived only from living in society.

2. Now let us have a look at the German textbooks. They were used to teach the science of administration somewhat later on. It was taught in various universities, especially in Göttingen, and was extremely important for continental Europe. Here it was that the Prussian, Austrian, and Russian civil servants — those who were to carry out Joseph II's and the Great Catherine's reforms — were trained. Certain Frenchmen, especially in Napoleon's entourage, knew the teachings of *Polizeiwissenschaft* very well.

What was to be found in these textbooks?

Huhenthal's *Liber de Politia* featured the following items: the number of citizens; religion and morals; health; food; the safety of persons and of goods (particularly in reference to fires and floods); the administration of justice; citizens' conveniences and pleasures (how to obtain them, how to restrict them). Then comes a series of chapters about rivers, forests, mines, brine pits, housing, and finally, several chapters on how to acquire goods either through farming, industry, or trade.

In his *Précis for the Police*, Willebrand speaks successively of morals, trades and crafts, health, safety, and last of all, of town building and planning. Considering the subjects at least, there isn't a great deal of difference from Delamare's.

But the most important of these texts is Von Justi's *Elements of Police*. The police's specific purpose is still defined as live individuals living in society. Nevertheless, the way Von Justi organises his book is somewhat different. He studies first what he calls the 'state's landed property', i.e., its territory. He considers it in two different aspects: how it is inhabited (town vs. country), and then, who inhabit these territories (the number of people, their growth, health, mortality, immigration). Von Justi then analyses the 'goods and chattels', i.e., the commodities, manufactured goods, and their circulation which involve problems pertaining to cost, credit, and currency. Finally, the last part is devoted to the conduct of individuals: their morals, their occupational capabilities, their honesty, and how they respect the Law.

In my opinion, Von Justi's work is a much more advanced demonstration of how the police problem was evolved than Delamare's 'Introduction' to his compendium of statutes. There are four reasons for this.

First, Von Justi defines much more clearly what the central paradox of *police* is. The police, he says, is what enables the state to increase its power and exert its strength to the full. On the other hand, the police has to keep the citizens happy — happiness being understood as survival, life, and improved living. He perfectly defines what I feel to be the aim of the modern art of government, or state rationality: viz., to develop those elements constitutive of individuals' lives in such a way that their development also fosters that of the strength of the state.

Von Justi then draws a distinction between this task, which he calls *Polizei*, as do his contemporaries, and *Politik, Die Politik*. *Die Politik* is basically a negative task. It consists in the state's fighting against its internal and external enemies. *Polizei*, however, is a positive task: it has to foster both citizens' lives *and* the state's strength.

And here is the important point: Von Justi insists much more than does Delamare on a notion which became increasingly important during the eighteenth century — population. Population was understood as a group of live individuals. Their characteristics were those of all the individuals belonging to the same species, living side by side. (They thus presented mortality and fecundity rates; they were subject to epidemics, overpopulation; they presented a certain type of territorial distribution.) True, Delamare did use the term 'life' to characterise the concern of the police, but the emphasis he gave it wasn't very pronounced. Proceeding through the eighteenth century, and especially in Germany, we see that what is defined as the object of the police is population, i.e., a group of beings living in a given area.

And last, one only has to read Von Justi to see that it is not only a utopia, as with Turquet, nor a compendium of systematically filed regulations. Von Justi claims to draw up a *Polizeiwissenschaft*. His book isn't simply a list of prescriptions. It's also a grid through which the state, i.e., territory, resources, population, towns, etc., can be observed. Von Justi combines 'statistics' (the description of states) with the art of government. *Polizeiwissenschaft* is at once an art of government and a method for the analysis of a population living on a territory.

Such historical considerations must appear to be very remote;

they must seem useless in regard to present-day concerns. I wouldn't go as far as Hermann Hesse, who says that only the "constant reference to history, the past, and antiquity" is fecund. But experience has taught me that the history of various forms of rationality is sometimes more effective in unsettling our certitudes and dogmatism than is abstract criticism. For centuries, religion couldn't bear having its history told. Today, our schools of rationality balk at having their history written, which is no doubt significant.

What I've wanted to show is a direction for research. These are only the rudiments of something I've been working at for the last two years. It's the historical analysis of what we could call, using an obsolete term, the art of government.

This study rests upon several basic assumptions. I'd sum them up like this:

1. Power is not a substance. Neither is it a mysterious property whose origin must be delved into. Power is only a certain type of relation between individuals. Such relations are specific, that is, they have nothing to do with exchange, production, communication, even though they combine with them. The characteristic feature of power is that some men can more or less entirely determine other men's conduct — but never exhaustively or coercively. A man who is chained up and beaten is subject to force being exerted over him. Not power. But if he can be induced to speak, when his ultimate recourse could have been to hold his tongue, preferring death, then he has been caused to behave in a certain way. His freedom has been subjected to power. He has been submitted to government. If an individual can remain free, however little his freedom may be, power can subject him to government. There is no power without potential refusal or revolt.

2. As for all relations among men, many factors determine power. Yet rationalisation is also constantly working away at it. There are specific forms to such rationalisation. It differs from the rationalisation peculiar to economic processes, or to production

and communication techniques; it differs from that of scientific discourse. The government of men by men — whether they form small or large groups, whether it is power exerted by men over women, or by adults over children, or by one class over another, or by a bureaucracy over a population — involves a certain type of rationality. It doesn't involve instrumental violence.

3. Consequently, those who resist or rebel against a form of power cannot merely be content to denounce violence or criticise an institution. Nor is it enough to cast the blame on reason in general. What has to be questioned is the form of rationality at stake. The criticism of power wielded over the mentally sick or mad cannot be restricted to psychiatric institutions; nor can those questioning the power to punish be content with denouncing prisons as total institutions. The question is: how are such relations of power rationalized? Asking it is the only way to avoid other institutions, with the same objectives and the same effects, from taking their stead.

4. For several centuries, the state has been one of the most remarkable, one of the most redoubtable, forms of human government.

Very significantly, political criticism has reproached the state with being simultaneously a factor for individualisation and a totalitarian principle. Just to look at nascent state rationality, just to see what its first policing project was, makes it clear that, right from the start, the state is both individualising and totalitarian. Opposing the individual and his interests to it is just as hazardous as opposing it with the community and its requirements.

Political rationality has grown and imposed itself all throughout the history of Western societies. It first took its stand on the idea of pastoral power, then on that of reason of state. Its inevitable effects are both individualisation and totalisation. Liberation can only come from attacking, not just one of these two effects, but political rationality's very roots.

THE TANNER LECTURERS

1976–77

Brasenose College, Oxford	Bernard Williams, Cambridge University
University of Michigan	Joel Feinberg, Brandeis University
Stanford University	Joel Feinberg, Brandeis University

1977–78

Brasenose College, Oxford	John Rawls, Harvard University
University of Michigan	Sir Karl Popper, University of London
Stanford University	Thomas Nagel, Princeton University

1978–79

Brasenose College, Oxford	Thomas Nagel, Princeton University
Clare Hall, Cambridge	C. C. O'Brien, London
University of Michigan	Edward O. Wilson, Harvard University
Stanford University	Amartya Sen, Oxford University
University of Utah	Lord Ashby, Cambridge University
Utah State University	R. M. Hare, Oxford University

THE TANNER LECTURES ON HUMAN VALUES, Volume II,
was composed in Intertype Garamond with Garamond Foundry display type
by Donald M. Henriksen, Salt Lake City.